MW00574326

The Ellipsis Manual

The Ellipsis Manual

ANALYSIS AND ENGINEERING OF HUMAN BEHAVIOR

● ● ●

Chase Hughes

© 2017 Chase Hughes
All rights reserved.

ISBN-13: **9780692819906 (Evergreen Press)**
ISBN-10: **0692819908**
Library of Congress Control Number: 2017900801
Evergreen Press, Virginia Beach, VIRGINIA

Table of Contents

Introduction

• • •

You'll soon discover this is about as close as you can get to having a super power.

The Ellipsis Manual was written for engineering human behavior and producing predictable behavior outcomes. The methods can be used in therapy, intelligence, sales, and almost any social interaction.

By using this manual as a therapeutic tool, providers will see much further into the problems and issues patients face and will achieve faster behavioral outcomes. These groundbreaking methods exceed the traditional methods taught to mental health-care providers.

Intelligence operatives will learn techniques for behavior engineering and human intelligence (HUMINT) operations that far exceed the current government-training curriculum. Field operatives can arrive at outcomes faster and can learn to influence behavior with an unprecedented certainty.

The skills you will learn range from previously classified, top-secret (CIA, 1964) intelligence techniques, interrogation tactics and covert hypnosis to advanced behavior-profiling methods. The training is designed to make you an expert at reading people, their behavior and using covert-influence techniques. You'll learn to use advanced linguistics to bypass resistance and implant thoughts and ideas into minds.

The first section of the manual describes how to profile body language and human behavior, how to develop a powerful social authority, how the human brain functions and its loopholes, how the brain socially adapts, and how our outward behavior and nonverbal communication signal thousands of valuable bits of information, which trained operators can interpret, use, and exploit to meet the needs of their assignments. You will also learn how to identify human weaknesses, fears, insecurities, and needs, enabling you to custom-tailor the skills taught in the second section.

The second section covers psychological techniques that can be applied in interactions. These techniques cross into what some consider to be a gray area of ethics. The use of these techniques is made more sophisticated, elegant, and powerful when paired with the knowledge you will have gained from the profiling techniques in section 1.

We all have hundreds of loopholes in our psychology, which you will very soon be able to access. Our brains are constantly on the lookout for ways to learn, create new routines, and lessen the amount of cognitive processes involved in our daily actions. No one wakes up wishing to be manipulated or controlled, but our minds are wired to do exactly that.

As you progress in your training, you will notice what will probably be a disturbing revelation about human behavior and how we are all wired socially: we are quite perfectly wired to follow, to obey, and to be programmed by our environment. If you're not doing the programming, you are being programmed.

The Understanding of Influence

When most operators and hopeful influencers approach behavior engineering, it's done the wrong way. It's common for even seasoned influencers to assume that there is a magic script or procedure to cause change. It's also common for them to assume that there is an easy way to learn influence with quick tips and tricks. If you were, just for a moment, to compare learning the piano to learning influence, you'll begin to see the depth; while there are tricks that can be learned to create something impressive for a short time, there's far more to mastery than tricks. Mastering the piano takes years of daily drive, patience and hands-on practice. The human instrument is far more complex, but somehow, the belief that there's an easy trick to bypass mastery still exists. The methods you'll learn here can be used immediately to produce change, but the depth that some of the methods require is something that takes practice to master. Whether your journey started today when you picked up this book, or the hands holding this book are those of a master, may this book serve you in your endeavor to live above the common level of life.

ETHICS IN PRACTICE

You acknowledge that this manual is for entertainment only and the methods herein are not to be used in any way. Be good to others. Remember Dr. Frank Olson.

DISCLAIMER

While every effort has been made to ensure the accuracy of citations, information, references and works cited, typographical errors or omissions may occur. In the event that any part of this document contains work cited to an incorrect source, please notify the publisher so that an immediate correction can be issued to the public. The information in this book is only to provide education to the public. Chase Hughes, Ellipsis Behavior Labs, its employees, principals, or agents do not accept any responsibility or liability whatsoever whether in contract, tort, equity or otherwise for any action taken as a result of information in this volume. No part of this manual should be taken as mental health advice. No part of this book is intended to provide therapeutic care or any form of advice for anyone.

The Ellipsis Progression

● ● ●

THE ELLIPSIS PROGRESSION IS A visual representation of the Ellipsis system. With their organic nature, conversations and interactions are impossible to reliably systemize. The Progression chart shows the average progression of obedience and thought control when using the Ellipsis system. Each section can be moved as necessary to accomplish the goal. The training in this volume follows along the progression.

Within the Ellipsis progression, there are three main sections on the top that detail the three parts of the interaction. The progression from top to bottom is a chronological process of control.

The left column shows what you can reasonably expect to see in the behaviors and attitudes of your subjects as the conversations play out.

In the middle, the boxes represent the phases of the actual Ellipsis progression, from the initial approach to the activation of full control.

The right column indicates the varied techniques that can be used on a subject. This is not an all-inclusive list of techniques but a progression with examples of techniques that can be used.

The Progression illustrates what takes place anytime agreement is made to take action on something you otherwise wouldn't' have. For instance, consider the last time you bought something from an infomercial that you regretted, or loved. Some of the steps may have been glossed over, but they were all touched upon to create the buying experience. In reality, the Progression shows how humans progress psychologically in anything from infomercials to full-blown brainwashing. As you move through the Ellipsis Manual, all the methods and techniques will fall somewhere in this timeline. Occasionally, techniques and phases will trade places or be omitted, but the Progression should be the go-to reference for planning and training.

Subject	Phase	Technique
Doubt	*Approach*	Autopilot Disengage
Interest		Profile Development
Focus / Curiosity	*Authority*	Physical Leading
Trust		Authority Development
Confidence	*Profiling and Pacing*	Activation of Scarcity
Deep Focus		Metaphor and Linguistic Focus Development
Advanced Agreement	*Linguistic Manipulation*	Linguistic Control of Emotion
Hyper-Focus		Anchoring Emotions and Negative Dissociation
Confusion	*Trance Development*	Full Linguistic Trance
Slowed Breathing and Fixed Gaze		Deepen / Suggestion
Fixation of Interest	*Deepening*	Hypnotic Linguistics
Unconscious Nodding		Intensity Focus / Future Pacing
Unconscious Agreement	*Needs Providing*	Deep-Focus Development
Willing Release of Control		Resistance Negation
Internal Discovery	*Thought Control*	Parts Creation / Praise
Esteem Building		Reassurance / Activation
Eagerness of Action	*Agreement Testing*	Suggestion and Testing
Esteem Reliance on Obedience	*Compromise*	Confirm Obedience

How to use the Manual

● ● ●

THE MANUAL IS LAID OUT to be studied in order, however, it can also be a choose-your-own-adventure book. It's both a reference and a training aid. Use a journal daily to log your training, and use a calendar to set reasonable goals to use each new skill you learn. As you read through the book, take notes, and write your own examples of every technique and linguistic method given to you. The journal, and an audio recorder will prove to be your best allies when you are training.

Knowing the methods in this book is great. Knowing how to USE them and being able to apply them in diverse scenarios is what will separate you from the masses. It's easy and comfortable to fall into the trap of becoming an information collector, just harvesting valuable or 'cool' information from a book to use later in conversation or to impress people with knowledge. Don't do it! Journal and practice daily. You CAN use this stuff every day. When you read through the techniques, imagine applying them in different scenarios. Many times, students will have a defined goal in mind and only train to accomplish that single goal. While this is admirable, your skills will unfold when you can use them in more than one or two scenarios.

If you've studied influence, you've seen the books that promise to teach covert methods that wind up being next to unusable in normal conversation. This is not that book. The methods here can be tailored and the techniques for inducing trance will not leave you feeling awkward when testing them out. Use them, tailor them and make them a part of your daily living.

Use a planning tool to manage your goals for the manual. Don't be concerned with perfect, be concerned with progress. Use a journal every time you read the book and develop your own examples of every example given. Commit to mastery and the book will serve as a guide for years to come, until you find yourself at the point where you create outcomes without having to plan, rehearse and concentrate on methods.

Analyzing Behavior

• • •

THE BEHAVIORAL TABLE OF ELEMENTS is designed to have multiple applications across unlimited platforms and to work in any environment. As an organic document, the table will continue to evolve and progress in complexity, accuracy, and applicability.

The system is designed for field operators of law enforcement and US intelligence agencies. Field operations place high demands on operatives. Without the aid of complex and sophisticated equipment, such as polygraph instruments and video-based behavioral analyses, operators need a system that produces *reliable* results—that is, a system that can be used expediently to deliver vital intelligence information to the front lines or can be used to determine causation in crime-related events.

The table is an invaluable piece of hardware that enables fast, accurate, and measurable training results, which can be replicated with ease across a broad spectrum of employees.

As an analysis tool, the table can be used—for the first time in human history—to mathematically break down interactions into accurate, universally understood gestures, behaviors, deceptions, and vocal indicators.

Whether you are reading this as a student, an analyst, or an instructor, this guide will help you understand that the behavioral table of elements is a simple system that exemplifies the best attempt to scientifically understand and categorize human behavior, in a way that can be shared and understood by anyone or can be presented in court. The deception-rating scale, discussed in the following chapter, was developed to account for variables and to automatically change numeric values in response to organic events in interrogations and conversations.

Every time the table is used, users develop a more intimate understanding of behavior and of the cell abbreviations and their important positions within the table. After three weeks of periodic use, most clients in a test group experienced significant results and could recall over 95 percent of the cell data and the relationships of behaviors. Field agents can use this table to eventually develop an intuitive competence that can save hundreds of lives.

An instinctive ability to use the table to profile behavior in real-world environments usually takes about nine to eleven weeks of exposure. The trifold wallet cards that accompany the advanced-training package are indispensable for field agents. You'll find that it is easy and enjoyable to take the table home and to use it while watching the news and TV shows and even while interacting with your children. Employees can take this table into their personal lives and use it in myriad ways that will vastly speed up the process of their familiarization with it and the development of their unconscious competence. In CIA and other interrogation schools, the first principle of interrogation is the suspension of judgment. As you progress, you will learn that judgment and opinions about a subject can have horrible effects on the outcome and can even cause a profile to be read negatively, ending up with somebody getting hurt. Suspend all judgment and become open to the ideas and the self-image of the subject. Keep this single thought in mind throughout your training, and let it stay with you during your operations.

The Behavioral Table of Elements

● ● ●

THE BEHAVIORAL TABLE OF ELEMENTS is widely available as an image online. Since you've purchased the Manual, you can download the interactive Table on www.ellipsisbehavior.com. Simply click on 'The Ellipsis Manual'. On the bottom of the page, there's a link called 'I bought the book'. Use the password 'twotwoonebee' to get instant access to all the offline documents and interrogation resources.

The behavioral table of elements (BToE) is laid out in a way that makes it easy to find a gesture. It is based on two axes. The vertical axis represents the body; the head is on the top of the chart, and the feet are at the bottom. The two sections at the far bottom are behaviors that take place outside the body; the top is how we interact with objects in our environment, and the bottom is our verbal-expression methods and syntax.

The left-to-right axis represents the lowest stress and deception likelihood on the left, gradually increasing to the right to end at the most stress- and deception-related behaviors and gestures.

The number in the upper left-hand corner of each cell refers to its position within the table, while the other data within each cell represent the qualities associated with the relevant behaviors.

The table can be used in almost any scenario. This field guide, while serving as the reference text for the table, is also intended for use by analysts who will perform systematic analyses of interviews and interrogations.

The Key

Just like what's found on a map, the key enables users to identify the specific data contained in each cell.

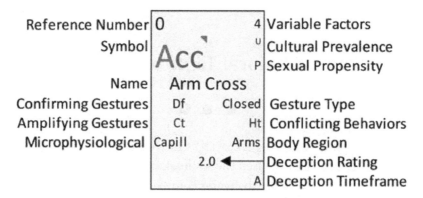

Each cell contains fourteen individual data points that provide reference and identifying data about each behavior:

* Reference Number
* Symbol
* Name
* Confirming Gestures
* Amplifying Gestures
* Microphysiological Amplifiers
* Variable Factors
* Cultural Prevalence
* Sexual Propensity
* Gesture Type
* Conflicting Behaviors
* Body Region
* Deception Rating
* Deception Timeframe
* Reference Number

Each cell contains a number in the upper-left corner. This number is used to identify the location of the behavior and relevant gesture in the table, not the gesture itself. As the table evolves, the numbers will remain constant in their location within the table. The reference number can be used to identify only a location within the table, not a specific behavior. As the table evolves and new cells are added or removed, the numerical system of numbering the cells will remain the same.

Symbol

Each cell contains an abbreviation of the name of a behavior. These abbreviations are used to identify behaviors. For instance, to refer in a report to the occurrence of an arm cross, the abbreviation "acc." is used to annotate it on the interview timeline provided in appendix 1. The same abbreviation is used to refer verbally to the gesture. Every effort was made during development to ensure the symbols within the cells would be easily memorized and easily intuited in their written and spoken forms. In training scenarios, symbols should be used as stand-alone objects and should be presented to trainees without the whole cells as often as possible to facilitate rapid absorption of the symbols and their associated behaviors.

Name

The name is given under the symbol in each cell. In some cases, for lack of cell real estate, an abbreviated form of the actual name is listed. The data file associated with the BToE contains the full name of each gesture and behavior.

Confirming Gestures

The confirming-gestures area provides the most closely related behaviors and gestures that confirm the translation or meaning of the main behavior. For instance, foot withdrawal (Fw) has confirming gestures of chair legs (Cl) and jewelry play (Jp). Both confirming gestures amplify and resonate with the original and intended meaning of foot withdrawal.

Any gesture in the confirming-gestures data point will confirm a diagnosis of the main behavior as indicating the intended message set forth in the table.

Amplifying Gestures
This area shows other behaviors within the table that can confirm the intended meaning but can also add more meaning or relevance to the behavior. For example, lip compression (Lc) is confirmed by jaw clenching (Jc) and digital flexion (Df). However, lip compression is amplified by chin thrusting (Ct) and self-hugging (Shg). The second two elements give us a sharper picture of what is going on and allow us to infer more data than would otherwise be available from the gesture alone.

Microphysiological Amplifiers
This section contains smaller and subtler cues to look for to either confirm a gesture or measure its intensity during interactions. Some microphysiological references may refer to a different gesture on the table, and some may simply contain a small bit of data. Sometimes, as in the example of an arm cross (Acc), capillary withdrawal is the microphysiological reference. Capillary withdrawal occurs when blood is forced from the tissue due to the application of pressure. Anything in this field can be easily missed but can play an important part in measuring the meaning and intensity of a gesture in question.

Variable Factors
This section refers to the number of different ways a gesture can present itself in human interaction, and the variations sometimes convey diverse behavioral messages. In the earlier example of the arm cross, the variable factors rating is four. As we have determined, people cross their arms in four common ways. Each arm cross can produce a different result, so the data table must be referenced to determine which variable was seen.

Cultural Prevalence

The cultural-prevalence section indicates whether a certain country or region of the world identifies a gesture with a different meaning than the one intended within the table. For example, people in some countries do not shake their heads horizontally to indicate that they mean no. This occurs in Bosnia and Croatia; it's common in the Balkans, Turkey, and Greece, as well. Where any cell has a particular country listed in the cultural-prevalence section, the data table will provide more information and the cited research for each datum. The *U* most commonly seen in this section means that most countries, with few exceptions, perform this gesture or behavior for the same reasons.

Sexual Propensity

The data in this field indicates whether the gesture is more common in women or men.

Gesture Type

Within this body of research, the behaviors are divided into four types of gestures:

* Open
* Closed
* Unsure
* Aggressive

Conflicting Behaviors

The conflicting-behavior field contains behaviors that are indicative of results other than what is described within the table. For example, we assume digital flexion (Df) is a stress and anxiety behavior. Humans do this in conversation when confronted with troubling, accusatory, stressful, or otherwise anxiety-producing information. However, the conflicting behavior listed is anger (Ag). Digital flexion with an angry facial expression is not in line with the meaning of digital flexion, per the table. The flexion in this case is caused by anger, not stress.

Body Region
This field shows the region of the body in which the behavior usually takes place.

Deception Rating
This field is a representation of each behavior's individual deception level. After using the deception scale (discussed later) and factoring in variables and influencing factors, the numbers in the deception-rating field of each cell can be added to form a total-deception rating for each response to a question or statement.

Deception Timeframe
Within an interaction, there are three times to look for deceptive behaviors:

Before a person answers a question or makes a statement (this includes the elapsed time from the time a question is asked to the moment the person begins to answer)

During the person responds or makes a statement

After the person has made the response or statement

Using these three times as guideposts, each deceptive cell has a rating of B, D, or A and shows the best time to observe a person for deceptive behavior.

*Anywhere within the table where a minus symbol (–) appears, this field indicates the lack of the associated behavior or gesture.

The Behavior-Analysis Process

● ● ●

ATTEMPTING TO LEARN INFLUENCE WITHOUT learning behavior analysis is a misguided endeavor; using covert influence methods with no knowledge of a subject provides minimal results. This book isn't designed to produce minimal results. Behavior analysis allows you to custom tailor your methods to the person you are speaking to. This makes the process of influence exponentially more powerful and creates a deep connection between the subject and your words. This connection is the difference between a subject who will entertain an idea and a subject who will willingly shove your idea into their subconscious and be happy about it.

Using the table—whether for training, interview analyses, interrogations, political debates, or even in pub conversations—is much easier than it appears at first glance. As you progress through this chapter, the table's potential for easy application to almost any environment will become clear.

Earlier, the form and shape of the table were explained. The key and the contents of each cell, with their characteristics and variations, were then described. Here, we will build a fundamental understanding of how to apply the table to real-world settings.

It's important to remember when performing analyses that an observed behavior is only as valuable as the stimulus that causes it. For example, a chronology statement, in which an interview subject describes a course of events in a seemingly memorized and rehearsed fashion in perfect chronological order, is rated a 4.0 on the deception-rating scale

(DRS). But if an interviewer pointedly asks that a course of events be described in their actual order of occurrence, the chronology statement would have no weight in the analysis of deception.

First, we will use an example of a post interrogation analysis using the BToE. Consider the following scenario:

For scenario purposes, the events that take place appear in italics. First, a single question and response will be documented and analyzed for deception.

You are a senior interrogator and have been informed that your staff has finished interrogating a suspect for child molestation. The video of the interrogation is available, and you sit at your desk with the BToE to perform an analysis of the interaction.

For analyses, the table provides the most useful method of obtaining data for any interaction. The table has variables (discussed in the next chapter) that shift the contents a bit, but the concept comes first.

The video is ready to watch, and you begin observing the behavior of the suspect. You've entered the variables into your initial notes on the BToE "quick notes page."

As the behaviors are observed, it becomes apparent that they take place in clusters. A person may make three or four small gestures or behaviors when giving one statement. These are called groups. A group is a series or collection of several gestures and behaviors that are performed within a very small timeframe and usually in response to a single stimulus. Conversational behavior—though most people observe only a single gesture at a time—often comprise groups of gestures that contain several unobserved movements in the face, fingers, feet, and body. As observations are made using the table, the observations should be recorded in these groups.

As the interrogation begins, your suspect, a male, is seated. After the interrogator introduces himself or herself and establishes the purpose for the suspect's having to be there, the interrogator asks the suspect the following: "Mr. Phillips, what happened when you were with Kyle Williams in your car last week?"

Whenever a question is asked, the clock starts when the first word leaves the mouth of the interrogator or interviewer. On the deception timeframe, "Before" is considered to be the time the question is asked and before an answer is given; "During" is the answering of the question; and "After" is the moments following the answer until someone speaks again.

In the current scenario, you notice as the question is asked that you see digital flexion (Df). One of the confirming gestures of Df is knee clasping (Kc). The suspect's hands are on his knees as he listens to the question, and you have both gestures to start formulating the group before he has even spoken a word to the interrogator.

Now the suspect begins his response: "I am a well-respected member of this community. My entire neighborhood knows who I am, and I'm an usher at our Presbyterian church. He and I did not do anything while he was in my car." As you observed the suspect's reaction and behavior, you noticed when he said "he was in my car" that his right shoulder raised as he shook his head to signal no and exposed his palm while answering. (In all likelihood, the suspect would have displayed associated facial expressions, changes in posture, blink-rate changes, rising vocal pitch, and several other behaviors while giving his "innocent" response to your junior interrogator's questions.)

Let's break down the above scenario.

The first statement he makes is a résumé statement.

The cell for this behavior is rated as a 4.0 on the deception scale. In the lower-right corner, the letter *D* is present, indicating that this behavior most commonly takes place *during* an answer, response, or statement. Confirming this gesture using other confirming, amplifying, and conflicting gestures should be saved for the post interview analysis.

Following Mr. Phillips's résumé statement, he makes a noncontracting rejection of any wrongdoing. This means he used two words to deny his actions instead of simplifying his language with a contraction. In this case, "did not" is used in place of "didn't."

This behavior is listed as 4.0 on the deception scale as well. It is marked as such in your notes, and it matches the deception timeframe with a *D* (during), as well.

In this block, also notice that there is only one variation of this behavior. This means that there is no other way to interpret this behavior. Now let's observe the other behaviors contained in his response to your interrogator.

The next behavior Mr. Phillips exhibits is a single-sided shoulder shrug (Ss).

This behavior is listed as a 4.0 on the deception scale. While by itself it may be completely innocuous, when combined with other high-rated deceptive behaviors, deception becomes glaringly obvious.

The next behavior exhibited by Mr. Phillips is the horizontal shaking of his head, or the "no" gesture.

This behavior is rated 1.0 on the deception scale and is noted as "no" in the notebook.

Palm exposure comes next, when Mr. Phillips is denying his involvement in anything corrupt or immoral. Humans frequently expose palms when they want to appear nonthreatening, trustworthy, or friendly.

This gesture has a 1.0 deception-scale rating and has a "deception not likely" tag (DNL). This also goes into the interrogator's notebook.

All of these gestures would be grouped as one in the notebook. Let's tally up the results and see whether Mr. Phillips is a monster:

Total score: 17.5

With a score of 12 being extremely deceptive, 17.5 is almost a sure bet. For the example above, we are identifying only a few of Mr. Phillips's behaviors. In reality, you'd identify many more behaviors. For example, in the final sentence of his statement to your interrogator, Mr. Phillips also engages in psychological distancing (Psd), a deceptive behavior that would add four points to his overall score. This will be covered later, but it is quite evident here that we are in the company of a dishonest man.

As you can see, a single question can cause several behaviors to occur. However, some of the behaviors are often innocuous and will not yield results.

As an interviewer continues through an interview, each question and statement should be recorded and analyzed separately. The interaction as a whole can have a total deception sum, but this type of calculation is usually reserved to a news interview or political debate.

BASELINING BEHAVIOR

In the behavioral-analysis community, much attention is paid to the baselining of human behavior, which is the careful analysis of people's behaviors while they are comfortable, expecting to be truthful about safe and easy conversational topics, such as the exchange of facts or a discussion about their employment activities. These early behaviors are later compared to their behaviors exhibited in the interviews, when the questioning and statements fathom their guilt or innocence; when faced by such questioning, subjects are most likely to be deceptive.

Many experts believe that baselining does not produce accurate results for several reasons: Subjects can anticipate the efforts of the interviewers and deliberately display conflicting or dishonest gestures in response to truthful questions. During the initial process of interviews, the intimidation, stress, or anxiety felt by subjects in the interrogation rooms will likely produce behaviors that appear deceptive. The baselining phase of interviews isn't measurable and thus cannot be a viable source of information for interviewers. Getting a false read while baselining subjects will produce faulty results and create confusion in both the interviewers and the subjects. Finally, interviewers' behaviors toward their subjects may cause the subjects to exhibit false red flags.

For the behavioral table of elements in the interview process, we will baseline all subjects (when possible).

Establishing a behavioral baseline is critical. Even if subjects know baselines are being developed, the information they nonverbally provide to the interviewers is still very valuable. Despite the beliefs and opinions of some psychologists, nothing related to human psychology and behavior is absolutely quantifiable. To collect data to the furthest degree possible, we should utilize any possible time we can to gather information about subjects' behaviors before the high-stress questions come up.

If subjects are deliberately being deceptive during baselining, the deceptive behaviors alone will reveal their intent. The conflicting gestures (listed in each cell) will start to raise red flags across the board when a gesture or behavior is deliberately faked.

As the interview progresses, the collection of information about idiosyncratic, behavioral mannerisms should never stop.

INFLUENCING FACTORS

Several factors can influence subjects' behaviors. These factors will always affect the results obtained using the table, whether the interviewers are parents of teenagers who might be using drugs or are seasoned government interrogators. From the temperatures in rooms to subjects' opinions about the races or sex of interviewers, such influencing factors will always be a part of the interview process. The structure of the behavioral notebook and the general formulas provided in this book are designed to serve as a mitigating and amplifying element. If analysts know what factors are influencing their interviews, they can shift the numerical values of the cells, can make more-accurate determinations of behaviors' inclusion or exclusion. This provides clearer pictures of the meanings of the observed behaviors.

Influencing factors are broken down into two groups: observation influencing and non-measurable effects

Observation-Influencing Factors

These are things that can be considered when performing analyses. These factors are events and circumstances within an interaction; when factored into the table, these events and circumstances affect the deception-likelihood analyses and stress analyses. There are six observation-influencing factors that can be somewhat accounted for in behavioral interviews:

* Temperature
* Interviewers' behaviors
* Subjects' emotional states
* Proxemics
* Handicaps or missing limbs
* Presence of others

TEMPERATURE

Rooms' temperatures always play a part in the interaction. In the table, some of the cells have blue lettering. These cells are behaviors that automatically increase as temperatures decrease. For every ten-degree increment below sixty-nine degrees, closed-type gestures lose one point on the deception-rating scale.

INTERVIEWER BEHAVIOR

The behaviors, attitudes, projections, and opinions of interviewers are factors that influence the outcomes and results of the analyses. Rating or scoring these factors are a judgment call for analysts, but the guidelines that follow help illuminate the decision to exclude or include the factors of interviewers' behaviors in the overall score or an individual behavior-response score. However, when human judgment is used to change a score, it should be noted in the report so that the human factors are obvious to other investigators who may read the report.

If interviewers begin interviews with behaviors that induce stress, they increase not only subjects' resistance but also their nonverbal and verbal stress indicators. At this point in the interview, there is no way to tell whether the behaviors that seem deceptive stem from induced stress or deceptive stress. Even when interviewers correct their behavior or modify their approach, the resistance remains constant, even though stress behaviors may decline.

An interrogator can easily destroy interviews that could have produced significant results. Every effort must be made to ensure that the behaviors observed and recorded are coming from subjects' emotions rather than their emotional responses to interrogators.

While it may be necessary in the process of an interview to become confrontational or accusatory, this shift must be accounted for in the observations to maintain accurate results.

For each confrontational or accusatory behavior exhibited by the interviewer, subtract two points from every 4.0-rated behavior and subtract one point from every 3- to 3.5-rated behavior.

EMOTIONAL STATE OF THE SUBJECT

The emotional state of the subject will always play a role in the interview. The following actions are the most common emotions that have a negative influence on the interrogation:

* Fear
* Aggression
* Defensiveness
* Unresponsiveness

Fear

This reaction is the most common in government and law-enforcement interviews. Even with innocent, nonoffending citizens, the anxiety produced by simply being in the interview room or sitting down with an interrogator can cause complex emotional reactions, which are hard to account for. An apprehensive, tense, or fearful subject will produce more fear-related gestures as a result. These gestures must be accounted for, and their values should be adjusted to increase analyses' accuracy. Ultimately, analysts or interviewers must judge or determine whether the stress reactions are due to emotional factors or to deception; no matter the cause, the appropriate annotations must be made in the notebook sheets.

Aggression
This emotional state can be caused by so many factors that there is almost no way to discern its origin. In interview rooms, Innocent people experience aggression as often as guilty people do.

Defensiveness
The overall behavior of subjects undergoing interrogation will almost always cross into defensive territory. A seasoned interrogator can discern the differences between feigned defensiveness of guilty people and defensive attitudes of innocent people. They each have a very unique texture. While this is not a text on interrogation, please note that innocent people, when questioned, often become defensive and vehement in their denial. Innocent people generally focus on denying their involvement, instead of describing reasons why they wouldn't have committed the acts in question.

UNRESPONSIVENESS
This is probably the hardest emotional element to defeat. Unresponsive subjects can appear to have no emotional reaction to the presented information and questions. Every effort must be made to emotionally involve subjects to the furthest extent. Unresponsiveness is the physical equivalent to a response of "I don't remember" from a subject. There's no way to refute such claims, and this behavior is the hardest for an interrogator to counter. In the table below, the behaviors associated with unresponsiveness also indicate when an emotional nerve has been struck—when the behaviors take place in exaggerated manners.

PROXEMICS
Proxemics is a subcategory of nonverbal communication that studies the way human beings use space—from personal space to the way a city is designed. The use of space in the interview room can either help subjects

to be more truthful or cause subjects to be closed or defensive. The personal space of the average person is one and a half feet in all directions, according to Edward T. Hall, an anthropologist and cultural researcher. In general, we allow only our close friends and family to enter this personal space.

When an interviewer (naturally an unfamiliar entity) occupies this personal space, the subject's reactions immediately dictate what outcome can be expected. In the short list below, the ranges of the proxemics show what behaviors will likely arise as the space is invaded, if the subject is closing off or becoming defensive.

Social Space (1.5–4 ft) Df, Lc, Cg

Personal Space (0–1.5 ft) Df, Br, Fw, Sh, Hd

According to the Lewis model of cultural types, different cultures have varying personal distances within which they normally conduct conversations, but the average is 1.5 feet. Cultures differ in their personal spaces, with Asian cultures being the most distant and Arab and sub-Saharan African cultures having the closest face-to-face, interpersonal comfort zones. Use caution when deliberately crossing the personal-space barrier.

HANDICAP OR MISSING LIMBS

Fifth on the list of observation-influencing factors are subjects who have missing limbs or handicaps that prevent them from making gestures in the same way an able-bodied person can. Any cell listed as a specific body part that is affected by a handicap should be completely dismissed and not used, annotated, or otherwise analyzed.

PRESENCE OF OTHERS

The presence of other people during an interview will impact the behavior of the subject in many ways we cannot measure. However, certain observations can be made to determine the possible effects that the presence of a person has on the subject. Every effort should be made (in the interrogation) to separate a subject from other sources of stimuli, human or otherwise.

Whether a child is being interviewed in the presence of abusive parents or a subject is being shown photos (that remain face up) of an abusive partner, the behaviors associated with this kind of social influence are almost always predictable and easy to spot.

If the presence of other people negatively affects the subject, the influence will become apparent quickly enough to correct the situation in most scenarios and will present the following indicators:

Cg, Jc, Df, Fw, Gp, Lc, Sh, Wt, and Jp

Behavior Reference Guide

• • •

THIS SECTION CONTAINS A FULL description of each cell. Each cell has its own page to make bookmarking and training easier. The behavioral table of elements is intended to have limitless use. There is no need to make notes when using it for live interactions or watching or reading body language in a video. The elements described below will help you understand the meaning of the behaviors within each cell and the relevant variations.

Throughout the cell-reference chapter, cell numbers are frequently shown before a behavior symbol to provide a quicker way of reading and referencing a printed copy of the BToE.

ARM CROSS—O

The arm-cross gesture is used universally and has four basic variations important to the interviewer. This gesture is frequently seen in magazines, detective shows, and books. These sources say the same thing: crossing your arms is defensive.

While there is a hint of truth in this translation, the actual meaning reveals much more. When seeing the performance of this behavior, note the closeness of the palms to the body, the direction the thumbs are pointing, the tightness of the cross, the flexion of the fingers, and the distance from the humerus (upper arm) to the torso. These variations all broadcast small but significant details about the gesture's true meaning.

Crossing the arms is something we do when we need assurance or warmth or when we feel threatened. Here are a few generalized rules to follow when making observations about arm-crossing behavior:

* The tighter the grip, the stronger the need for reassurance.
* Palms go toward the body in such a way that we hug ourselves when needing reassurance.
* Thumbs protruding upward is an almost certain sign of confidence, despite the crossed arms.
* Digital flexion increases in sync with the level of anger experienced.
* Crossed arms, when grouped with postures and facial expressions, is a sure sign of pride.
* Hands wrapped around the upper arms with the associated display of Ag or Co is an intimidation attempt.
* When women cross their arms during socially stressful situations, the act is almost always accompanied by Sh.
* When the fingers wrap around the arms and pull toward the sternum, look for Ag. This is a warning sign. If you see this with Wd, your subject is about to become violent.
* The dominant hand is almost always the one on top, while the dominant arm is on the bottom.

The four variable factors to be annotated in the notebook are as follows:

* Arms crossed with palms touching body: Acc1
* Arms crossed with hands wrapped around arms: Acc2
* Arms crossed with palms touching body and thumbs pointing upward: Acc3
* Arms crossed with clenched fists, with or without amplifying digital flexion: Acc4

Head Tilt—1

The head tilt is an open and vulnerable gesture. We tilt our heads for a variety of reasons: we may be feeling curious, wanting to flirt, or attempting to appear innocent. This is why this gesture is listed with Sq, Ye, and Ip. You'll see Pe appear when someone is explaining a point he or she wants communicated very clearly in a friendly environment.

The first conflicting behavior listed is Jc. This behavior indicates that the gesture could be a sign of anger or aggression, or it could be a challenge. Males (and sometimes females) sometimes expose vital parts of their bodies to appear fearless to their adversaries.

The second conflicting behavior is Tp because a head tilt sometimes reflects boredom. Head tilts accompany feigned boredom much more often than they do actual boredom.

Some research, including that of Desmond Morris, details the possible or observed differences between the leftward and rightward tilts of the head. Thus far, no significant study has been conducted to validate these observations, so the direction of head tilts in the BToE is irrelevant.

Chin Thrust—2

The chin thrust is a gesture that has cultural implications in the Middle East and some southern countries of Asia, such as the southern part of Ukraine and the Slavic Republic. In the exceptional regions, the chin thrust is communicated very regularly in conversations to indicate agreement and to point directions; Americans, on the other hand, extend a finger and arm to signal directions.

In the BToE, there are two variations: one is used as a deliberate movement in conversation, and the other is a seemingly involuntary and short-lived microgesture.

In the first variable, most chin-thrust behaviors are made to communicate anger, dissatisfaction, or challenges toward human competitors. Because chin thrusts deliberately expose vital organs to another person, the gesture is usually registered as a challenge in the United States.

The second variable is actually a ventilating gesture used mostly by men. This type of chin thrust is a way for men to adjust the collar of a collared shirt without having to use their hands to do so.

You'll notice that the sexual-propensity field contains "1U/2M," meaning that variable one is universal and variable two is performed by mostly men.

Eyebrow Flash—3

The eyebrow flash is common among developed cultures. When performing this gesture, subjects quickly raise and lower their eyebrows, usually upon greeting another person. Anger makes the face crumple and lowers the eyebrows significantly. This gesture raises the eyebrows and conveys friendliness, trustworthiness, and vulnerability.

Constantly raised eyebrows can indicate anger and fear; this gesture is used frequently to communicate an important point with emphasis. Parents frequently do this when scolding children.

This gesture has two variations:

Eyebrow flash: Ef1

Constantly raised eyebrows: Ef2.

Please note that when a person sees another give an eyebrow flash, an unconscious reflex takes place: the gesture is returned unconsciously. Most people do this, and most aren't even aware of their having returned the expression.

Head Downcast—4

The downcast head has multiple meanings depending on contextual references, but most of these gestures are used when a subject is experiencing shame, guilt, submissiveness, and personal anger.

The "~" symbol before the *U* in the sexual-propensity field indicates that both sexes perform this action, and it is sometimes used more often by women, especially during early stages of flirtation and courtship.

Gpr is indicated here to show that this behavior displays contraindications of typical downward-head behavior. This is seen regularly in abused spouses, sexually abused children, and children frequently bullied in school.

Lip Compression—5

There are several gestures that involve lip compression, but this expression predominately indicates that someone is suppressing opinions. This action creates a barrier that prevents an individual from speaking, and you'll see this in conversations on a daily basis. While lip compression is usually performed when someone is holding back information, it doesn't necessarily mean that deception is present. Social rules and norms, peer pressure, and societal influences cause us to hold our tongues regularly in conversations. The only time the gesture is significant is if an interrogator is recounting a hypothetical timeline of a crime or telling the suspect about possible reasons the crime that was committed is an acceptable offense given the circumstances. Seeing lip compression at this time should sound alarms in your head and increase the Lc deception likelihood number to 3.0. The above scenario is simply an example and should not hinder an analyst from making a judgment call on a behavior involving Lc that seems deceptive in nature.

Teeth Sucking—6

This behavior is universally antisocial in conversation; thus, it is an aggressive behavior when deliberately performed in the presence of others. This behavior is usually performed to challenge another person or to express latent disrespect or contempt.

Sucking teeth as a deliberate antisocial act: Ts1
Sucking teeth as a hygienic gesture: Ts2

Turtling—7

Turtling is when the shoulders draw upward and the head is lowered downward simultaneously. This behavior protects the neck and other vital organs and is a fear-based gesture. Children who have been abused frequently display this in interviews and when unknown strangers approach them (Darwin, 1872). These children also turtle their bodies reflexively when abusive parents make sudden movements (Schutz, 1958).

The gesture occurs in adults when fear is present, so it should be contextually relevant and rouse suspicion of deception in interview scenarios.

This is a temperature-affected behavior and is more common in colder temperatures.

Object in Mouth—8

When a subject puts something into their mouth, it is not likely to be a deceptive behavior. This behavior is performed mostly from a need for reassurance or from a sense of uncertainty. Men and women do this equally (Caro, 2003; Bryan, 1971; Navarro J., 2011). A good rule of thumb is to assume that when an object or finger passes the barrier of a subject's lips, the person needs reassurance.

This cell also includes a particular way subjects bite their lips: the lips actually pass their teeth and go into their mouths.

A simple "lip" can be annotated in the comments section of the accompanying gesture block in the interrogator's notebook.

Jaw Clenching—9

This nonverbal cue is seen in the jaw muscles and the temple area. Most of the time it suggests a subject is withholding aggressive actions or feelings, and it can also signify latent hostility or anger at what is being done or discussed.

Nostril-Wing Dilation—10

All mammals require oxygen to survive. As our hearts beat faster in response to stressors, our bodies send a signal that more oxygen is required to meet the needs of the impending adrenaline rush. In conversation and social settings, instead of a subject taking a giant breath, the slight flaring of nostrils often occurs. This is a way for us to increase blood oxygenation by taking in a larger volume of air.

Situations that create physical or emotional arousal produce some of the same neurochemicals as stress. Likewise, you may observe *wing dilation* (the scientist-speak nonverbal term for nostril-wing dilation) in emotionally aroused subjects engaged in conversation (Ekman P., 1994). You'll see more wing dilation in attraction and arousal scenarios when subjects are listening to people whom they are attracted to or aroused by.

Confirmation Glance—11

During an interview or conversation, subjects tend to look at people or a group of people to confirm that a statement has been understood and sometimes to confirm that they, the subjects, are being believed. Following a statement, a subject's cursory glance at another party in the room to verify that his or her story is "working" is called a confirmation glance.

While this behavior occurs before, during, and after a statement, it is more likely to occur just after a statement, an answer, or a denial of guilt in an interview setting.

In social settings, you'll see that confirmation glances always tend toward the most socially influential or powerful person in the group while people are engaged in conversation.

YAWN—12

While yawning is commonly associated with boredom and tiredness, it is likely a sign of anxiety and sometimes deception. The letter symbol in this cell is colored red, meaning that once it is mixed with another 4.0-rated deceptive behavior, the yawn observed will also be a 4.0. When no deception is present and no other signs of deception are observed in the current phase of the interview, the yawn is likely nothing more than a sign of boredom.

Yawns that originate directly from boredom or tiredness tend to last almost twice as long as yawns caused by anxiety.

In some cases, a false yawn is produced prior to questioning. It has not been proven yet, but guilty people almost exclusively exhibit this behavior (Navarro, 2011).

HAPPINESS—13

This facial expression and its associated microexpression cause the upper parts of the face to draw upward, causing wrinkling of skin in the outer corners of the eyes and causing the eyelids to draw closer together.

A fake (or social) smile is mostly done using only the lower face and can appear to have unequal muscular contractions on both sides of the face.

FLUSHING—14

Flushing is a natural reaction in all humans as a result of an adrenaline spike. The adrenaline produced during an embarrassing moment causes vasodilation and opens up blood vessels to receive more oxygen (Darwin, 1872; Ekman P., 1992; Vrij, 2001).

In interview settings, the appearance of blushing may be due to embarrassment, guilt, or fear. The other gestures observed within a group should tell you which meaning the subject is communicating.

Other causes of blushing or flushing to be aware of are alcohol, sexual arousal, and the consumption of certain party-related drugs.

HEAD BACK—15

Tilting the head back can have multiple nonverbal translations when the context is considered.

First, many people unconsciously tilt their heads backward while looking upward to retrieve information. When asked to recall data about remembered events, subjects tilt their heads back while attempting to retrieve information, whether it's true or false.

Tilting the head backward also exposes the vital part of our necks. Males typically perform this movement while challenging another person physically or while preparing for a fight. Exposing vital parts of the body to an adversary in the animal kingdom shows that one has no fear of being harmed by the other.

Variations

Head back to recall data: Hb1

Head back to expose neck: Hb2

LIP RETRACTION—16

Lip retraction closely resembles lip compression, but the two have very different implications. When subjects draw their lips into their mouths, as mentioned in Oi earlier, they are signaling a need for reassurance or even uncertainty about what is being discussed or what they are being questioned about.

This occurs equally in men and women alike.

OCULAR ORBITAL TENSION—17

This behavior regards the muscular tension that occurs around human eyes. When we experience things like curiosity, focus, and intense conversational emotions, the muscles around the eye contract and appear to make the ocular opening smaller. Squinting developed in humans to temporarily allow the eye to see things with slightly clearer focus by slightly modifying the shape of the eye and reducing the amount of light taken in by the pupils.

Orbital tension classical: Ot1

Orbital tension associated with disgust: Ot2

Eyebrow Narrowing—18

The narrowing of the brow is typically associated with anger in Western cultures and is almost universally recognized as being connected to deep levels of concentration as well. It usually presents itself before and during the question and answer phase and, depending on context, indicates an angered emotional response to the current topic or indicates an emotionally related thought during the question phase of interview.

Narrowing brow associated with anger: Bn1

Narrowing brow associated with contemplation: Bn2

Ventilation—19

As heat builds up in the body—owing to increased stress, anxiety, and adrenaline spikes commonly associated with deception and stress—subjects perform various behaviors intended to lower their body temperatures. Sweating is common among the guilty and innocent, but the need to ventilate physically is far more common in deceptive and high-stress subjects.

Using clothing and other objects, ventilation behavior may appear in several forms:

* Pulling or tugging a shirt collar to force air into the shirt to allow heat to escape (most commonly seen in male subjects)
* Pulling the front of a shirt to ventilate heat

- Moving long hair away from the back of the neck to allow airflow
- Adjustments in which subjects lift their bottoms from chairs for unusually long periods

Regardless of the type of ventilation behavior exhibited, all are intended to pacify the same need. All ventilation behavior is thus grouped into a single category without variable fluctuations in the upper-right corner of the cell.

ADAM'S APPLE RAISE—20

The sudden rise of the Adam's apple can indicate disagreement and stress.

The gesture that conflicts with the above meaning is the facial expression of fear. The Adam's apple, in this instance, is directly associated with the reticular activating system, a precursor to the fight-or-flight response.

Adam's apple jump associated with swallowing: Aa1

Adam's apple jump without an immediate swallow: Aa2 (emotional reactive)

GUIDING—21

The guiding gesture is used when telling or showing someone where something is or where to go. When someone points to an object or a direction or emits any form of nonverbal communication with the intent of guiding the gaze or direction of travel of another person, it is considered a guiding gesture. This gesture is frequently made by a hostess at a restaurant to signal to guests to follow him or her to their table.

Guiding with hands: Gg1

Guiding with head motion: Gg2

Guiding using the removal of the self from the path: Gg3

Baton Gestures—22

While speaking, the gestures made to accentuate syllabic, emotional punctuation are all baton gestures (Morris, 1979; Morris, 1970). These hand motions keep time with speech rhythms. Important things to take away from the observation of baton gestures are intensity, and whether the baton gesture is in synchronous rhythm with the spoken words.

An asynchronous baton gesture indicates a rift between what is being felt and said. Subjects often gesticulate and express statements that coincide with this type of gesture. When there is a timing gap, the emotion is almost never genuine.

82Df is listed as the conflicting gesture here, not because it implies different meaning but because it implies a different emotional state. 82Df will serve as a gauge that indicates anger, stress, anxiety, or negativity associated with 22Bg.

Vertical Head Shake—23

This is the vertical head-shaking motion we all use to indicate yes in the United States and most other countries.

The conflicting gestures here are protective and barrier behaviors. These include covering the body, closing the legs, and protecting the genitals. Look for these only to occur simultaneously and to be associated with 5Lc and an increase in 26Br.

Head Support—24

Though this behavior is performed by an arm-hand movement, the head is listed because of its body-region priority. The support gesture involving the hand resting has two basic identifiable variables:

The chin rests on the hand: Hs1

The head is tilted to rest on a hand near the ear: Hs2

The amount of skin-to-skin contact in variation 1 above often indicates the level of boredom or the intensity of fatigue in subjects. When boredom is feigned, it is far more likely to see a more upward gaze and slightly less hand-to-face contact.

Variation 2 involves a 1Ht and the tilting of the head to expose the side of the neck. The associated meanings conveyed by 1Ht are also conveyed here; a subject is likely feeling trusting or curious or is attempting to show defiance if the gesture is performed during an interviewer's asking questions or making remarks.

SURPRISE (FACIAL EXPRESSION)—25

The most authentic facial expressions of surprise cause the eyebrows to rise, exposing the sclera (white part of the eyes) above the iris. Also, the lower jaw drops in genuine surprise. Even when surprise is being suppressed, a small but noticeable drop of the lower jaw can be seen in a subject's face (Beattie, 2003; Hess E., 1975; Ekman P., 1994; Ekman P., 1993). It takes countless hours of training and practice to successfully conceal surprise on the face.

EYE BLINK RATE—26

The blink rate (the number of times a subject blinks per minute) varies with exposure to emotional and physical stimuli. Being a variable cell, the Br factor is given a 1.5 rating found below in the table.

When humans are captivated, interested, or otherwise curious about something in their fields of view, the blink rate will slow and gradually decline as the interest peaks. Conversely, an increasing or rapid blink rate indicates high stress and is associated with low levels of concentration and interest. Watching a great movie causes blink rates to decline, and taking the SAT causes a marked increase in blinking (Pease, 2006). During courtship, increases in blinking can be attributed to attraction. Rapid blinking during conversation can be interpreted as a feeling of superiority and contempt.

2Ct is listed as a conflicting gesture because of the deliberate decrease in 26Bl due to anger or physical threats or challenges.

A blink rate should be recorded with the numerical value immediately after the gesture name in the interrogator's notebook—for example, "Bl3."

Pupil Dilation—27

The pupils have only one physiological function: to control the amount of light passing into the eye. However, when humans experience emotional fluctuations, the pupils can respond by signaling the emotional response to a subject, person, or photograph that is present.

In response to pleasurable emotional or visual stimuli, the pupils expand and dilate. Babies looking at their mothers will do this. Prospective mates will show pupil dilation, and even exposure to photos of baby animals can cause the pupils to dilate significantly (Hess E., 1975; Vrij, 2001; Pease, 2006).

Exposure to disgusting, repulsive, ugly, or traumatic images and causes subjects' pupils to constrict, and given a consistent light source, this is rather easy to spot.

The documentation of pupillary constriction is annotated as –Pd. As with all cells in the BToE, the preface with the minus symbol indicates a lack of (or the opposite of) what follows.

Pupil dilation: Pd

Pupil constriction: –Pd (notice the presence of the minus symbol before Pd)

Eye Squint—28

Squinting the eyes has so many Hollywood connotations, but it is rarely seen in real life. Eye squinting is primarily a response to stress, disagreement, or anxiety (Navarro J., 2011). A squint can also signify incredulity, confusion, or deep concentration. If the squint is seen simultaneously with a head tilt and raised eyebrows, it's almost certainly incredulity. If the head is tilted while the person is squinting and the eyebrows are narrowed or lowered, deep concentration is more likely to be the cause.

It is important to note the difference between orbital tension (17Ot) and the squint (28Sq): the squint involves a more pronounced rising of the cheek muscles (levator labii superioris and zygomaticus). The cheeks will seemingly lift when a squint is performed, and the small degree of muscular tension in the ocular and orbital muscles rarely raises the cheeks in such a way.

Shoulder Shrugging—29

The shoulder shrug has been continually documented since Darwin first wrote about the gesture in his journal musings in the late 1800s (Darwin, 1872). Today, the shrug is widely accepted to mean one of about four possible things, depending on context:

* Uncertainty, amplified by 1Ht
* Surrender, amplified by 3Ef
* Fear, amplified by 32Fr
* Denial of guilt, amplified by 45No

While some books and research articles interpret this gesture as being possibly deceptive, others have considered it to stem mostly from fear (Goffman, 1963). The single-sided shoulder shrug, however, is much more likely to be associated with deception in an interview scenario (Navarro J., 2011; Morris, 1979).

Sadness (Facial Expression)—30

The sadness facial expression is nothing more than a pronounced effect of gravity on the face and a full relaxation of the facial and ocular muscles. The conflicting element listed here is jaw clenching (9Jc) because of its likelihood to immediately precede anger or violence.

Disgust (Facial Expression)—31

This facial expression is seen when someone is experiencing emotional or physical disgust. If you were to imagine putting your nose into the mouth of a jug full of spoiled milk, this expression would show on your face, where all parts of your face would draw toward your nose. When this facial expression is seen in social and interview settings, the subject being discussed is usually responsible for the expression. Subjects almost never feign this expression, and it is highly reliable for observation.

The conflicting gesture listed here is nostril-wing dilation (10Wd), which may indicate a need for air more than disgust.

Fear (Facial Expression)—32

The facial expression of fear causes the eyes to widen, exposing the sclerae around the top and bottom of the irises. The lips stretch horizontally backward, and the eyebrows rise outwardly.

Conflicting gestures listed here are subjects' arms being behind their backs (51Bb) or their arms being in the air (57Ia). These two behaviors indicate to some degree that the facial expression stems from pride smiling (in the case of 51Bb) or intense excitement (in the case of 57Ia) (Mcneil, 1998; Ekman P. N., 1975; Ekman P., 1993; Ekman P., 1992; Ekman P., 1994).

Contempt (Facial Expression)—33

The contempt facial expression is the only genuine facial expression that shows stronger on one side of the face. Contempt is best described as a self-assured feeling of moral or social superiority.

This expression became popular in recent television shows such as *Lie to Me* and *Criminal Minds*. Though it is a recognized human expression (Ekman P., 1994; Ekman P., 1992), our recent societal influences and shifts have made it a gesture that is now commonly seen in flirtatious and courting behavior.

ANGER (FACIAL EXPRESSION)—34

This facial expression forces the eyebrows down and compresses the lips together. What's more, 40Pe is listed as a conflicting behavior not because it negates anger but because it implies that anger stems from innocence, the result of innocent protest to an interviewer.

PROTECTING GESTURES—35

Protecting gestures involve one or more of the limbs crossing over the body to cover a vital area or piece of property. This is associated closely with anxiety, insecurity, and uncertainty with a person or subject. It is, however, a closed gesture because it allows limited access to the body. When a protecting gesture is observed with 9Jc, it is usually a masked-anger behavior and directly conflicts with the meaning of the given 35Pr (Schutz, 1958; Weisfeld, 1982; Wolfe, 1948).

SWALLOWING—36

In the context of deception-detection research, the act of swallowing is inconclusive at best. We do know that excess saliva is produced during the activation of the reticular system and during the spike in adrenaline that immediately follows. There is no way to determine whether the act of swallowing is due to stress, anxiety deception, or something else. It has a red color code because if we start to see several other 4.0-rated behaviors exhibited in the same behavior group, we can assume it is associated with the deceptive mind-set. Exceptions to this, of course, would be excessively thirsty or dehydrated subjects and subjects who swallow regularly (in the baseline). Some drugs can cause drying of the mouth and produce the swallowing behavior.

ELBOW CLOSURE—37

This behavior occurs only in seated subjects. It involves the inward drawing of the elbows as they sit on the table. This drawing-together instinct has its origins in the same place as protective gestures. It is designed to bring nonvital body parts in front of vital ones. This is especially common in acts of deception occurring in police interrogations that have been studied in the United States.

This gesture indicates discomfort, insecurity, and a need for protection.

Temperature affects this behavior, as represented above in the color scheme.

SINGLE-SHOULDER SHRUG—38

The single-shoulder shrug represents predominantly doubt and disbelief. The deception timeframe specifically states that this gesture is seen chiefly during verbal expressions rather than at any other time. Alone, this gesture is not enough to warrant a flag—other high-rated deceptive behaviors must accompany it.

When subjects shrug a single shoulder, they are expressing disbelief in what they are saying or what is being discussed at the moment the gesture occurs.

DIGITAL EXTENSION—39

This behavior refers to the action of the extension of the fingers. It reflects a relatively low level of stress and anxiety and is not associated with deception. This may occur anytime and in any position, seated or standing.

The extension of fingers and opening of the hands signifies openness and relaxation. In some cases, this behavior is also used when fearful, as seen above with 73Gpr (genital protection).

PALM EXPOSURE—40

Palm exposure and wrist exposure are in this behavioral cell. Both occur when subjects desire to appear trustworthy, nonthreatening, or honest (Szas, 1978; Rappoport, 1995). Both are frequently seen in denials and excuses made by teenagers and adolescents, but this gesture continues well into adulthood. It is just as common to see it in a murder investigation as in a missing candy quest with children.

In interviews, deceptive palm exposure occurs with less bodily and facial involvement. The absence of raised shoulders, facial expressions, and noticeable vocal shifts indicating emotion indicate more likely deception.

Chin Stroke—41

This behavior, when subjects stroke or rub their chins, is mostly contemplative, indicating curiosity, thought, and internal processing. When associated with 33Co (contempt), the behavior indicates contemplative ownership or deviant thought about a subject's audience.

Pupil Constriction—42

The constriction of pupils is a relative measurement in the interview process. Regardless of pupils' initial size, any decrease in pupil size qualifies to be registered as a 42Pc.

The pupils normally constrict to restrict the amount of light coming into the eye, but they also respond to emotional stimulus. Our seeing or hearing something we have a serious aversion to causes the pupils to constrict. Some subjects experience more-drastic contractions than others, and there is no way to measure this or identify how a subject will respond before an interview begins.

It is especially difficult to note the shifts in pupils' sizes in subjects with dark-colored irises. This should be noted if desired in the notebook.

Elbows Out—43

This cell refers to three types of variable behaviors related to the outward motion of the elbows. This is an opening gesture. This gesture exposes vital organs and is seen when subjects suddenly become confident or feel more secure in their environments.

Elbows moving outward less than shoulder width apart: Eo1
A single elbow shooting outward during interview: Eo2
Elbows moving outward farther than shoulder width: Eo3

POSTURE—44

Being so variable, the posture, like other behaviors, should be recorded not only if a shift occurs within an interview but also if the behavior is observable. Posture cannot be attributed to a root meaning because it is a baseline behavior that does not often play a part in the current mood of subjects.

Posture becoming vertical: Ps1
Posture becoming convex: Ps2

No—45

On 90 percent of our planet, this behavior, the horizontal shaking of the head, indicates no. However, its relevance here is that it can occur when subjects are affirming statements or attempting to confirm something. As the subjects are saying that something is true, their heads shake side to side—revealing the truth of what they are actually thinking. For instance, while a subject (a male) is describing that he loves his wife, he expresses the no gesture, indicating his disagreement with his statement.

LOCKED FINGERS—46

This behavior in itself does not indicate stress or anxiety unless you confirm microphysiological indicators and make a determination as to which gesture is being seen. Variation 2 is likely indicating stress and anxiety and, if associated with other high-scoring behaviors, should be moved to 2.0. Subjects who lock their fingers are revealing their attempts at self-restraint, and they may also exhibit other restraining behaviors, such as shallow breathing or wrapping their legs around the legs of their chairs. It's important to note the degrees of digital flexion when subjects lock their fingers.

Locked fingers loosely and restfully laced together: Lf1

Locked fingers with visible signs of capillary withdrawal or muscular tension: Lf2

STEEPLING—47

This is seen when subjects are seated. The palms of their hands face each other, and the tips of their fingers touch. The steepled-finger gesture is a sign of internal confidence in a social setting or in a subject matter. The three variations of this gesture are listed below. A subject holding his or her steepled fingers high is far less likely to listen and absorb than a subject holding his or her steepled fingers close to the surface of a table or at a near-waist level (Ellyson, 1985; Collett, 2003; Caro, 2003; Pease, 2006).

Steeple at head height: St1

Steeple at chest height: St2

Steeple at waist height or lower: St3

BEHIND HEAD—48

This behavior exhibits false confidence usually and is closely associated with feelings of contempt and insecurity. This is a deliberate gesture of dominance, which subjects use to appear less concerned with the situation around them. Subjects may clasp their hands behind their heads, indicating that they feel ownership over people with whom they are socially engaging.

ARMS ON HIPS—49

Subjects' placing their arms on their hips indicates several potential meanings that depend on contextual variations. For a male, the thumbs going backward may represent a desire to appear in charge; for a female, the same gesture may represent a desire to present her body to a mate. Context plays the largest role in determining the meaning behind this behavior. Thumbs' positioning can help sift through the potential meanings; for example, thumbs pointing forward indicate an emotional tendency toward curiosity and interest.

Arms on hips with thumbs facing backward: Ah1

Arms on hips with thumbs facing forward: Ah2

Self-Hug—50

This differs from the arm-cross behavior because it involves both arms actively embracing a subject's body, with the palms facing the body but with the thumbs *not* pointing upward. This is a closed and uncertain gesture subjects use to soothe themselves, a gesture that calms them when stress or anxiety is high. This self-hugging behavior is slightly more common in women.

If a subject's thumbs are facing upward and if the palms are making contact with the body, the subject is exhibiting confidence and relaxation.

Arms behind Back—51

The placing of the arms behind the back indicates one of two basic categories of associated thoughts:

The subject holds hands behind back: Bb1. This indicates confidence and sometimes superiority.

The subject holds a wrist or part of the arm with the opposing hand: Bb2. This indicates self-restraint in times of anger, and the higher the grip on the opposing arm, the higher the level of anger. While it is sometimes displayed for confidence, it is much more likely to be a display of restraint.

CONSTANTLY RAISED SHOULDERS—52

This can happen for a few different reasons, depending on contextual influences, but it mostly is a sign of social fear or self-consciousness. The raising of the shoulders is a vital-organ-protection mechanism that occurs automatically when subjects experience fear of any kind.

SINGLE-ARM WRAP—53

Performed mostly by women, this behavior is a self-conscious signal and involves the crossing of a single arm across the midsection of the body. Women typically display this behavior in social settings, where they know few people or are feeling threatened or insecure. This is common among new students in schools during the first several weeks of class. As the females in groups begin to socially connect with others, the arm-wrap behavior begins to diminish respectively.

FREEZE—54

When the cognitive system in a subject becomes loaded with scenario management and behavior regulation during deception, the movement of the body sometimes comes to a near halt. The amount of mental energy exerted to manage the deception leaves little room for authentic gesture management. The exception here is the facial expression of fear, in which the reticular-activating system in the brain overrides movement to focus on more-important things, such as threats to safety (Vrij, 2001; Beattie, 2003).

FACIAL TOUCHING—55

Perhaps no other gesture has gained so much notoriety for being deceptive as the facial touch. Touching the face, as noted in several behavioral studies (Vrij, 2001; Morris, 1979; Navarro J., 2011), has been shown to be the most common behavior displayed in study subjects during deliberate deception. As with all elements, the facial touch is no more important than others. In study settings, the gesture may become more prevalent, which may be attributed to a lack an interrogation scenario. Decreased stress levels that cause no leakages elsewhere on subjects' bodies, or the overall "safety" of knowing that a study is being conducted, caused participants to relax more than if they were lying about a more important legal matter.

Throat Clasping—56

Clasping the throat is nearly identical to facial touching, with the small difference that this gesture is associated with fear and grave consequences. Though an operator may assume that a subject is feeling all of the associated meanings of facial touching, this gesture is specifically related to fear.

Arms in Air—57

The visible comfort displayed when the arms rise during a Sunday football touchdown is a great example of this behavior. Comfortable subjects have no problem exposing their underarms or moving their arms where they feel comfortable with fluidity. This demonstrates comfort, elation, and excitement. Subjects using this while telling stories are demonstrating a high level of comfort with the operators and those involved in the conversation.

Figure-Four Leg Cross—58

This seemingly American body movement is associated with comfort, relaxation, and trust. The crossing of one ankle over the other knee is frequently seen around the world as the sociogestural tolerance spreads. Owing to the exposure of the sole of the foot, this movement is not acceptable in many countries throughout the Arab world and most of Asia.

Listed here as 90Kc, this conflicting gesture (whether in a figure-four position or traditionally crossed) communicates apprehensiveness and a desire to end the conversation.

Pelvic Tilt—59

When a subject is being observed, this variable movement should become visible almost immediately. It is often overlooked, but it can provide crucial information to smart observers. This is primarily an observation that should be made while a subject is standing but can be made if the subject is in a seated position as well, if the pelvic tilt is visible.

The pelvis can tilt forward and backward. The forward motion of the pelvis arches the lower back and pushes the groin to the rear. The backward motion of the pelvis brings the groin forward and rounds the lower back.

The forward-rotated pelvis is seen in confident subjects, especially when they experience situation-related emotional confidence.

The backward-rotated pelvis indicates a lack of confidence and the associated emotions.

Facing—60

When subjects are standing, their pelvises often follow the objects of their mental focus, even when their upper bodies are not facing the direction where they are paying the most attention.

Variations:

Facing away from interviewer: Ff1

Facing interviewer: Ff2

Hands in Pockets—61

Subjects sometimes place their hands into their clothing pockets or sit in this position, and this movement or posturing provides vital clues to their internal thoughts. There are three variations in this behavior set:

Hands in pockets with thumbs inside pockets: Po1. This indicates a lack of confidence, uncertainty, and willingness to show deference.

Hands in pockets with thumbs protruding or thumbs in pockets with fingers out: Po2. This indicates situational confidence and (in certain contexts) sexual availability.

Hands in pockets with only fingertips inserted into opening: Po3. This indicates readiness or reservation or both, depending on the context.

Chest Touching—62

The touching of the chest is a behavior commonly seen in movies and made by women while they receive bad information from a sheriff. This is an unsure and nervous gesture performed in response to stressful or anxiety-producing stimuli.

Double-Leg Cross—63

The double-leg cross is quite different in meaning from a figure-four cross or a traditional cross at the knees. The double cross is when the legs are crossed in the traditional over-the-knee manner and when the foot crosses once more around the lowest leg. This is a very distinct gesture that indicates withholding and probable concealment.

Tapping—64

Tapping fingers on a table has multiple meanings. It is contextually dependent and can indicate boredom, inner thought, nervousness, and tension release. There is no specific tapping movement that indicates one or the other. Context must be taken into account before making a judgment on the scenario or scoring an interrogation.

FIDGETING—65

While this gesture can be performed by subjects with or without an object, it typically involves the seemingly nonproductive movement of hands and is not intended to accomplish a specific task. The farther a body part is from the head, the harder it is to control during times of anxiety and stress. The accumulation of nervous energy and the buildup of adrenaline cause the body to need to "burn off" the excess by making small muscular movements in the extremities.

TWO-HANDED GRASPING—66

In this behavior, a subject grasps an object with both hands. It can be a thigh, a leg, an object, a piece of clothing, or any other object. This is a closed gesture but may be displayed during anxiety, indicating a need for reassurance and control. Women who are untrusting or overly cautious about their environments do this to their purses.

HANDS ON BACK OF THE NECK—67

The hands draw rearward to the back of the neck on occasions that present the subject with stress, anxiety, or deep, contemplative thinking.

LINT PICKING—68

This self-conscious behavior manifests in the form of picking lint (real or imaginary) from clothing or nearby objects. This behavior shows nervous energy and insecurity. A person in an uncomfortable lull in a conversation may pick at his or her clothing to do something "productive" as an excuse for not talking.

WRIST TO FOREHEAD—69

This behavior is identical to the ventilation gestures because it communicates a need to pacify stress or a need to reduce internal conflicts or anxiety. Subjects use this behavior to calm themselves when the need for self-assurance arises.

Barrier Gesture—70

This behavior is somewhat difficult to pin down in a social context. The arms move in various directions throughout a conversation, but the barrier gesture is a behavior that specifically involves an arm coming in a direct line between the interviewer and the subject. This is a subtle and mostly unconscious gesture that sometimes occurs in fragmentally significant increments. Subjects use this behavior to feel more secure and protected in environments or social contexts that cause them to feel slightly threatened or insecure.

Barrier Cross—71

This differs from the figure-four cross and the traditional crossings of the legs. In this position, legs are mostly pointed toward the interviewers and are crossed with the calf muscles placed over the knee. This is a closed gesture, and where other leg-crossing gestures indicate comfort and relaxation, the barrier cross indicates a withholding or concealment of something. This may also be nervous tension associated with the appearance of the interviewer or being interviewed.

Palms Down—72

This occurs for various reasons and indicates a lack of willingness to be transparent, honest, and forthcoming in an interview. It is a lack of a subject's willingness to show his or her hand, so to speak. During interviews, this is typically seen when subjects become threatened or operators begin to expose flaws in subjects' statements. In social scenarios, this may be as harmless as a subject disagreeing with the operator but not wishing to voice his or her opinions. Subjects who are withholding information perform this while listening to questions before they speak.

GENITAL PROTECTING—73

This behavior is unconscious and indicates subjects' immediate needs to protect themselves when verbal, physical, or psychological threats are presented to them. Imagine a man who isn't keen on public speaking, on standing on a stage while being introduced to a large crowd. The need to cover the genitals is innate in most men and occurs when subjects are feeling vulnerable, threatened, or otherwise insecure.

HUSHING—74

Barbara and Allan Pease (2006) coined this behavior term. Subjects' bringing their hands to their faces or their performing any behaviors that cover their mouths, are considered to be hushing gestures in the BToE. Hushing occurs when subjects become nervous or self-conscious about what they are saying or thinking. Three normal variations exist for this behavior:

Hushing by covering mouth to cough: Hu1
Hushing by covering lips with fingers: Hu2
Hushing by scratching the nose: Hu3

GROIN EXPOSURE—75

When subjects open or part their legs toward interviewers, they are showing trust, vulnerability, honesty, and a willingness to communicate the truth.

LEG CROSSING—76

This behavior is when legs are crossed in the traditional way: one knee is crossed over the other, and the legs remain mostly together. This indicates of trust and comfort. Subjects typically cross their legs toward the people they trust in a social scene when first sitting down (Scheflen, 1976; Pease, 2006).

Though this gesture is important to note while in an interview, its opposite is of even more value: legs being uncrossed indicates the opposite of the meaning above.

Toes Up—77

This is an antigravity gesture frequently seen with arms-in-air gestures, usually representing relief, celebratory, and exclamatory gestures. The toes-up gesture indicates elatedness and happiness. This occurs when the toes of a subject's shoes are lifted off the ground slightly by the toes. The common rise of the feet is one inch or less.

Breathing Rate—78

Subjects' breathing rates fluctuate during interviews. The average breathing rate is twelve to twenty breaths per minute for a healthy adult. Breathing rates typically increase in relation to the amounts of stress subjects experience.

Torso Facing—79

While this sounds much like the previous behavior of twisting torso, it refers specifically to the direct frontal or away facing of the torso. For instance, the torso is pointed slightly away from the interviewer at the beginning of a question group, and the question causes the subject to immediately face his or her full body toward the interviewer while either answering or listening to the question. Conversely, the complete opposite is the second variation, where the torso is turned completely away from the interviewer.

Facing torso at interviewer: FcT

Facing torso away from interviewer: FcA

Postural Tilt—80

Within any social encounter, especially one involving only two parties, the tilt of the torso toward and away from one another is a constant and revealing behavior from both people about their thoughts. A person's leaning toward another person expresses interest in the second individual. When two people lean toward each other, they are communicating mutual interest. When one leans in and the other leans back, the person leaning back is showing his or her lack of interest, comfort, higher status, or trust.

Posture leaning toward: PtT

Posture leaning away: PtA

KNEE HUGGING—81

This is a rare occurrence in interviews, but this is when subjects, in seated positions, wrap their arms around their legs, which are pulled up to their chests. Knees have been considered to be an imaginary person that subjects can hug when real people are unavailable, thereby pacifying anxiety or stress (Morris, 1970; Morris, 1998; Morris, 1979).

DIGITAL FLEXION—82

The flexion (drawing-in) of the fingers toward the palm is a fantastic in-the-moment barometer of the anxiety of the subject in that specific moment. Noticing a small movement of the fingers in an interview can produce a lot of information when paired with the associated verbal and emotional content within the question group. The farther the fingers draw into the palm, the more momentary anxiety the subject is feeling.

BINDING LEGS—83

This occurs when the legs come together and show no relaxation. This behavior frequently brings the feet together to touch. This is associated with secretiveness, fear, anxiety, worry, and mistrust.

LOCKED ANKLE—84

This occurs usually when the ankles are locked under a chair. Subjects who are unwilling to provide a lot of information or are withholding or concealing something do this. It is best to deliberately modify this behavior by asking subjects to stand or move in a way that causes their ankles to unlock.

GROOMING GESTURES—85

Any behavior conducted to improve physical appearance or visual presentation is a grooming behavior.

These behaviors exhibit themselves in various forms, and they are relevant to a degree when connected to the stimuli that caused them. Subjects' upbringing can increase or decrease the frequency of these gestures; subjects with upbringings that favored neat appearances revert to grooming behaviors during times of anxiety.

CLASPING THE THIGHS—86

While clasping the thighs is more prevalent in women, men also do it. This autocontact behavior is commonly displayed during physical attraction and sexual arousal. Women do this in a similar way to a pacifying behavior, in that the hands take the place of another person, and instead of soothing them, they are caressing themselves.

In interviews, subjects perform this behavior to control themselves and to minimize the amount of stress they feel. While it isn't a pacifying behavior, it serves a similar purpose. Imagine the thigh clasp as another (imaginary) person inside the subject inflicting slight discomfort to prevent the release of information or deceptive behavior.

WRIST TOUCHING—87

Wrist touching is another form of autocontact behavior. It is listed as a closed gesture because of its barrier-creating properties and its meaning in social contexts. This behavior is used as a barrier and comforting movement, and it gives subjects a sense of protection and security when they experience social pressure, nervousness, or anxiety. Wrist touching is often seen in men in public in the form of reaching across and using one hand to adjust the wristwatch or shirt cuff of the other hand. Performing this same behavior to pop knuckles, rub hands, adjust a sleeve, or any other similar action is considered 87Wt. The second variation is when a subject physically grasps the wrist of his or her opposite hand. This is an anger-related and self-restraining behavior that sends a completely different signal (hence the red lettering).

Adjusting: Wt1

Grabbing: Wt2

Inward Toe Pointing—88

This happens slightly more often in women than in men, and it indicates self-consciousness and, when paired with barrier behaviors, indicates concealment, mistrust, or withholding. People's toes point inward when they feel insecure or when they wish to occupy less space. What's more, this behavior offers some protection to the genitals and can be read as a response to threatening scenarios or social environments.

Eyelid Rubbing—89

This is another hand-to-face gesture that shows signs of concern in addition to the stress immediately identified by the hand-to-face gesture. Eyelid rubbing is mostly performed by men and indicates the need to stop thinking of something or to end a train of thought.

Knee Clasp—90

Knee clasping reveals an inner desire to leave or end a conversation. This movement takes place only in seated positions. In this gesture, subjects (usually with both hands) take hold of their knees, and a long breath inhalation usually follows the movement.

Foot Withdrawal—91
Occurring in seated positions, this movement is the sudden withdrawal of the feet during a conversation. The feet withdraw underneath a chair (Navarro J., 2011). This movement indicates the sudden and immediate need to withhold something, such as a subject's sudden loss of trust for the interviewer or self-consciousness.

Finger to Nose—92
This variation of a hushing gesture has the added meaning of concealing the instinct to cover the mouth. This is a high-rated behavior because it is one of the most deceptive in all of nonverbal deception research (Wolfe, 1948; Pease, 2006; Morris, 1979). While this behavior by itself does not score high enough on the scale to be qualified as deceptive, when it is seen in interviews, it is almost always accompanied by a similarly rated gesture.

Interaction with Others' Property—93
Subjects who want to physically interact with the property belonging to unfamiliar people reflects the subjects' comfort levels, sometimes indicating the presence of contempt for those around the subjects. Typically, subjects handle others' property in the same manner they feel toward the people. If subjects are careless with others' property, they are not likely fond of those people. For the BToE observations, we only note any willingness to interact with other people's property, if it is present and accessible to the subject.

Voluntary interaction with belongings: Opi

Unwilling to interact, even when presented the opportunity to do so: –Opi

Object Interaction—94

The ways subjects interact with objects and furniture are highly accurate indicators of their comfort and confidence levels. Subjects' willingness to touch objects or move chairs to suit their comfort level shows how willing they are to take charge of their environment. Subjects wishing to put on the best show of deception of their lives do everything possible not to disturb their environments. This in itself is not deceptive, because the guilty and innocent always show different baselines of confidence and comfort.

Shoe Removal—95

The willingness to display the removal of footwear, the partial removal of footwear, or the unconscious fidgeting with footwear are signs of comfort, confidence, and trust. Shoe removal occurs in numerous ways and should be interpreted as a sign of subjects' comfort and trust when seen.

Belonging Carelessness—96

This behavior refers to subjects' carelessness with their property. Whether conscious or unconscious, displays of carelessness communicate a careless attitude and an aloof nature, and remote dispositions do not augment interviews. This behavior manifests in various ways: tossing a purse onto a seat, yanking a chair out to sit, throwing a jacket onto a chair back, or throwing a phone, keys, or objects onto a table.

Watch Checking—97

This behavior is commonly understood and easily spotted by novice interviewers. Pay particular attention to whether the checking of the watch involves two hands and whether the opposing hand creates an unusual amount of tension while holding the watch for the subject to view it.

Jacket Buttoning—98

This is more common in males because of the type of clothing men regularly wear. The buttoning of a jacket usually indicates a stopping point in trust, withholding, and anxiety. Temperature heavily affects jacket buttoning.

Clothing Covering—99

In clothing covering, clothes are pulled or adjusted to improve the coverage of the body. For example, women may pull their shirts down to cover themselves, lift their sleeves to decrease breast exposure, or pull on their sleeves to better cover their wrists. Temperature affects this behavior.

Object Barrier—100

This movement involves covering the body with any object. Walking to school holding books across one's chest, holding a drink at a bar in front of the body, using a book or clipboard as a barrier on a table by raising it, and putting objects (even cups) between subjects and interviewers—all examples of this behavior. It indicates insecurity, a need for protection, and sometimes a subject with withdrawn social behaviors.

Chair Arms—101

This involves the wrapping of the hands around the arms of a chair. This is a sign of self-restraint and can indicate that information is being withheld. Make note of the pressure with which subjects grasp the arms of chairs and whether one hand is tighter, showing more capillary withdrawal than the other. Discerning the meaning of this behavior without associated behaviors is almost impossible.

GROIN SHIELD—102

This is a barrier gesture, but it differs from object-barrier behaviors in that the same behaviors are made to cover the genital areas. This carries the same meaning as groin shielding: the behavior is unconscious and indicates subjects' immediate need to protect themselves when a verbal, physical, or psychological threat is present.

PERSONAL BELONGING SECURITY CHECK—103

This occurs when subjects visually or physically interact with objects belonging to them to check the objects' safety, presence, or exact location. Security checks strongly indicate the presence of mistrust, nervousness, and insecurity. This behavior occurs in common ways in interviews; for example, female subjects unconsciously grab their purses and pull them closer to themselves without looking. Other common examples include men's reaching back to check on their wallets, their pulling their phones on tables closer to them, and their patting shirt pockets to ensure that valuable objects are still there.

FISTS ON TABLE—104

This highly aggressive behavior is actually shown equally in both deceptive and genuine people. Discerning the difference between deceptive and honest subjects exhibiting this behavior must be done in real time, while watching for associated behaviors and ensuring the timing coincides with the behavior. Honest behaviors happen simultaneously, and deceptive behaviors tend to happen microseconds apart from each other, as they all have to come from different parts of the brain instead of one.

OBJECT CONCEALMENT—105

This behavior is when subjects conceal something from view or attempt to do so. Subjects, when approached, may tilt their phones' screens away, close an open purse, or unconsciously draw their hands over a phone screen. Object concealment is also seen when subjects hold their phones at the sides of their bodies, unconsciously angling their phones away from the interviewers. This behavior indicates a desire to conceal information not actually contained on a subject's phone or similar objects—that is, such objects are functioning as surrogates for the actual information being withheld.

JEWELRY PLAY—106

The jewelry most people wear is closely associated with identity and self-image (Vrij, 2001; Pease, 2006). Playing or fiddling with jewelry is a way some subjects pacify themselves during social stress or anxiety. This is frequently seen in women who play with or reach up to grasp their necklaces or bracelets.

FEET AROUND CHAIR LEGS—107

When subjects wrap their ankles around the legs of chairs, as if to stay put should someone try to pull them upward, the behavior is marked as Cl. This behavior is a self-restraint gesture and mainly indicates the withholding of information and unwillingness to openly participate in conversation. This is an underresearched behavior but has been seen more commonly in young adults during interview scenarios.

VOCAL HESITANCY—108

The hesitancy seen before an answer is usually a time gap; this pause allows subjects to process their stories in their minds to ensure their stories' success, before they answer out loud. This occurs in only one way: subjects display a distinct pause prior to answering questions or making statements.

Psychological Distancing—109

This occurs when a subject euphemizes the crime or offense in question and replaces it with a less-severe word. Examples include using *hurt* instead of *kill*, *take* instead of *steal*, *relations* instead of *sex*, and *touch* instead of *molest*. This is a very common deception tactic employed by the subconscious to lessen the guilt experienced in the presence of interviewers. It is a psychological way of reducing the amount of nonverbal stress that shows in the body during interviews.

Rising Vocal Pitch—110

The stress of deceiving an interviewer and the anxiety caused by fear of failure with high stakes cause the muscles used in vocal production to tighten and raise the natural pitch of the voice during testimony and conversation. This is measured only as a deviation. If this is a baseline element, it must not be recorded as a 4.0-coded behavior.

Increase in Vocal Speed—111

This observation requires interviewers or analysts to establish vocal baselines, to note the cadences with which subjects speak. In an attempt to "get it over with," subjects frequently speed up the rate of speech to lessen the amount of psychological stress experienced and exude less nonverbal signs of deception during the deceptive statement.

Nonanswer Statement—112

This occurs when a subject replies to a question with a lengthy response that does not answer the question. Any reply to a question that doesn't answer the question is considered a nonanswer statement. For example, if an interviewer asks whether the subject went to a liquor store on the previous night, the subject might respond by saying, "I don't even drink."

Pronoun Absence—113

Deceptive statements sometimes lack pronouns because of the load placed on the cognitive faculties during deception. An example of this is a subject, after being asked to recount events, saying the following: "Well, woke up around two, went to the ATM at the gas station, left the bar around two in the morning, and got back to the house around two thirty." You will see the absence of pronouns come up more regularly in conversations if you begin to listen more to regular, daily conversations you have with others.

Résumé Statements—114

This verbal expression is commonly used as an answer to an allegation or a question involving the suspicion of wrongdoing. Subjects may express themselves to the interviewer by talking about all the reasons that they aren't capable of the act, the volunteer work they do, where they went to school, or their positions within a community. After being questioned about a theft, a subject may reply, "I am a well-respected member of this community, and I volunteer at the church. My wife and I both give our time to help the homeless, and our neighbors will tell you the same thing." This statement doesn't answer the question, and the subject is attempting to manage the way the interviewer sees him or her by listing good qualities and civic involvement.

Noncontracting Statement—115

When subjects deny or reject an accusation, to make the statement easier to believe, they may decline to use contractions, using *did not* instead of *didn't* and *could not* instead of *couldn't*. By doing so, subjects feel they are communicating more clearly to the interviewers. What's more, noncontracting statements are made on a subconscious level. In essence, subjects' subconscious minds are doing their best to remove ambiguous forms of communication to make statements sound more matter-of-fact.

QUESTION REVERSAL—116

This is an aggressive reversal of questioning by the subject. When asked a question, subjects may respond by asking questions that imply guilt lies in the interviewers or that attack the motives of the interviewers for having asked the main questions.

AMBIGUITY STATEMENTS—117

This occurs when subjects answer questions by providing vague statements about the relevant incidents or by vaguely recounting the pertinent events.

POLITENESS—118

This behavior specifically involves a shift in politeness level within the conversation. When a subject frequently answers questions with "yeah," "yep," and "mm-hmm" then follows other questions with a sudden "yes, sir" or "no, sir, I didn't," the subject is shifting in the level of politeness from the subject's typical behavior. The presence of politeness alone does not warrant the rating of 118Pol in analyses.

OVERAPOLOGIZING—119

When subjects continually apologize for things that occur during interviews, such as their not being able to provide more information, their lacking adequate detail, or their not having what they think the interviewers are looking for, the act is a subconscious apology for other things that need to be uncovered. The sudden presence of apologies in conversations is very much a red flag, regardless of their associated reasons.

MINICONFESSIONS—120

These take place in the form of confessions that aren't about the events for which subjects are being questioned. In these subjects' minds, if they confess to a few small things, they will appear to be more open and honest, encouraging the interviewers either to eventually trust them or to forget to ask them the bigger questions. Miniconfessions often seem to be genuine confessions of small and insignificant wrongdoings.

EXCLUSIONS—121

Words that seem to answer questions but deliberately exclude information are exclusions, which are polite ways of withholding information from interviewers. Examples include the following phrases: "as far as I know," "to the best of my knowledge," "basically," "probably," and "I suppose."

DIRECT CHRONOLOGY—122

This behavior is difficult to spot because interviewers have the potential to inadvertently trigger it, therefore making the behavior void and unrecordable. When subjects recount stories or chains of events in perfect chronological order, this is a 122Chr. Emotional stories are often jumbled, and the subjects almost always start with the most traumatic parts of such stories. However, if interviewers directly ask subjects to recount events in the order they occurred, the chronology of subjects' statements are basically irrelevant.

51.523772 -0.158538

Section II

• • •

ESTABLISHING AND MAINTAINING CONTROL OF THOUGHT,
BEHAVIOR, AND EMOTION

IN SECTION II, YOU WILL learn to take your profiling and people-reading skills (which are now above the level of an FBI interrogator) and apply them in tandem with the most advanced psychological-control techniques in the world. Understanding how to spot weakness, needs, fears, and insecurities is the first building block of this section. All other techniques are based on a vector determined by the information you gather about your subjects. After learning about the human social-profiling methods, you will be given the master key to the human mind—the "weaponized" part of this program.

Imagine your subjects standing at the wheels of their own large ships. The steering wheel is in their hands, their ships seeming to move just as they want them to. In reality, you actually have control of the rudders, *not* the wheel. The wheel only provides the semblance of control to your subjects; you control the movement. In such cases, you will rarely get credit for making behavioral changes, and your subjects will assign responsibility for their actions to themselves.

Human Needs and Profiling

● ● ●

BECOMING FLUENT IN BODY LANGUAGE is only the start of your training in human-behavior analysis. The behavioral table of elements provides meanings of gestures and behaviors, while the map of humans needs and the chart of human weaknesses provide detailed information about the human qualities that allow the largest door to be opened into the human mind. The seventeen needs on the map are like seventeen small loopholes that allow access into the private areas of the human mind when used correctly. The problem is, not all humans have the same loopholes or needs.

In this section, we decided that the outdated version of the map of human needs should be kept in the book. The revised version will immediately follow.

The human needs you will learn about are the following:

* Appreciation
* Approval
* Acceptance
* Protection
* Freedom
* Strength
* Respect
* Intelligence

* Pleasure
* Comfort
* Privacy
* Pity
* Caretaker
* Attractiveness
* Uniqueness
* Admiration
* Success

The map of human needs is a designed map created specifically to aid your memory and training. Your recall of the human needs will be easier in the field if you learn to visualize yourself inside the "house" on the map.

The chart of human weaknesses is designed to allow quick access to the psychological leverage that can be applied to a subject to allow more behavioral plasticity. While the techniques you will learn are almost universally applicable to all subjects, they are sharpened and exponentially more effective when applied through needs and weaknesses. The techniques reach a much stronger level of sophistication and personalization when used with the needs and weakness aids.

HUMAN NEEDS MAP©

Using the Human Needs Map

The map of human needs is designed to be memorized by operators. It is one of the most valuable tools you will have when operating on subjects; what's more, it will be powerful in regular social settings because it will show you the humanity and frailty of the people with whom you'll interact—especially those who would otherwise be intimidating. In the appendix, you will find a full-page copy that can be removed and placed into your journal or training folder for reference.

As you begin to commit the map to memory, start to imagine yourself actually *in* the house while looking at the different needs. For example, while looking at the caretaker need, imagine being inside that kitchen and seeing the stove, table, and the sink around you. Also, make mental notes of the red needs closest to you as you stand in this kitchen.

The needs on the map are laid out in a way that shows similar-minded people are likely to be in the same or nearby rooms. A person who needs to feel attractive will likely seek friendship from people who are in the adjacent bedroom. The closest red shaded need is likely this person's most fundamental need.

Fundamental needs (in red) are the foundational needs of all social human beings. When you're able to place people on the needs map by using the profiling training that follows, the closest red needs to their needs are their fundamental needs. The weaknesses associated with their needs and corresponding fundamental needs are on the weakness chart.

At first glance, the map seems simple. While simply designed and easy to learn, it is the most powerful tool that can access the needs of your subjects when used with profiling information. The needs on the map aren't direct needs in themselves; some of them are a need to be *perceived* or *seen* a certain way by others.

The Needs
Appreciation
The need for appreciation is a fundamental need. Subjects with this need tend to exhibit behaviors that benefit others, improve others' environments, or enhance the well being of those around them. This need to feel appreciated drives their behaviors, without their knowledge, to seek appreciation from people around them. Something as small as a compliment or a thank-you is enough to fuel their need temporarily. They also respond well to comments about how much they improve the lives of others; such comments create positive and more-relaxed mental states in them.

APPROVAL

We all seek approval on different levels. For subjects to be in this room on the map, however, their behavior and needs must be stronger than normal. Subjects with this need perform several acts to seek approval from others. They change their positions to get approval when someone disapproves of their views. They typically ask permission to do things when it is not needed and sometimes coax or coerce people into giving them compliments to feel good. They are less likely to complain when they receive bad service at an establishment and pay insincere compliments to those around them to gain approval from them. Their language patterns contain unnecessary apologies such as "I'm sorry, but…" You will also see these subjects' reluctance to admit they don't know about a topic when they are pressured or feel unaccepted. They typically act as though they know more than they do about something. These subjects respond strongly to disapproving or indifferent attitudes of authority and work harder to gain approval from this behavior.

ACCEPTANCE

The behaviors exhibited by subjects who need acceptance are very similar to the behaviors of those seeking approval. The difference is revealed in subjects' willingness to change their behaviors, speech, mannerisms, and dress to be accepted by a group or culture. The behaviors of approval-needing subjects are similar, but instead of seeking a social thumbs-up from a person, acceptance-driven subjects typically focus their efforts on a community or group of people whom they would like to either belong to or become accepted by.

PROTECTION

The subjects with this need are in need of feeling protected. Actual protection may or may not be what they truly desire, but the feeling of being guarded against a threat is their biggest concern. These subjects have extra locks on the doors, look around before using ATMs, carry defensive weapons, have long and confusing Wi-Fi passwords, and can be easily persuaded by anyone offering them information or goods to increase their personal level of protection.

FREEDOM

People who need freedom want to feel free. These subjects make decisions that empower them and champion ideas and interests that empower people to make their own choices. These subjects may bend the rules in traffic while other people are waiting in their lanes, may feel that almost all rules are excessive, and may behave rashly when constrained or given too many regulations to govern their behavior.

STRENGTH

This is a need to be seen as strong and to feel strong. These subjects typically seek confirmation of their strength from anyone they interact with. They talk about their strength and typically have clothing, stickers, and objects on their persons that show others that they are strong. This need is driven mostly by a fear of harm and an internal fear of being dominated or publicly exposed as weak and insignificant. Any offering of information to enhance their social standings and images of physical or personal strength will open doors no one else has access to.

RESPECT

The need to feel respected by others derives from a fear of being disrespected publicly. This need, when it's a driving need, is usually formed in the early years of life and governs and colors almost all of a subject's choices. These people will go out of their way to ensure they feel respected by others. They exhibit behavior that is domineering, controlling, or posturing in social settings and typically talk about accomplishments and achievements in public forums.

INTELLIGENCE

This is a need to be seen as intelligent. These subjects collect books and keep them on display in their homes. A need to feel that others see them as intelligent drives their behaviors to show others how smart they are and to seek verbal confirmation of their intellectual prowess from those they interact with. Subjects with this need typically use large words followed by a short pause to see whether you will ask what they mean or to witness your facial expression when you don't understand them. They are very eager to demonstrate their knowledge when asked about subjects they are most familiar with. You should notice a visible change in their demeanors and facial expressions when you elicit information about topics with which they are familiar.

PLEASURE

The pleasure and comfort needs are very similar. Subjects with both needs place personal enjoyment over other "lower" priorities in their lives. The difference between them is that the subjects with pleasure needs seek pleasure openly and are more prone to want to enjoy themselves in large crowds, in public places, and in the company of many members of their social circles. These subjects display behaviors and make choices that are typically short sighted, and place personal satisfaction and enjoyment over responsibilities in their lives.

COMFORT

Subjects with comfort needs show this desire in many ways, such as in their choices of vehicles, clothing, movement speeds, speaking styles, and personal products. Their vehicles have added features for comfort, and their homes are likely to have numerous items designed to aid their enjoyment of a relaxed lifestyle. These subjects also usually exhibit behaviors that are highly social when discussing their preferences and giving advice on life.

PRIVACY

This is a need to be seen as a private person. Whether or not subjects are completely private people, you will see behaviors aimed at communicating their needs for privacy and their abilities to manage themselves. Subjects needing privacy have paper shredders in their homes, always hide valuable objects when parking their cars, and typically glance over their shoulders when typing their PINs into machines for their purchases. This need, when validated by others, can produce a wealth of personal information and open up an otherwise closed-off subject quickly.

PITY

These subjects want attention. You will hear them telling stories of their misfortunes, their bad luck, and how they have been victimized by people and organizations. When in conversation, these subjects show their need by replying to your comments with "related" stories of how they had it worse than you did or have otherwise not had the opportunity to enjoy such a lavish and perfect life as you have. These subjects are usually quiet and reserved, often waiting for someone to ask them about their plights or for someone to offer condolences for how poorly they have been treated by the world. If you offer any sort of advice or guidance to subjects when they are in this frame of mind, they will likely try to retract or break rapport. You need to be bring them out of this frame of mind by applying more-elegant linguistic solutions, which are explained in the following chapters. The solution to opening most pity-need subjects is to confirm their statuses as victims and to offer condolences for their bad luck.

CARETAKER

This is the need to be seen as the go-to person for enjoyment and comfort. These subjects exhibit behaviors of taking care of others. They carry extra items in their purses for those in need on the go, keep the back seats of cars cleaned, cook often for others, and always ask others about their days. Caretakers also need to be seen by others as a source of inspiration and livelihood. They talk to others in an inspirational way and keep updated on social information to update others with the latest news around town.

ATTRACTIVENESS

Being seen as attractive is something we all desire. On the needs map, however, attractiveness must be a driving force in subjects' decision-making processes. Subjects with this need ignore responsibilities and long-term hazards for the short-term gain of looking good. Their needs are only fulfilled (temporarily) if they are validated and confirmed by other people making advances on them or complimenting their appearances. Their behaviors, too, also reflect this need by the confirmation-seeking actions that tie into the need for approval. The attractiveness need and the approval need are closely related, and both types of subjects can be mentally accessed using the same set of techniques. When others confirm their attractiveness, they lower their defenses and open up. Some of those with this need are the opposite, however: they seek confirmation desperately when it is not given freely to them.

UNIQUENESS

This is a need to be seen as unique. These subjects go out of their way to purchase items and clothing that deliberately set them apart from the current trends and fads. They typically change their desires and focuses regularly to become or embrace the newest thing they've found to set themselves apart. Nothing works quite as well to access their minds as confirming how unique, interesting, and practical they are. For these subjects, seeing other people mimic or copy their styles or choices is the ultimate form of needs fulfillment. These subjects often go to seemingly extreme lengths to stand out from the crowd.

ADMIRATION

Admiration-seeking subjects are usually very open about their victories, strategies, successes, and achievements. They are driven to purchase products and services that increase their status levels (in their minds) and cause people to look up to them (in their minds). Success- and admiration-needing subjects are similar; they both seek attention and typically make purchases to confirm their sense of status. The difference lies in the personal level of satisfaction. Admiration subjects allow control when they feel admired and appreciated. Nothing opens their barriers more than a genuine compliment or someone acknowledging their behavior as being admired and looked up to.

SUCCESS

Subjects who need success focus their activities or behavior on showing themselves that they have achieved something great. They are motivated and driven by their definitions of success and are less prone to seek confirmation outside themselves for their sense of status. They have a need to be admired like the admiration-seeking subjects but differ in a certain way: their self-admiration comes from reaching a level that they admire and view as successful. They sometimes compromise their values to feel as if they were staying ahead of others in their peer groups and social circles.

THE UPDATED NEEDS MAP

Appreciation	Primary	These subjects will exhibit behaviors that tend to benefit others, improve other's environments or enhance the well-being of those around them. This need to feel appreciated will drive their behaviors without their knowledge to seek appreciation from people around them.
Acceptance	Primary	The difference between these subjects and appreciation-seekers is in the subject's willingness to change their behavior, speech, mannerisms and dress to be accepted by a group or culture.
Approval	Primary	These subjects will perform several acts in order to seek approval from others. They will change their position in order to get approval when someone disapproves of their views. They will typically ask permission to do things when it is not needed and will sometimes coax or coerce people into giving them compliments in order to feel good.
Intelligence	Secondary	Subject has a need to be seen as intelligent and will exhibit behaviors that elude to education, facts and academic achievements.
Pity	Secondary	Pity-seeking subjects will discuss pitfalls, tragedies and misfortunes in hopes of gaining sympathy and support.

| Admiration | Secondary | Subjects will behave in ways to harvest envy from others with their property, achievements and life circumstances. |
| Power | Secondary | Power-seeking subjects don't need power. They have a need to FEEL powerful, and for others to SEE them as such. |

In 2015, the needs map was updated and replaced with the one seen here. It contains only the most critical information. Students expressed a desire to use the older version so frequently that we decided to leave it in the manual and let you decide which to use.

Every conversation you will ever have will expose some forms of your subjects' needs, whether through nonverbal means or language. Using the needs in behavior engineering and constantly being on the lookout for need-profiling opportunities are usually what make the difference between successful and unsuccessful operators. While this map is only a brief stop in the manual, it is vitally important, but it is typically a point of failure when it's ignored.

Try using this as soon as you can, utilizing online videos of interviews and conversations in movies and television. The learning curve is steep for needs identification and most students can use it fluently within a few days. Next, examine the social weakness profiling chart and see how many correlations you can find within the conversations you used to train on the Needs Map.

Profiling Social Weakness

Social Weakness Chart		
Timidity	**Assertive**	**Aggressive**
Verbal/vocal		
Soft spoken	Confident tone	Forcibly loud
Frequent pauses	Even, fluent speech	Attention-seeking behavior
Filler words	Declarative speech	Profanity
Rapid speech	Downward-inflected statements	Flat tone socially
Interrogative tone		
Confirmation-seeking language		
Gestural and behavioral		
Limited eye contact	Comfortable physical contact	Glaring/staring
Tense facial muscles	Relaxed, straight posture	Exaggerated posture
Fear expressions	Open hands	Tense jaw
Fidgeting	Slower movements	Chin thrusting
Hands fully in pockets	Comfortable pausing	Impassive
Nervous gestures		Closed hands
Frequent facial contact		Rigidity
Shifting weight or touching chest when beginning to speak		Personal-space invasion
Downcast head		Orbital tension
Rapid head turn when name called		
Raised shoulders		
Feet together/toes inward		

The chart of social weaknesses provides operators with a quick reference to establish nonverbal profiles for subjects and to place them in the appropriate social-behavior categories. The chart is simply a rule of thumb and should be used only in situations where time is critical and an opportunity to form a complete social profile is unavailable. Understanding the locations on the chart allows operators to determine where interactions need to be guided to control the outcomes.

Human Weaknesses Associated with Needs		
	Needs	Fears	Weaknesses
1	Appreciation	Abandonment	Rejection and loss
2	Approval	Dissent	Approval creates windows for change
3	Acceptance	Ridicule of ego	Willingness to shift values to blend in
4	Protection	Weakness	Will sacrifice personal resources to feel protected
5	Freedom	Imprisonment	Loss of autonomy
6	Strength	Social weakness	Social or authoritative confirmation of strength
7	Respect	Ego death	Social or authoritative confirmation of respect
8	Intelligence	Dismissal	Confirmation and compliments on intellectual abilities
9	Pleasure	Loss	Will go out of their way to avoid discomfort
10	Comfort	Drastic change	Avoidance of change and conflict
11	Privacy	Loss of privacy	Willing to sacrifice and comply, to remain undisturbed
12	Pity	Social ridicule	Will completely allow control once pity is confirmed and nurtured
13	Caretaker	Loss of loved ones	Allows control when seen as an unmatched provider
14	Attractiveness	Disfigurement	Becomes off balance and easily influenced when attractiveness is not confirmed by others
15	Uniqueness	Dismissal	Will go to extreme lengths to stand out
16	Admiration	Contempt	Allows control when they feel admired and appreciated
17	Success	Failure	Compromises personal values to stay ahead of others

PROFILING SOCIAL STABILITY FOR INFLUENCE

The Hughes social-stability scale is a reference that helps operators comprehend the basic profiles of subjects. You've learned to read body language and pinpoint needs, and the following step is to evaluate subjects' social stability. Place the subject in sections 1, 2, or 3 in the columns in the chart after identifying the needs. For instance, within about ten minutes of conversation, you should be able to identify a subject by using this chart. He or she would have a few needs, and the associated numbers with each column. For instance, a subject might be listed as "Appreciation, Comfort, Uniqueness: 131." This number would refer to the location within each column from left to right.

Once the needs have been identified, move to the right and make estimations on the subject's locus of control, following behavior and esteem. Usually, a social stability score can be estimated within five minutes or so, as you start applying this more often, it will be easier to form a stability profile.

A sample stability profile would look something like, Approval, Power, 1, 3, 2.

This profile would allow you to see several mental loopholes present in your subject. He has a need to feel powerful, will respond to approving statements, and is most likely to *follow* your lead instead of *telling* him that he should.

Training for using the Social Stability Scale can be done easily by watching talk show hosts interview guests, and people describe themselves online. Every conversation you have from this day forward will allow you to place stability profile values on the speaker.

The Hughes Social Stability Scale

Identify Needs	then...	Make Estimations on the Social Stability Scale: Rate 1-3 in each column				
NEEDS		**Locus of Control**		**Following Behavior**		**Esteem**
Appreciation Acceptance Approval Intelligence Pity Admiration Power	**1**	External locus of control. Uses victim language. Assigns blame to external forces for life events and feels out of control.	**1**	Absorbs behaviors and attitudes of people around them. Unable to feel congruent emotions unless they observe it in others.	**1**	Low esteem. Will seek self-identity in opinions of others. Uses coercion to gain compliments. Behavior to impress or intimidate others.
	2	Locus of control shifted depending on context. Blames some events on circumstances. Able to take responsibility.	**2**	Will adopt emotions of others with high intensity. Able to make decisions using own set of values instead of group.	**2**	Average esteem. Positive beliefs about self and others. Needs little verbal encouragement and seeks little validation.
	3	Completely internal locus. Assumes responsibility for their life and takes action. Assumes responsibility for well-being of others in social circle.	**3**	Able to fully insulate emotions from the outside world. Not influenced by emotions of others except for empathy. Able to stay positive during intense negativity.	**3**	Has positive beliefs about self and will admit mistakes and openly seek advice. Able to endure criticism without creating identity from it. Seeks no validation.

The Structure of Covert Influence

• • •

How to Control Behavior and Engineer Outcomes to Achieve the Best Possible Outcomes for Subjects, Patients, and Clients

There have been several attempts to develop a concrete timeline in which social influence or covert manipulation takes place. The problem, however, is that the interaction between a masterful operator and a subject is organic; nothing can fully be calculated in the interaction with any degree of certainty. At the outset of this chapter, you are already more advanced in communication than most of the world.

Your mastery of the full Ellipsis program is crucial, and you have more tools at hand now than any other human has ever possessed. Having a few of these skills might be "neat" at a party or business meeting, but the mastery of these methods will bring you power that you can feel. It is a power that is nothing short of true magic, but it carries a tremendous responsibility. Using behavior engineering (BE) methods will prove to be both applicable and powerful in all aspects of your life.

As you make your way to becoming a well-studied master operator, you see that there are far more influencing factors in our lives than most people are aware of. Your new skills will require you to control and manipulate the environment to gain compliance and control. This section includes training on methods dealing with the hypnotic and linguistic control of human behavior, thought, and emotions.

In the coming chapters, you will learn how to use your body to influence, how to speak in conversation using hypnosis methods, and even how to create alter personalities.

What's most important, perhaps, is a small chapter about authority. This chapter may be the most important one in the book for you. It explains the glue that holds all of the other methods together and the fuel that drives the behavior of others. It's easy to overlook, but authority, as you'll soon recognize, is immensely more important than most assume.

This section of the book takes time and frequent practice to fully utilize. Consider the human being to be a complex instrument, that takes everyday practice to master. Covert influence works in hidden ways, convincing the subject that they made the choices that led to your outcome. It's a human trait to assume our brains are little impenetrable forces, but the truth is, we have no firewall. The belief that we can't be easily manipulated is also what causes subjects to reverse-rationalize that their actions were of their own choosing.

Before we move forward into psychological processes, let's cover how our behavior and body language controls the direction we steer others' thoughts.

Gestural Markers

● ● ●

GESTURAL TENDENCIES IN EVERYDAY CONVERSATION are varied and mostly random when observed. However, gestures indicate small pieces of intent and meaning in our speech with other people. Over the years, several pioneers (such as Jeffries) have developed methods to use gestures to control and change the subconscious meaning of words and phrases.

As we speak, our fingers, hands, and arms move naturally and sometimes make meaningful references to objects, directions, or motions. We do this to communicate and assist our language to get a specific theme or idea across. These gestures in conversation go completely unnoticed most of the time. As we speak, we don't monitor or consciously process gestures and behaviors of our arms and hands. As humans, we process all the meaning of our gestures in our conversations at an unconscious level.

This tendency in humans to be unaware of most hand and arm gestures can be exploited to use these gestures to signify a very pointed meaning. Since gestures are processed only at an unconscious level, the meanings we signify with them are mostly absorbed unconsciously. Here, we will give examples of hijacking this unconscious process to deliberately create scenarios that promote favorable outcomes.

Along with the other training you'll receive, this can be used in many scenarios, such as the following:

* Job interviews
* Traffic tickets or police stops

- Getting upgraded to first class on an airplane
- Interrogation in law enforcement
- Seduction and intelligence gathering (while this is not seduction training, any highly advanced training in communication and behavior is inherently applicable to seduction)

Imagine a conversation between two people about a restaurant. Think about these key phrases you might hear when they speak positively about the restaurant:

- "Absolutely the best thing I've seen"
- "Wonderful service"
- "Trustworthy people"
- "Something you just want to have all the time"
- "Absolutely perfect"
- "Comfortable place to be"
- "Want to go there all the time"

These phrases are simple examples you may hear in such conversations. As you think about the phrases, you may imagine that there is not much gestural movement while people are saying them. Now imagine that if you were able to attach all of the above phrases to yourself within a conversation while speaking them, you could quite literally mold and shape the images of yourself in a subject's mind in almost no time at all. Here is a list of abbreviations you'll find in the coming chapters that show the directions in which the gestural references are being made (or to which objects):

OP
Gesture to the operator

OMP
Gesture to the operator's mouth

SP
Gesture to the subject

SFP
Gesture to subject's face

EP
External gesture (away from you and the subject)

IP
Gesture to an item

GP
Genital gesturing

Making a simple and subtle gesture toward yourself (torso) with your hands and fingers eventually builds unconscious recognition in subjects, causing an unconscious marker to associate the phrase with the focus of your gestures. The gesture should be performed with relaxed hands and a smooth, fluid motion; it should not be quick or dramatic, to prevent subjects' gaze from shifting to your hands.

Thinking along these lines, imagine yourself associating traits with your subjects that you might want them to associate with the conversations. You can gesture toward subjects when you want to associate phrases with them. Doing so helps to control their behavior and can change their mental state by itself. With the following phrases, consider the implications of making subtle gestures toward your subjects' torsos as you speak to them about a local doctor's office you frequent:

- "Always comfortable [sp]"
- "Knowing you are safe [sp]"

- "Completely able to trust [sp]"
- "Always knowing you are taken care of [sp]"
- "Having that feeling of knowing you're in the right hands [sp]"
- "Feeling absolutely comfortable [sp]"
- "Trust completely [sp]"

These phrases, when associated with subjects in a gestural context, begin the process of unconscious association. The gestural markers create a tie between the object of the gesture and the spoken phrase.

Next, imagine speaking about an episode of *The Bachelor* and using the following phrases in a HUMINT (human intelligence) gathering or seduction scenario:

- "Become completely attracted [sp]"
- "Get so curious about this [op]"
- "Start to realize you're addicted to something [op]"
- "Feel that sense of fascination [sp], and then the commercial break comes [lean back], and all you want to do is find out what happens next [now gesturing back and forth between subject and operator]."
- "They look at this guy [op] and just feel so compelled [gesturing to subject] to do whatever it takes to get him [op]."
- "She feels herself [sp] realizing this growing feeling of…just… what do I [sp] have to do to be with this guy [op]?"

Triggering the association is easy, but this gesturing method requires practice. No training manual or mental rehearsal can substitute for this.

SPECIAL GESTURES

There will undoubtedly be special gestures you develop on your own to use in specific scenarios. Ellipsis uses three special gestures that are more or less culturally understood when they are made, even if on an unconscious level:

The "Now" Gesture

This gesture has two parts. First, within sixty seconds before you use it, make contact with your wristwatch. Then, as you want to indicate "now" without saying it, point your finger at the ground as if you were an executive saying the words "right now" to an employee.

The Removal of Something Old

This gesture is used in situations where you are convincing subjects by using linguistics that they need to move forward or get rid of some old beliefs they have. To perform it, simply make a washing motion with your hands as if you were washing them in a sink, followed by a dismissive gesture that you are getting rid of something.

The Corridor

This gesture is used to build focus or connection with subjects. Your hands are placed flat and fingers are extended vertically. Your hands should be placed about six or seven inches apart and somewhere in front of your face, as if you were measuring a fish. You should move your hands back and forth between you and your subjects. This can be done conversationally, and it must look and feel natural to keep subjects from focusing their attention on the gesture instead of the message you are trying to convey.

ACTIVATING TRUST

Whether you are operating in a bar or an interrogation room, the development of trust and sometimes endearment is essential to the production of actionable HUMINT, confession comfort, and interpersonal trust. This method relies on generalized and accepted gestures and assumes the ubiquity of basic gestural associations in Western countries.

When you live in a Western country, some gestures are universal. In the United States, we place our hands over our hearts to signify a promise, indicate sincerity, and pledge our allegiance to our country. In all Western civilizations, this behavior of putting the hand to the heart is also a common sign of deep feelings and sincerity. Imagine a woman hearing news of a heartwarming story coming to a perfect ending. This gesture is seen in both sexes, but women tend to do it 9 percent more often than men (Morris, 1978). It is also commonly associated with a slight degree of head tilt to the left.

Imagine replicating this gesture during a conversation using when the following comments are spoken by the operator:

Interrogations

- "You can finally open up. Know you're completely safe."
- "Know that you did the right thing and you're a good person who deserves to get your side of the story on the record so people understand."
- "Just let go of the old beliefs someone gave you."
- "Realize you're with someone who is only here to help and whom you can trust."

While these comments may not include every scenario and while some of the conversational behavior-engineering elements seem to be left out, you must understand the gestural reference concept before you move forward in the training.

- "Become completely vulnerable"
- "Realize how small we all are, how fragile life is"
- "Finally understanding how things work and seeing all your old beliefs for what they really are"
- "Knowing when you can truly let go and trust, all the way"
- "Letting yourself finally trust someone"
- "Completely allowing yourself to just feel what's happening"

* "So many people zone out, but it's good to meet someone you know you can trust, who is here now"
* "These superstitions about behavior hold so many people back; it's so different to meet someone who doesn't wear the handcuffs of restraint, who can just let go."

This block is meant only to illustrate the capacity of this technique to change behavior as a short reference. When you learn, in the next chapter, to incorporate this technique with the next method, you will be able to do a lot more. From getting free coffee to getting huge discounts at stores, the next chapter covers limited-timeframe behavior engineering, and it is important to grasp this concept before moving forward.

Identifying Strengths

● ● ●

IN COUNTLESS BUSINESS BOOKS, YOU'LL find ways of identifying the strengths and work styles of people. These books typically revolve around a common theme: when you know someone's strengths, it enables you to more effectively task that person and communicate with that person to produce greater effectiveness. While these books have proven to be a valuable reference for managers and business leaders, they don't address the important issue of self-identity.

In any behavior-change scenario, the person's self-identity is placed somewhere in the middle of the interaction. When we speak about self-identity, it simply means how people see themselves and what good traits they want others to see in them.

In behavior-engineering operations, the traits people want to be seen as having are often more important than the traits they actually have. When you can discern what people want to be seen as, you can steer the direction of their behaviors much more quickly than you could if you knew what their good traits actually were. Your making subjects feel powerful and effective makes them work much harder to live up to the reputations you have given to them. After gaining this determination, they will naturally excel in the directions you've set for them, and their actual strengths will come out naturally and on their own.

Imagine this scenario: you encounter two employees in a store at different times while shopping, and you'd like to get a particular behavior outcome from each of them.

The first employee, a male, seems to be a hard worker, and his physical appearance is neat and well groomed. You ask him about the location of a particular item, and he responds by describing how he has just finished reorganizing that aisle and by pointing out exactly where your item is located. Hearing him speak about his organization, you immediately know he seeks approval. Whether he is particularly good at organizing is irrelevant. Simply knowing he wants to be seen as a hard worker and a great organizer means that you can now use this information in the behavior-engineering process.

As you speak to him, you use phrases that trigger his need for approval/acceptance/appreciation (from the needs map) for the traits he has demonstrated to you. Here are a few examples of phrases that could trigger responses from his needs:

"It's great to see someone who has such an awesome work ethic and drive. There are so many disorganized people nowadays who have no ability to see the valuable opportunities that come their way [op]."

"I'm glad you're so in tune with the store. That would have taken me an hour to find. Thanks. It's good to see someone who takes pride in his or her work. Such people know they will succeed because they [sp] always know when they have an opening to focus on something important [op]."

"I can tell you've got bigger plans, and you seem as if you'll be extremely successful someday. I'll bet, with your work ethic and skills, that you're the type of person who can spot tremendous opportunities [op]—that is, opportunities that hundreds of others [ep] would miss."

These examples take the power of these subjects' beliefs and direct their pertinent desires and drive in any direction you choose. This profiling method is rather easy to master and requires only that you tune in to what you hear and see when you communicate with subjects in the field.

The second employee, another male, has a more disheveled appearance and seems to be lazing around, leaning on a shelf. As you begin to speak with him, his attitude makes it apparent that he doesn't like his job and lacks motivation, drive, and enthusiasm. As you request assistance and see him lazily move to assist you, his drives on the needs map should become apparent. While someone else may judge him as lazy, unambitious, or trashy, you observe the way he sees himself and decide to capitalize on his needs and use his perceptions to your conversational advantage. Here are a few examples of phrases you can use in this scenario:

"I'll bet the manager makes a ton of money and expects everyone to be as happy as he is. Not many people would tolerate it as you seem to. It's always interesting to see all the people who don't know how to just relax and live, so busy all the time, for nothing. They have no ability to just let go and realize that the present is the most important moment, not the future."

"My niece works at one of these stores. Says they don't take very good care of people. It's good to see someone who doesn't kill himself for a worthless master. You're obviously using only a fraction of your potential. I can tell you're the type who'll be famous someday."

"You've got the look as if you already know you're headed off to bigger and better things. It's amazing how many people are happy working at a place like this [ep]. It's refreshing to see people who have the sense to see opportunities [op] and rare experiences [op] when they come along."

While reading the above examples, you probably observed how easy it is to access the "back door" of the mind when someone's desires, needs, and self-image are on apparent display. Your training should become easier when the judgment stops.

Let's explore a few more examples from actual case studies. In the following examples, you will, just like an interrogator or behavior operator, be given the data from a first impression of a subject. You can walk through the data using the needs map or analyze it on your own. These are taken directly from the behavior logs of Ellipsis Behavior Laboratories.

SUBJECT 1: a seemingly upper-class man with impeccable hygiene and what looks to be a thousand-dollar watch on his wrist. His car keys have a large Jaguar logo on them, and his nails appear to be manicured. Within the first few minutes of conversation, you hear the following sentence: "My wife and I are planning to buy a castle in Scotland that hasn't been open to the public for almost three decades."

While some (if not most people) would be disgusted by the flagrant form of communication and such a desperate desire to show it off, as you suspend judgment, the needs reveal themselves. Judgment would have utterly clouded your ability to identify this person's needs. Your dealing with this personality becomes instantly easier because you have suspended judgment and have chosen to focus on his desires and self-image. This man views himself as being appreciative of the finer things, of having good taste, and of being generally envied and looked up to by others. This information alone can produce immediate changes in behavior if used correctly. Consider the following examples of comments that could be made:

"It's not very often I meet people [sp] who genuinely have a taste for the finer things and know what they like. I've always found it interesting when I meet people who have no appreciation for things. They always have no ability to let go and fully commit to new opportunities [op]. You know what I mean?"

"Every time I meet someone [sp] whom I know others look up to, like the type that is just a natural leader, it is amazing they all have the same thing in common [insert the trait you'd like them to start behaving with as if they had it]."

LINGUISTICS

This section is the hypnosis section of the book. Everything from formal to covert-hypnosis methods will be covered. Applications ranging from getting free products at a store to creating absolute obedience (so absolute that subjects would injure themselves on command) are possible. From curing phobias to creating the perfect outcomes for clients in therapy, this section is where the "meat" is.

HYPNOSIS DOESN'T EXIST

The term *hypnosis* has been around since the 1840s. Before the term came about, it was widely referred to as *mesmerism*. Several healers and physicians attempted to use this force to help people with physical and mental ailments. In the 1840s, a Scottish surgeon named James Braid coined the term hypnosis in his unpublished "Practical Essay on the Curative Agency of Neuro-Hypnotism" (1842) as an abbreviation for *neuro-hypnotism*, which means "sleep of the nerves." Following his death, hypnotism lost some of its momentum and popularity until around 1890, when the concepts of hypnosis were passed around by surgical doctors and mental-health professionals. It had its first widespread medical applications in the US Civil War and was declared as "the calling of Satan" by the Catholic Church. In the 1900s, hypnosis began to draw more medical attention and eventually became recognized in the United Kingdom and in the American Medical Association. It is widely accepted today as a valid and scientifically based approach to therapy and behavioral change. The *practice* of hypnosis is still used in well-respected psychotherapy, psychiatry, and forensic applications, but there is no specific *place* people go that can be classified as "hypnotized." The trancelike state of hypnosis is a natural occurrence, and the hypnotist merely serves as a laser-focused guide into that trance and implants suggestions and retrieves information using sophisticated linguistics and psychological methods.

When people are hypnotized, they enter what's referred to as a trance, a state in which people's focus and attention are directed to subdue competing information and stimuli, creating a state of heightened suggestibility and the reduction of mental reservation. Clinical hypnotherapists use this state to implant suggestions to better the lives of their patients and to instill confidence in the abilities of the hypnotists. With overt hypnosis, subjects' beliefs that regard whether the therapy will work or their expectations come together to form the actual outcomes for the subjects. In Ellipsis hypnosis, subjects have not given consent to be hypnotized and remain unaware that they are being hypnotized; the beliefs and expectations they form are the ones you program into their minds.

We all enter and exit trance states several times a day. The time between sleeping and waking, the deep thoughts that occur while commercials play on television, and the phenomenon of having driven for several minutes with no ability to recall the turns made—all are classic examples of the daily trances we all enter. All human beings are in some degree of trance 90 percent of the time.

Knowing that most subjects are already in some form of trance, your leading subjects into hypnotic trances becomes only a task of guiding them into the deeper levels of the trance they are already in. Subjects who already know how to enter a trance throughout their days need only the application of a few well-sharpened skills to bring their minds back into that state. After achieving this hypnotic-trance state in subjects, you are welcome to deepen it as much as you see fit using the covert methods in this section of the manual.

We've learned more about the human brain and its components in the last five years than in the last five thousand years. Neuroscience and hypnosis are now joining hands to make your trip more scenic and enjoyable on your way to mastery. If you had to imagine a single region of the brain that you would be directly talking to and dealing with, it would be the amygdala. This part of the brain deals with emotion, impulses, fear, and making critical decisions. It's also sometimes beneficial to imagine speaking directly to this part of the brain while in conversation, picturing the brain inside of the subject's skull and visualizing how your words are affecting it. Your words are activating electricity and waking up neurons that would have otherwise been inactive.

As humans, we all experience trances regularly. You already know that almost every decision people make is based on emotional content, regardless of how logical they try to make their decisions sound. Emotions, fears, feelings, and weaknesses drive decisions and behavior. That last sentence is worth underlining or copying into your notebook. Look at the following chart:

There are levels, each of which allows a greater degree of compliance, suggestibility, and unconscious obedience. Your first goal in most interactions is what we call *attentional captivity*. This is where subjects become focused to the point that outside noises and distractions temporarily fade in their conscious awareness. The same phenomenon happens when we see a movie that keeps us unaware we are in a theater full of people. The movie is so interesting that it produces attentional captivity.

Clinical Hypnosis
Even though the process of clinical hypnosis will not be used within this system, it is important for you to develop a familiarity with the process. Your knowing the process of clinical or classical hypnosis will help you to form a clearer picture in your mind of how the pieces that follow fit together.

In a clinical setting, patients are typically seated in a waiting room before seeing the hypnotist. Inside of the waiting room, there are several objects designed to prime subjects for authority, trance, trust, and relaxation. Several framed certificates should line the walls to create a sense of respect and trust in the patients. The presence of these certificates on the wall encourage patients to trust the practitioners. Awards and news articles may be placed around the waiting room as well. These objects further the cause of creating trust and authority. They help patients to view hypnotists as professionals, and they remove several doubts they might have carried with them into the office. The forms that patients need to fill out while in the waiting rooms are written in a way to increase their positive expectation of the therapy. The phrases used on the form should presuppose that patients will have positive outcomes and will have no trouble settling into trances while in the hypnotists' offices. The waiting room should not include anything that could induce anxiety in patients. Professional hypnotists generally avoid including photos of aircraft, deep bodies of water, and anything else that might cause apprehension in patients. Small items placed around the waiting room can also serve to calm patients down and increase their positivity—for example, small rock gardens, fish tanks, and well-placed magazines or articles that discuss the positive benefits people experience with hypnosis. Setting up this anticipation and expectation in the patients is crucial for practitioners and saves hundreds of hours of having to alleviate fears or worries that would otherwise surface and interfere with the hypnotic process.

Once subjects are called in to see the hypnotists, the hypnotists then greet them. By this time, most patients are unaware that the process of hypnosis and inducing trances has already begun!

Hypnotists, when greeting new clients, take several small actions verbally and nonverbally to enhance and strengthen their patients' abilities to enter trances. Small questions are asked, such as, would you prefer to go into a trance in this chair or that one? Questions such as these are called *double binds*, and they force clients to go into a trance. With either choice that clients make, they are deciding and agreeing to go into a trance. There are hundreds of these small linguistic tactics that can all be equally applied within the Ellipsis model as well.

As the clients sit, they can see even more certificates and degrees on the wall, furthering their comfort and trust.

Next, pretalks between hypnotists and clients commence. In this preliminary talk, clients' issues are discussed, which alleviates fears, dispels myths, and gain hypnotic rapport. Well-trained hypnotists use several linguistic trance techniques in this phase to start the induction into the trances.

At this point, hypnotists typically use scripts suited to the clients' particularities, or hypnotists reference their personal mental resources they have gained through years of practice and training. A good example of a script a hypnotist would use for a session can be found anywhere on the internet. Reading through several induction scripts is recommended as it illustrates the different ways a clinician can bypass the critical factor of the conscious mind of the client.

After the sessions are completed, clients should be reassured that they did a terrific job and that everything that took place in their hypnosis sessions will certainly affect their daily lives. Some therapists tie in the suggestions they've made by telling clients that certain things they encounter will revivify what took place in their hypnosis sessions. For example, a client's seeing a red car or hearing a certain sound may bring back the hypnotic suggestions that were given during his or her hypnosis. Using this technique, clients can later recharge their therapeutic batteries and may reexperience the initial effects of the suggestions made in their trances. Good practitioners leave their clients happy, positive, and completely relaxed after their sessions, and the above technique enables clients to feel those feelings again. Think of the feeling you had immediately after watching an amazing movie or hearing a compelling story. Though short lived, such feelings are positive—they make you feel good inside. Later, when you are reminded of that movie by a poster or commercial on television, the feelings return, even if only briefly.

Following their therapy sessions, clients usually follow up within a week or two and schedule appointments to make adjustments to their hypnotherapeutic treatment.

This is the basic structure of clinical hypnosis. The Ellipsis system utilizes many similar techniques. The exception is that subjects do not give consent to enter hypnotic trances; they enter this state without their knowledge—that is, they remain unaware of their entering any hypnotic trances. Subjects do not need to go into a deep trance to be affected by these techniques. Many of them work extremely well on their own, but the trance state multiplies the effectiveness and power of the techniques.

Hypnosis isn't the only tool you will use. Many of the techniques you will learn in the coming chapters involve highly modified psychological techniques designed to change thought patterns and behaviors rapidly. With your current level of mastery, you can choose to use them with or without inducing trances in your subjects.

Factors driving all human decisions		Factors you will master control of in your subjects	
	Emotions		Emotions
	Fears		Fears
	Feelings		Feelings
	Weaknesses		Weaknesses

Consciousness

• • •

The Reticular Activating System

The reticular activating system (RAS) is responsible for human arousal, focused attention, and responses to threats. It will serve you best to think of the RAS as a gatekeeper or security guard protecting the unconscious. It screens information to help us focus on what is most important and relevant. The brain is inherently lazy; it filters out any information that isn't essential to living, and the RAS is the decision maker for this action. If information or stimuli are high priority, they will activate the RAS and multiply the focus on them. When you're in a crowded room filled with the sounds of conversation, the RAS activates when your name is called. All the information that triggers the RAS is programmed into a guest list of sorts. As soon as high-priority information that's on your RAS guest list is present, the RAS automatically turns on the focus and attention parts of your brain. Human brains are overwhelmed with data and information; the RAS helps to filter out what are unimportant, boring, harmful, or otherwise nonuseful information and stimuli. During normal periods of consciousness, the RAS is on autopilot, making tiny decisions and letting you perform tasks you've done hundreds of times. However, when something disrupts an otherwise normal routine, the RAS automatically establishes focus and makes you pay attention to the stimuli causing the activation. You will learn all of the methods to hijack the RAS in the chapters to come.

The Science behind the RAS

The RAS is composed of several neuronal circuits connecting the brain stem to the outermost layer of the brain (the cortex). The RAS contains both cholinergic and adrenergic components, which exhibit synergistic as well as competitive actions to regulate thalamocortical activity and the corresponding behavioral state. Thalamocortical activity is one of the main building blocks of human consciousness and working memory. This activity is a brain activity that you will learn how to control and regulate in other people during conversation.

What You Need to Know

When the RAS senses something as extremely unusual or important, it redirects conscious awareness toward whatever is causing the switch to flip. In a sense, it can block out all stimuli, thoughts, and objections to pay attention to a single thing, person, or event.

Nothing is quite as important as something threatening our lives. Imagine, for a moment, that you're driving down the highway and that the giant tanker a few cars ahead of you explodes. Nothing in your life, no matter how important, can trump this explosion. The RAS makes the decision that this is a priority, allowing you to focus on absolutely nothing else. In social settings, the RAS works in much the same way: it focuses the brain's attention and awareness toward the most socially attractive people. If you are talking with someone and your favorite celebrity walks into your conversation, your attention is automatically programmed to shut out everything and pay attention to the celebrity—not because the celebrity has some high status, but because your brain is programmed to respond to high-value people in this way. The celebrity may not be high value to anyone else, but you view him or her in this way, causing your RAS to respond immediately.

The RAS and your understanding of it are critical to your development as an operator. The tactics you will learn to bypass and regulate a subject's RAS will require a substantial amount of study and elegance.

The Nature of Psychological Obedience

In July of 1961, a Yale University researcher and psychologist named Stanley Milgram began a series of experiments that would later be included in the pages of every basic psychology textbook in the world. These experiments measured the willingness of subjects to obey someone they perceived as an authority figure who instructed them to do things against their own desires and morals. Participants were asked to repeatedly deliver shocks to a person on the opposite side of a wall when the person answered a question incorrectly. The authority figures in this experiment, dressed in lab coats and carrying clipboards, continually told participants to deliver higher and more dangerous levels of electric shocks to the person on the other side of the wall. The number of participants who complied with the authority figures' request was shocking. Some students continued despite protests, even while weeping for the victim in the other room.

Charles Sheridan and Richard King hypothesized that some of Milgram's subjects might have suspected that the victim was faking (he was), so they repeated the experiment with a real victim: a cute, fluffy puppy who was given real—albeit apparently harmless—electric shocks. They found similar findings to Milgram's: half of the male subjects and all of the females obeyed to the end. Many subjects showed high levels of distress during the experiment, and some openly wept (Milgram, 2009).

In 1955, a similar study on obedience was done to see whether people would be more likely to disobey a law or regulation when they witnessed a high-status person break the rule than when they witnessed a low-status person doing it. In this experiment, a model wearing a business suit and polished shoes stood at the crosswalks of several intersections in downtown Austin, Texas. When the model disobeyed the "do not cross" signal, the chances of people at the intersection following his actions were drastically higher than when the model did the same action wearing wrinkled and soiled street clothing. Simply perceiving someone to have higher social status drastically altered the behavior of subjects at the intersections. Class counts.

While all of us would like to believe we are in control of ourselves and make our own decisions, our choices are mostly the results of outside influence. Our subconscious picks up on subtle cues and overt actions alike. From a radio commercial, you think you're ignoring to a random headline you skip over while walking past a newspaper stand, these seemingly innocent and powerless things have the ability to change the course of your personal history. We are bombarded with advertising, messages, flashy banners on web pages, and constant marketing hype throughout almost every day. It's an endless sea of nauseating requests for you to part with a little bit of your money.

Human beings are programmed to seek direction in most things that we do. Even if we aren't aware of it or we'd like to deny it, our brains search for shortcuts and loopholes all the time. They help us to make sense of the world, and our seeking directional cues from the environment on an unconscious level actually helps us to manage how much of our mental capacities we are spending on seemingly mundane tasks and thoughts. If you had to consciously think about which direction to drive every day instead of unconsciously following the lines on the road and the flow of traffic, driving would be more stressful than combat.

Imagine an iceberg adrift near the North Pole. A seemingly large, mountainous mass sits above the surface. As far as we can visually determine, the iceberg ends at the surface of the cold water in which it sits. However, the largest part lies below, reaching to unknown depths—it is exponentially more massive than what we see above the surface. Our consciousness is very much the same. The amount of cognitive processing we are actually aware of is dwarfed by the hundreds of thousands of incredibly complex processes governed by the subconscious mind.

The term *subconscious* was coined by French psychologist and psychotherapist Pierre Janet. He argued that there is a limit to the amount of information the brain can process at any given time. Much like a computer's CPU, he argued, what is seen and processed on a conscious level is only a tiny fraction of what is required for us to function in our daily lives; there are hundreds of processes running in the background to keep things running smoothly. Hence, he believed, a vast storehouse must be present to handle the multitude of data we encounter, remember, and process.

Though there may be skepticism as to whether the subconscious exists or whether it is a separate part of our minds, it will serve you best to think of it as a real and separate entity within your own mind and the minds of the subjects on which you will be operating.

In the context of behavior engineering (BE), we visualize the brain as a medieval castle. Let's take a quick tour of the castle to become familiar with its notable parts. The castle is equipped with guards, villagers, rooms, an underground level, a king, and the assistants who serve him.

As you approach the castle grounds, you can see only what has been designed for you to see from the outside. This is the same way our minds work; all of us have a façade or mask that we wear to present an image to the public.

Coming up to the doors of the castle, you encounter the guards, who are the conscious and critical factor of the mind. Their job is to screen incoming people, information, ideas, and experiences. They decide who gets through the doors and into the castle. The critical factor within the conscious mind decides what gets accepted and let into the unconscious or vulnerable side of the mind.

After you use techniques to bypass the guards and get yourself into the castle walls, you see villagers are everywhere. These people aren't guards per se but have tremendous influence if they notice you behaving in a way that seems threatening to their way of life or their friends. When you move through the inner workings of the castle, the villagers occupy every room you travel to. They aren't suspicious unless you give them reason to be. They are very accommodating and assist you in whatever task you are doing if they believe you're there to help and your presence makes sense to them.

The rooms inside the castle all have different intended uses and functions. There are rooms to serve almost any function. There are rooms for data storage, entertainment, relaxation, sleep, sex, nourishment, and sciences. This is the cortex, or outer layer of the brain. It's what separates us from animals for the most part and what makes all of us human. Throughout your entire training program, you will spend a great deal of time walking around the rooms of people's castles without their consent or knowledge. The feeling that comes from having the ability to bypass the castle walls is incredibly addictive. It is amazingly easy to become fascinated with the inner workings of the people you speak to every day.

The king of the castle comprises the needs, desires, insecurities, and fears of an individual. The king governs the morale and decisions of the village, basing his decisions on his own personality; even if it is weak or broken, the king's behavior sets the tone for how the villagers function and the daily life of the community. He dictates responses to environments, and his views are what constitute the vast majority of reactions to events. Just as people's fears and beliefs can completely control the ways they behave in almost all situations, the king can greatly alter the way the community behaves and how it reacts to events. In a few chapters, you will learn how to identify the needs, fears, and insecurities of people simply by looking at them. This will provide invaluable intelligence before you decide to enter the castle.

The assistants who serve the king tend to his every need. They are similar to file clerks, fetching information and bringing new viewpoints to light when needed. The king's viewpoints allow only certain information to be retrieved and certain viewpoints to be entertained. Within the mind, the information we all make decisions with is completely filtered by our needs and insecurities. Our social and situational fears alone can drastically change the type of information we choose to ignore and what memories and facts we bring to the table when we need to make a decision. The brain's memory and data-retrieval system are very much like the king's assistants, bringing up only information and recalling only data that gel with the king's beliefs. In this way, people are fairly certain they have all the information they need, when in reality they recall only information that confirms their beliefs and keeps their beliefs unchallenged.

Moving farther into the castle, you have access to the underground levels. This is the subconscious mind. While the villagers are always around, they are far fewer the deeper you go underground. The underground, like the subconscious, is where the hidden parts are, the parts that most of the inhabitants of the castle have no access to. These deep recesses of the underground contain the most powerful information in the castle. Here in these levels of the subconscious, control of decisions and covert influence on behavior are possible. Getting to these parts of the mind's castle is what *The Ellipsis Manual* is all about. Your training will take you to each part of the castles of each mind you will interact with. Different techniques and methods can be applied covertly and overtly to each inhabitant of the castle, and you will soon learn the methods for engineering your way into almost anyone's subconscious mind.

Authority dictates your ability to create behavioral outcomes. When experimenting, try to exaggerate to see what you can get away with. It will surprise you.

The Autopilot Mode

As you've learned, the brain functions in ways that conserve resources. It is inherently lazy and may become entrenched when it experiences tasks and events that it's already seen several times. When the brain becomes familiar with a routine or task, such as driving to work or pumping gas, it stops becoming conscious of a lot of information and relies on imprinted memories to keep a person functioning without having to consciously process every detail. Imagine if you had to process the entire method of tying your shoes or typing on a keyboard. Those simple tasks alone would exhaust the cognitive processes within your brain. To keep from having to process every single bit of data we encounter, our brains become familiar with routines, objects, and events, thus needing fewer faculties to accomplish the same tasks.

With this autopilot functioning throughout our lives, it's easy to become entrenched in an activity, no matter how entertaining it seems.

Your first lesson in advanced behavioral engineering will cover how to shut off or bypass the autopilot function in the minds of your targets. Bypassing the autopilot is nothing more than shutting off a subject's habitual behavior thought patterns and creating a small opening into which you can insert linguistic phrasing.

The autopilot is a critical function of the brain. Without it, as you now know, seemingly ordinary tasks would occupy almost all of our mental resources. Imagine walking into a big-box electronics store. The employees in the store have a mode that their minds shift into when they are at work. As they deal with customers every day, their minds begin to form habitual behavior patterns that allow them to navigate the conversation, to talk about products, and to eventually sell items to customers. Short of someone coming into the store in a gorilla costume, their interactions are all pretty much the same when they deal with customers, and their brains, in turn, develop an "I'm at work" autopilot behavior, helping them function at work and deal with customers and coworkers.

It's best to use this example of being in a role to understand how autopilot behavior works. Let's imagine a young lady named Sarah; she has a normal life and works in the mall at a cell phone booth. As she wakes up in the morning, her mind shifts to the autopilot mode of "Sarah waking up." She gets into her car and shifts into the role of a person driving in traffic, dealing with life according to what she's previously experienced during the hundreds of times she's made this same trip. As she arrives at work, her mind knows she's about to start her work day and automatically shifts into "I'm an employee." Again, these modes are based on the thousands of days she's been at work, and her mind has become conditioned to be at work.

As her day continues, Sarah shifts into several other autopilot modes. When going home, working out, and heading to a nightclub, her mind continually shifts into an automatic response mode connected to her previous experiences of the same environments.

Imagine Sarah at work now. She's obviously in her work mode, and she acts according to the appropriate autopilot mode. If a man wearing jeans and a tee shirt approaches her at the mall kiosk, she automatically treats him like a customer and deals with him in this way. If the same man wearing the same clothing approaches her in the nightclub, her autopilot generates a different response to his presence.

For a moment, try to imagine both Sara's and the man's autopilots speaking to each other in the mall. Both of them are running automatic programs: one of them is running a customer autopilot; the other, a sales associate autopilot. Short of an unusual or shocking event occurring, their interaction is much like the thousands of similar ones that have occurred before. They are in their roles and will stay in them unless something disrupts the patterns of their behaviors.

Roles are the easiest and most effective way to view the functions of the autopilot. Our brains become habituated to recurring scenarios. This is also why highway hypnosis occurs; that is, hours of driving with repetitive sounds and sights lull the mind into a deep level of low attention. Think about the last time you drove your car to work and went several miles before realizing that you hadn't been paying attention. The brain does this with interactions and social functions as well.

If you know the power of the environment to lull our minds into states of diminished attention and to create patterned behavior, hijacking this brain function to use it to your advantage becomes exponentially easier. When a stimulus that presents itself deviates from the patterned experiences we have stored up, it triggers the RAS, and we automatically focus and shift to a high-attention mode to make sense of the unusual or new stimulus. Something in the brain says, "This is different," and it focuses to identify and gather information on the new experience.

In the Ellipsis system, bypassing the autopilot function and shutting it off are the first order of business for any behavior engineering you wish to accomplish. There are several ways of doing this, but all of the methods revolve around a central theme: to create a situation that deviates from a subject's normal experiences in a given environment to trigger the RAS.

First, you must consciously identify what environments subjects are in and make educated hypotheses about their likely interactions in those environments. Doing so allows you to know the loopholes that you will later exploit.

Second, your next objective is to deviate from their normal routine enough to trigger a small RAS activation and then to use the small window of high attention to establish attentional captivity. Establishing attentional captivity is easy once you've opened the window.

Your knowing the routines of subjects is critical to identifying the methods you will use to bypass their autopilot functions. Bypassing a sales associate's autopilot will involve much different behavior than when you want to bypass a coworker's autopilot.

Here are several examples of creating a hypothesis of what a subject experiences depending on his or her role. Let's use Sarah again. You will see what each situation is likely to bring to her conscious mind during her normal day. Sarah's roles are listed instead of her activity. Roles are more important than what a person is actually doing.

As a person waking up, she probably doesn't want to be disturbed, thinks about tasks that need to be completed during the day, notes her appearance in the mirror, and thinks about family.

As a person driving to work, she thinks about the rudeness of drivers, goes over tasks in her head, thinks of friends who have cars similar to the ones within her view, changes stations when a commercial comes on, and drinks coffee.

As a person arriving at work, she thinks of things needing to be done, slowly drifts into employee mode, and becomes more socially alive as she greets coworkers.

As an employee in customer-interaction mode, she needs to sell accessories to make quota, helps strangers find stores in the mall, greets customers, uses the cash register, checks the time, and talks to customers.

As a visitor to nightclub, she views guys not as customers but as people who need sex or attention, acts socially alive and friendly with her friends, and wants to enjoy herself.

As a college student, she needs to be seen as intelligent, interacts more socially than she does at work, and focuses on class work and exam notes.

Hacking the Human Autopilot

As ridiculously simple as the preceding descriptions may sound, they are absolutely critical to your understanding of behavior. Understanding that we socially function in roles when we are in public is what will set the foundation of all of your BE training.

Once the general idea of what role a person is functioning in is established, you can decide which technique to use to shut down the autopilot to begin BE. There are three main technique categories for autopilot-shutdown methods:

- Unusual speech
- Unusual behavior
- Authoritative presence

These three methods have several subsets of techniques within them. Let's break each section down and describe the techniques, and we will follow up with examples of how to use them for several scenarios in the field.

Unusual Speech

There are six techniques you can apply within the unusual speech method to shut down autopilot and create focus. They are listed here, and their uses and examples follow.

Volume

Using a different volume than a person would expect to hear in a given role or scenario creates a different experience and turns on more focus than usual.

Tone

Shifting the tone of your voice in an unusual way creates a small pocket of mental focus. The tone shift is a subtle technique that most outsiders are unable to identify in crowded places.

Word Choice

Choosing words that are unusual or unrelated to the situation creates a shift in attention. The word choice may reflect your BE goals for priming (covered later) or can be a seemingly meaningless choice of words inserted into a sentence during an interaction.

Confusion

Asking the brain to accomplish a task it doesn't normally do at work confuses the brain, causing it to shift its focus to the task and to simultaneously turn off or suspend the autopilot response.

Unusual Comments or Questions

Posing questions that people have not been asked in their particular roles causes them to use an "outside the box" mental network that they don't commonly use at work or within their habitual autopilot behavior. Commenting on something unusual or something no one has ever complimented them on before has the same effect.

Accent

The use of a well-placed "foreign" accent automatically causes someone to pay more attention than usual—if not to better understand the language, then simply because it's novel and different.

Unusual Behavior

The presence of any type of behavior that deviates from what subjects experience on a regular basis in their usual environments produces focus and temporarily turns off autopilot behaviors. There are six types of unusual behaviors within this category.

Unusual Behavior

Exhibiting behavior that deviates even slightly from the commonly experienced behaviors seen by subjects in their current routines causes autopilot suspension.

Unusual or Exaggerated Gestures

The use of abnormal gestures and movements that are counter to what is normal in that environment focuses attention to the gesture but requires additional tactics to fully bypass the autopilot.

Unusual Gait

Even the presence of a limp or a shift in the way you normally walk can draw the attention away from the normal states of mind of subjects. This also requires the application of additional tactics to achieve full bypass of the autopilot.

General Gestures That Don't Suit the Environment
Using seemingly normal gestures that mismatch the general tone of the conversation creates a small opening for a larger technique to be used. This amplifies the psychological effect of the secondary technique.

Touching
The use of touch by strangers in conversations immediately focuses all of the subjects' attention and psychologically pulls them away from the surrounding environment, muting their self-talk momentarily. This technique requires elegance and observation of behavior.

Appearance
Your physical appearance can completely alter the course of an interaction. It can also serve to bypass someone's critical mind-set or cause a "second look," in which other bypass techniques can be applied.

AUTHORITATIVE PRESENCE
Authority, which is discussed in great detail in the chapter to come, is the absolute cornerstone to every technique, tactic, and method you will learn throughout your Ellipsis training. The full list of techniques, qualities, and methods for obtaining authoritative presence is fully covered next.

Authority

● ● ●

It's an incredible thing to see our species; all of us are somewhat flawed and broken, standing in judgment of others.

As you learned in the introduction, humans respond obediently to figures whom they perceive as having social authority. In this chapter, you will learn loopholes in human psychology and the tactics you can start employing today to begin using your new authoritative presence.

Imagine walking into a large piano store. The room is large and full of beautifully crafted grand pianos. If you were to approach any piano in the store and firmly strike the middle C key, it would send out a sound wave. The waves travel outward to eventually fill the room with a specific frequency that the string is designed to emit. The middle C string is made to vibrate at 261.626 hertz, which fills any room with the same sonic frequency. The dozens of other pianos in the store are tuned to the same key. With this harmonic frequency being broadcast into the room, the sound wave causes the C string on every piano in the entire store to vibrate. The sound waves then become resonant with each other. Although they do not vibrate enough to become completely audible, the striking of the C key on a single piano produces enough of the sonic frequency to cause every other C string in the store to vibrate. This theory is called Social Coherence, and is also referred to as the Energetic Field Environment by the HeartMath Institute.

Although it may be scientifically disputed (or completely inaccurate), the metaphor above provides a much more useful and productive view of the human mind than traditional explanations of interpersonal psychology. Our social behaviors and the way we feel about people that we meet are very much dependent on the nonverbal signals they send and the feeling we get when we meet someone. A lot of the signals we get from people are broadcast on a level far below our conscious awareness. We all broadcast subcommunicated feelings, emotions, and thoughts with our nonverbal behavior. Thinking back to the piano analogy, imagine two people interacting as two pianos. Our subconscious processes feelings about a person based on what "strings" start to vibrate in our unconscious minds. When you interact with someone and are secretly feeling devious, dishonest, nervous, unconfident, worried, or fearful, all of these emotions and thoughts you are processing are "plucking strings" in your unconscious. The unconscious of your subject has an open line of communication with your unconscious. When your unconscious sends out a frequency, no matter how well you may think you've covered it up, the subject experiences that frequency on an unconscious level. In this regard, it is extremely important that you commit fully to making the training you receive in this chapter a part of your everyday life. You will be astonished at the changes that will occur in your interactions on a daily basis, and this chapter alone will dramatically increase your level of social influence, authority, and conversational dominance.

Authority, and your ability to project it, is more important for you right now than the techniques that will follow. You learned about the Milgram experiment and it's results earlier. In the Milgram experiment, no REAL authority was used to force a person to follow orders to the point of killing other person, it was only perceived authority. A man in a lab coat at Yale University was able to convince a stranger to basically commit murder in less than a few minutes for no other reason than him having on a lab coat. This perception we have of authority allows for what Stanley Milgram called an 'agentic shift', where our actions are no longer our own. We become an 'agent' acting out the wishes of another person. Authority is so powerful that it overrides decision centers in the brain and literally shuts off our sense of personal responsibility.

Consider the difference between two persuaders: Milton Erickson and Charles Manson. Milton was the worldwide expert in clinical treatment, covert influence and hypnosis. Manson knew nothing about these techniques, but he had a following that would kill and die for him. This is a socially exerted influence of perceived authority.

The use of social authority alone is MORE powerful than the use of any of the techniques in this book by themselves. However, once this social authority is paired with covert influence methods, the results and possibilities with human behavior are exponentially increased.

Authority beats skill.

The training in this chapter has the most-condensed, powerful, and useful information on social authority that you will ever encounter. The ethics of use are your choice as an operator and dependent on the regulations governing your operational tasking or directorate.

The training in this chapter is in two main sections: Managing Your Personal Life and Managing Your Behavior.

Managing Your Personal Life

Your training calendar will incorporate some of the lessons in this section, but the integration into your personal life is far too organic a concept to sensibly fit into a one-size-fits-all training plan.

The choices you make on a daily basis reflect, on an unconscious level, several things about your character, trustworthiness, authority, and leadership abilities to everyone you meet. Even the choices you make that feel private and secret will eventually leak out in your unconscious communication with subjects when you are operating. The following training on developing extreme social authority and leadership is comprehensive because it contains guidelines for behavior on and off the clock of operations, so that your unconscious communications are governed appropriately, regardless of the interaction or operation.

Inner Conflict Management

Something as small as leaving laundry and responsibilities unattended while you go to a party can send an unwanted message. There's a part of our minds dedicated to reminding us of unfinished business, things we've put off, and otherwise unfulfilled responsibilities. Even in the heat of an exciting social event or a crucial business meeting, this part of your brain is still active, sending soft reminders of the undone tasks awaiting you. Any part of your life that isn't congruent with the image you wish to project will eventually leak out in your behavior on an unconscious level. The section that follows will show you how to modify your behavior to eliminate or minimize your leakage of inner conflict while operating.

Imagine a plane crashing into the ocean safely near a deserted island. As the survivors, afraid and confused, struggle to shore, the only thing shared among them is the certainty of an uncertain future. As they struggle to find out what lies ahead in their future, all of them will naturally gravitate toward one person whom they've likely never met for guidance or leadership. People can feel when they need to follow or listen to someone; such instincts are based on hundreds of thousands of subcommunicated signals, behaviors, and gestures. The model that follows is the easiest to incorporate and includes the most-accurate and proven methods for absolute social authority, which automatically trigger the following instincts of subjects.

The model for influence relies on five key concepts: Control, Discipline, Leadership, Gratitude and Enjoyment.

The five categories above are the determining factors that create a social personality designed to influence, persuade, lead, and control. From a cult leader to a company's charismatic CEO, these qualities and behaviors are found in every influential and authoritative person. When individually present, none of them can act as a magic key to the mind; when combined, they are extremely powerful and compound covert hypnosis and behavior-engineering success in the field. Let's unpack the five sections listed above. It is best to define ten things directly applicable to you under each of the five sections. Under each section, choose ten behaviors or actions you need to change or modify. This will aid in the journaling of your transition into a master-level operator.

CONTROL

It is important that you make the distinction first between being in control and being controlling. This section refers to being in control. Being in control in conversations means having the ability to govern all of your behavior and thoughts to keep them natural, controlled, and calm. There are several lessons within this volume that will require you to control aspects of your behavior during certain situations. Your breathing, speech patterns, gestures, and several other aspects of your presentation will all come into play as your training progresses. Possessing the ability to control yourself to remain calm and caring will change your results if you do nothing else that follows.

Your breathing must be slow, natural, deep, and controlled.

Posture should be straight. Hold your ears above your shoulders and your shoulders above your hips.

Movements, even small ones like reaching for a pen on the table, should be slow, natural, and controlled. Imagine yourself moving while underwater, the slow movements of your limbs moving in the directions you wish, but never hurry or move too fast. Rooted in evolution, rapid movements display insecurity; they were originally a way for us to ward off attackers and appear more alert and ready. Only small, insecure dogs feel the need to bark and move rapidly in the presence of others. Natural leaders don't need to make a show of their stress, anxiety, and readiness.

Hygiene and personal grooming should be impeccable and resemble the socially accepted image of someone successful, respected, and conservative. Your grooming should not draw more attention than the behavior and linguistic tactics you decide to employ. If you look as if you have authority, you will increase drastically your chances of accessing obedient states of mind in others.

The speed you blink (not the rate) indicates your levels of nervousness and can broadcast the wrong signals when you are operating in the field. Slower and calmer blinking movements indicate personal comfort and confidence.

Exercise control over your schedule and time as well.

DISCIPLINE

Personal discipline is the hallmark of authority. Exercising discipline over yourself gives you a mental edge that very few of your subjects will have. Having the ability to follow through and completely control yourself when needed creates a mental state that subconsciously broadcasts your confidence and personal authority. Starting your day by waking up early or by maintaining a well-regulated fitness regimen will instill you with confidence throughout your day; you will know that the subjects you speak to probably don't have the same level of discipline as you. Your personal level of discipline will show through your communications every time you speak.

LEADERSHIP

The word *leadership* is very popular online and around the business world, and everyone you might ask would have a different definition of the word. To be simple and precise, leadership is the art and ability to automatically produce followership in others. Anything else falls under management.

A combination of your behaviors, lifestyle, confidence, humility, grace, and silent power will communicate thousands of unconscious messages to your subjects, which will make them trust you and want to follow your lead. Humans' natural gravitational pull toward people with this type of magnetism is almost irresistible. Here are the quick-reference reminders for maintaining this magnetism in your daily life. Keep in mind that these behaviors should never be something you have to "put on" while operating. If you don't weave them into your life, they will not subconsciously appear to be congruent and authentic—that is, they will trigger red flags in subjects who would have complied otherwise.

Here are the twenty factors that have been determined to produce the most effective social results:

* Keep interested and focused on your own wellbeing.
* Maintain a healthy sense of self-discipline.
* Plan your days and your life in advance to reduce anxiety.
* Prioritize your plans and desires to reduce anxiety.
* Work hard to make everyone you encounter feel like an interesting person.
* Never put another person down in the presence of others. The leader's goal with any group of people or animals is not to put others down but to lead and guide them.
* Exercise humility in all you do. While it may become tempting to talk about your new skills, qualifications, and achievements, be humble.
* Remember that all humans make choices of whom to trust and admire; these choices are based on how those people make them feel, not on how perfect or well qualified those people may be.
* Continuously plan ahead in your mind. Be present with your actions, and always have an alternate route or location in mind when in the company of others.
* The first person to suggest something is usually the pack leader in a group.
* Admission of faults and mistakes will not make you seem weak or incompetent; such admissions will often have the opposite effect of making you more genuine and authentic.

* Express genuine concern when dealing with others to create rapport and trust.
* When you're confronted with a problem, it is best to view it as a test.
* Find a mentor who is in the place you'd like to be in life. Become a mentor for those who need the guidance you needed to get where you are.
* Keep calm in all situations to train yourself and to display balance to others.
* Make an agreement with yourself to always display behaviors you would want your leader to have. Keep this constant in all situations and encounters.
* Listen to others.
* When subjects display any form of negative emotion, do not go down with them. Stay on top with empathy; be the reliable structure others can depend on.
* Never complain.
* Never criticize unless absolutely necessary.

GRATITUDE

The inner feeling of gratitude shows outwardly and resonates with the gratitude "strings" of the subjects you will encounter. Gratitude is the most powerful feeling you can have and will take the place of negative inner conflicts that can ruin an operation in the field. There are six points to creating this feeling, and they will prove invaluable to managing your unconscious emotional leakage in the field. These are ways you can incorporate gratitude into your daily life to modify the unconscious signals you are sending out.

Whenever you are experiencing something most people would be stressed about, find as many things around you to be thankful for as you can; imagine how many people around the world would trade places with you to have the life that you have.

Firmly believe that things are stressful only when you compare them to something much more desirable.

In social settings, become intensely aware that everyone around you has fears, insecurities, and conflicts. Fully process the fact that the people around you are vulnerable human beings with families that love them. They experience struggles, conflicts, social fears, and uncertainty just as you do. Be grateful for the fact that you are connecting with frail and imperfect people, regardless of how toxic or aberrant their behavior is.

Become aware of each moment's gift. While this may sound esoteric, focusing on the aspects of each situation that are good and provide you with anything enjoyable can shift your negative feelings and prevent them from being broadcast once you've developed this ability.

Get used to the awareness of depth; the small aspects of each situation are deeper than anyone realizes. When you are eating, for example, remember the lettuce in your taco salad was grown on a farm that provides income for a family somewhere. This farmer has taken care to nurture the lettuce into a full plant, and several people were involved in tilling the land before it was grown, providing care for the plants as they grew, harvesting them, bringing them to market, cleaning them, delivering them, preparing them, and finally making them into the meal you are now enjoying. Every moment provides an opportunity to become aware of its depth. The depth to which you become grateful will eventually change the way you converse with subjects; you will become able to see past their social masks and gain the ability to think deeply about their demeanors and backgrounds. The habit of depth awareness is easy to develop and will provide rewards in areas far outside of your operations.

Every day, practice saying "thank you" in your mind for everything you can identify that you've overlooked and for the small things you've previously taken for granted. This mental shift will be a visible change when you interact with subjects.

ENJOYMENT

The social magnetism of people who enjoy themselves is undeniable. People gravitate to those who are having a good time because the happiness is contagious. People want to feel good, so they attempt to absorb good feelings from highly positive operators. The gratitude lessons above will provide the foundation upon which your enjoyment levels will be built. Without one, the other cannot stand. Make it a daily practice to enjoy what you are doing. Whether you're on a ride at an amusement park or cleaning the baseboards in your bathroom, the ability to enjoy the process is limited only by your perception of the action, not the actual task itself. The more you can develop the skill of experiencing enjoyment at will, the more you will notice the social attraction of subjects when you're in that state of mind. Enjoy.

MANAGING YOUR BEHAVIOR

The nonverbal signals you send out can either confirm or negate the linguistic tactics and phrases you are using in the field. The skill to congruently communicate verbal and nonverbal signals must be cultivated and sharpened frequently to maintain a mastery level of linguistic and psychological prowess. While your confidence in your abilities and the belief in your skills will usually create congruent communication, the following list of nonverbal points will assist in your transition to communicative mastery:

* Never criticize others.
* Never complain; focus on gratitude.
* Maintain impeccable hygiene.
* Keep your speech unhurried and deliberate (you will learn how to speak hypnotically in the chapters to come).
* Develop a genuine interest in the subjects you communicate with.

- A tilted head while listening can communicate sincere interest to subjects.
- Using the needs map, ask subjects questions about what they love.
- Combine physical touch with compliments to increase the level of sincerity.
- Do not touch your face or use 3.0 or higher gestures (from the behavior table of elements) when you are speaking unless you are setting social traps or deliberately using nervous or insecure gestures to modify the defensive mechanisms of your subjects (techniques for this are covered later).
- Be humble; resist the urge to talk yourself up or discuss your achievements.
- Eye contact is critical. Show interest or give a genuine smile while making eye contact with others to eliminate the animal-challenge response.
- Nothing is more important in the field than keeping your goal in mind. When interacting with subjects, practice visualizing a large HD television over their shoulders with your goals and notes on it. Playing a movie on this television of the subjects complying at the end-stage of an operation is helpful to keep your behavior and manipulation tactics sharpened to the specific needs of the operation.
- Communicating behavioral authenticity requires the complete removal of insecure behaviors, so keep yourself loose and natural in conversation.
- Keep cold drinks in your left hand to prevent cold handshakes when meeting subjects.
- Keep your feet pointed at your subjects when you want to display interest.
- Cross your legs toward your subjects when building rapport and sitting beside them.

In almost all circumstances, you will not need to intimidate others to get the outcomes you desire. On the extremely rare occasion that you need to do this, it's important to note that it should be environmental intimidation and that it should use the quotes of others instead of your own words. Situations such as placing yourself in a position above someone or where a person look almost into the sun to see you are examples. You'll often find that any use of these methods is for the personal validation of the operator, not for the achievement of any planned outcomes.

Building Rapid Rapport

● ● ●

THERE ARE COUNTLESS BOOKS THAT offer rapport-building skills and training. You will learn a condensed version of about 130 different techniques here. Some of the methods in this chapter have never been released to the public.

LINGUISTIC HARVESTING

To build trust, you must convince subjects that you are like them. If you perform well-executed rapport-development efforts, subjects will like you and focus on you. When you hear someone speak, he or she will use a wide array of words to communicate. While traditional neurolinguistic programming (NLP) training focuses primarily on sensory-word identification, the expanded and more sophisticated methods offered here have been proven to be exponentially more effective than traditional approaches offered by simple NLP methods.

There are two methods of profiling the linguistics of subjects in the Ellipsis system. You will first learn to interpret *what* subjects are saying, then to analyze *how* they are speaking.

When subjects are speaking, they reveal dozens of useful and revealing behavioral cues, regardless of what they talk about. This chapter alone is enough to take to the field and begin social experimentation. The amount of hidden information concealed within our daily speech is astonishing. You will gain a brand-new skill set by the end of this chapter, and while it can be addicting to constantly process speech in conversation to peer behind the curtain of thoughts and social masks of your subjects, it is important to let this skill develop. This skill should be sharpened simultaneously with other linguistic behavior-control methods.

There are five phases of this training module. Large lists of words and what might seem like a college-level English lesson are to be studied next, but rest assured that none of what follows needs to be fully committed to memory. However, keeping the reference handy, to access when needed, will prove to be invaluable.

ADJECTIVES

The description words subjects use to define, explain, or otherwise communicate anything reveal the words you will need in phase 1 of the linguistic-analysis process. Adjectives are very important when collecting behavioral intelligence for the covert hypnotic phase of your interaction with subjects. Adjectives tell us how our subjects color their worlds. The descriptive language they use should provide you with information about how they think about negative things and the ways they view positive ones. As you converse with people, begin by letting the adjectives they each use come out of their language and fly onto the screen you've imagined over each of their shoulders. If you imagine the words as they say them, you will recall them more easily in the deep-level hypnosis phase of the interaction. The following is an example statement similar to something you might hear in a conversation on a normal day. See how many adjectives you can spot.

And it's usually like that too. There are so many disgusting things happening in our world. I'm just extremely glad we live in such a free country. I think a lot of us take our ability to live comfortably for granted. Watching the news only makes people grumpy and nervous. I don't like to watch the news. I'm relieved at the end of the day, when I can still feel calm and be in such an agreeable mood when I walk into my old house.

Let's take a look at the ramblings above and find the adjectives in there. We will further break them down into negative and positive words.

NEGATIVE
Disgusting
Grumpy
Nervous
Old

POSITIVE
Extremely
Free
Comfortably
Relieved
Calm
Agreeable

The adjectives the subject used above can later be applied to conversational control tactics. If you wanted to create negative feelings toward anything, you can use the negative adjectives above to pepper your hypnotic language. Conversely, the positive words can be powerful when you need to create positive emotions or when you are creating obedience and control routines for a subject. It's not imperative that you keep your internal record button pressed throughout a conversation. Attempting to memorize too many things before the skill set is fully developed will only lessen the effects of the other techniques you are using.

Imagine that concentration in the field is like spending money. You have only a hundred dollars to spend, and the more experienced you become at a skill, the cheaper it becomes. So while you may have to spend thirty dollars on the linguistic-harvesting process in the beginning and another fifty dollars somewhere else, every time you purchase something, a few dollars gets shaved off the price the next time you use it. Eventually, you will spend only a dollar or two on each skill and will get to the point where you have plenty of extra money to spend on more-advanced methods, bringing more sophistication and elegance to your skills.

The following table is an example list of specific adjectives divided into twelve types, which you can begin reading through to sharpen your ability to pick them out at the speed of conversation. Keep in mind that it's not necessary to collect every single adjective that subjects communicate. You should focus not only on anything they discuss with emotional content but also on the moments their behavior shifts to more-animated gestures and expressions. A full list of adjectives is provided in the appendix for mastery-level study.

Appearance	Color	Condition	Feelings (bad)	Feelings (good)	Shape
adorable	red	alive	angry	agreeable	broad
beautiful	orange	better	bewildered	brave	chubby
clean	yellow	careful	clumsy	calm	crooked
drab	green	clever	defeated	delightful	curved
elegant	blue	dead	embarrassed	eager	deep
fancy	purple	easy	fierce	faithful	flat
glamorous	gray	famous	grumpy	gentle	high
handsome	black	gifted	helpless	happy	hollow
long	white	helpful	itchy	jolly	low
magnificent		important	jealous	kind	narrow
old fashioned	Quantity	inexpensive	lazy	lively	round
plain	abundant	mushy	mysterious	nice	shallow
quaint	empty	odd	nervous	obedient	skinny
sparkling	few	powerful	obnoxious	proud	square
ugliest	full	rich	panicky	relieved	steep
unsightly	heavy	shy	repulsive	silly	straight
wide eyed	light	tender	scary	thankful	wide
	many	uninterested	thoughtless	victorious	
	numerous	vast	uptight	witty	
	sparse	wrong	worried	zealous	
	substantial				

Sound	Time	Taste/touch	Touch	Shape	Size
cooing	ancient	bitter	boiling	broad	big
deafening	brief	delicious	breeze	chubby	colossal
faint	early	fresh	broken	crooked	fat
hissing	fast	greasy	bumpy	curved	gigantic
loud	late	juicy	chilly	deep	great
melodic	long	hot	cold	flat	huge
noisy	modern	icy	cool	high	immense
purring	old	loose	creepy	hollow	large
quiet	old fashioned	melted	crooked	low	little
raspy	quick	nutritious	cuddly	narrow	mammoth
screeching	rapid	prickly	curly	round	massive
thundering	short	rainy	damaged	shallow	miniature
voiceless	slow	rotten	damp	skinny	petite
whispering	swift	salty	dirty	square	puny
	young	sticky	dry	steep	scrawny
		strong	dusty	straight	short
		sweet	filthy	wide	small
		tart	flaky		tall
		tasteless	fluffy		teeny
		uneven	freezing		teeny tiny
		weak	hot		tiny
		wet	warm		
		wooden	wet		
		yummy			

Gestural Hemispheric Tendency (GHT)

The movements and gestures of your subjects will always vary with their emotional levels, thoughts, and feelings. Before you modify their thoughts and feelings, pay attention to their gestural habits, which will provide you with data you can later use to deliver covert commands and make subconscious decisions for them during the control phase of the Ellipsis system. If subjects gesture mostly with their left hands when referring to negative or disliked topics, they will likely gesture to their left using their hands, eyes, head movements, and general postural shifts when discussing other negative things. Each of us uses one side more than the other when referring to negative or positive things. This behavior proclivity provides you with information, but it should by no means be relied upon to make outcome-affecting decisions. The information you receive from observing this behavior will assist you in the decision-control phase and can serve as a strong support for the other techniques you're using with a subject for an engineered outcome.

After making a mental note of the side of the body that the subjects use or gesture toward, you can later use this information to perform the same gestures on the mirrored side to cause them to feel negatively or positively about a certain subject (in combination with other techniques). Let's walk through a couple of examples:

While discussing a politician, subjects may use a single hand and may slightly lean in the same direction when speaking of something they dislike.

Subjects who appear to be emotionally healthy may begin to speak passionately about the level of dishonesty at their work. As they do this, their right hands seem to be more animated, and they gesture to the right in outward dismissive motions when talking about their coworkers. When speaking of the more honest people at their work, their right hands move closer to the center, and their left hands become more expressive.

A woman you are speaking with shows a tight-lipped expression while using her right hand to describe another woman with whom she's had a disagreement. Her face becomes natural and more expressive as she uses her left hand to describe the behaviors and qualities of one of her close friends.

As the above examples show, such subjects express negative associations on the right sides of their bodies. This in *no way* means that *all* of their negative references will be relegated to this side of their bodies. However, as our only sample of behavior from which to draw information, the above two examples show us that these subjects have associated negative things with their right sides. This information becomes more powerful the more you are able to verify them by using a reference to a particular side of the body.

Let's say we want them to associate a thought or an idea with negative feelings. We will give this example that implements only this single technique, so it won't be polluted with excess data for the moment.

We know the right side of their reference points is associated (sometimes) with negative feelings. You can move your body to your left (their right) a few inches to get their heads to start turning in the negative direction and can eventually use expressive gesturing with your left hand, causing them to look farther right to increase their feelings of negativity. You can move and gesture in the opposite direction to increase the chances of a positive response as well. While there are multiple books and chapters dedicated to the use of this single technique, this is all a successful operator needs to know about using it. The training to come will be far more advanced than anything you've ever come across, and this seemingly interesting collection of techniques in the beginning of this volume will become distant.

During conversation, making brief and small physical contact with subjects' hands or arms to regain attention can also be very effective in controlling the direction of thought. If you sense you've begun to lose a small amount of attention in the conversations, touching the hands associated with the positive side of the subjects will allow them to physically reconnect to the conversation.

Also, subjects will often reestablish focus during conversations when their names are used in a sentence.

Listen for key phrases that also indicate preference. People who use the expression "you know?" frequently will respond well to language preceded by "most everyone knows that…"

SENSORY CHANNELS

The word choices of subjects reveal the sensory inputs they are using to process information, and these word choices will provide, over time, a map of how they process information and through which senses they prefer to receive that same information. In neurolinguistic programming, the sensory systems play an important role in the structuring of language, increasing its impact on subjects' subconscious minds. There are four main representation systems—or channels, as we will hereafter call them—that we use to gather information. All subjects you will meet should have one or two dominant channels through which they unconsciously prefer to receive information:

* Visual
* Auditory (hearing)
* Kinesthetic (touch or hands on)
* Audio-digital (inner feelings and sensations)

VISUAL

Visual subjects tend to learn by watching, are typically not easily distracted by sounds, and find it difficult to maintain focus when listening to long verbal instructions. They typically make decisions based on how things look. They will use words and phrases like:

see, look, view, appear, show, picture, hazy, foggy, dawn, reveal, hidden, vision, visualize, illuminate, clear, focused, colorful, appears to me, short sighted, mental image, mind's eye, see to it, under your nose, upfront, clear as day, perspective, naked eye, looks right, scope him out, foggy ideas, staring into space, looks like, the way I see it, colorful language, face-to-face

AUDITORY

Auditory subjects are typically good listeners and are swayed dramatically by the tone of operator voices. They can follow long trains of conversational thought and are musically inclined or enjoy discussing music. They will use words and phrases like:

question, listen, earful, sounds, rhythm, harmonious, tuned in, all ears, silence, resonating, humming, sounds great, hear me out, express it clearly, give me your ear, listen for a minute, grant an audience, quiet mind, silent partner, tuned in, voice an opinion, loud and clear, unheard of, clear as a bell, tell me, I hear you, you hear me, speaker, well informed

KINESTHETIC

Kinesthetically oriented subjects breathe more slowly into their lower lungs. You will be able to see their bellies moving while breathing. They respond well to physical touch and rewards and stand slightly close during conversation. They will use words and phrases like:

feel, solid, grasp, touch, scraped, get a hold on, slipped through, catch on, tap into, unfeeling, hard, cold, warm, concrete, immoveable, contact, turn on, feels great, touched me, hold on, slipped through my hands, a load of this, heavy information, hard ball, pain in the ass, heated argument, cold hearted, scratch the surface, get it handled, fall into place, handle the elements, smooth move, bumpy road, rough time, felt weird

AUDIO-DIGITAL

Audio-digital subjects tend to be inwardly focused and have traits of the other three channels. They also look downward while processing information and talk to themselves more often than other subjects. They will use words and phrases like:

feel, sense, consider, ponder, wonder, understand, think, change, insensitive, analysis, learn, process (v), motivated, distinct, test it out, see how it feels, preference, exchange ideas, emotional, facts, planning, diligence, laws, does that make sense, conference, according to research, what criteria, understand the basics, get all the info, business first, professionalism, what's the bottom line

The language subjects use to communicate will show you what sensory descriptions you will later use in the hypnotic and psychological control phrases and the weaponized linguistic phase of the Ellipsis system. As you speak with subjects, keep an attentive ear to the language they use; doing so will provide great rewards in the end. Subjects' behaviors are much more likely to be swayed by the language of their thoughts, so the phrases they use, such as the ones in the previous tables, will give you all the ammunition you need to accomplish your goals.

SPEECH-CHARACTERISTICS ANALYSIS

You learned the skills to analyze the content of subjects' speech in the previous section. This section, while brief, will introduce you to the process of hearing the characteristics of speech, in addition to simply listening for content.

Before getting into this short lesson, consider the differences among these responses to the following question:

"What was your favorite Christmas?"

* "I think my favorite Christmas was probably when I was thirteen. My family and I went to Florida, and it was amazing. I loved that trip."
* "When I was fourteen, I got a new bike and a bunch of clothes I wanted."
* "When my family all went to my grandma's house together."
* "Not sure. They all were pretty good. Got a lot of cool stuff every time!"

The first response contains the frequent use of the pronoun "I." This is used by those who feel themselves to have lesser status than others, as well as children. There is an undertone of the importance of the holiday being about family and time well spent.

The second response uses "is" less than the first response. However, within the language, it becomes apparent that the subject describes the holiday only in terms of what was "got."

The third response also indicates a love of family but lacks group pronouns, such as "we," "our," "us," and "ours." This person may be family oriented, but we can also see that self-pronouns are the only ones the subject uses.

The fourth response is cold, distant, and unconcerned. The absence of pronouns shows either the subject's distance from the event or from the operator. The absence may also indicate that the subject is withholding something or being deceptive.

The contextual cues within the speech of subjects can show how they process information about their lives. Their processes of retrieving memories are also affected by this filtering system. As an exercise, try watching an interview or a candid conversation online. Divide a piece of paper into two columns, and as you watch the videos, begin picking out sensory channels and adjective usage, writing them in the left column, and keep track of the contextual needs and pronoun usage on the right. You will become familiar with the moods and life priorities hidden within the language you hear every day, with practice and casual exercise in social settings. Your training doesn't require you to engage in endless drills or exercises to become proficient. Simply having the knowledge of the linguistic-harvesting techniques in this section will eventually shift your awareness into a natural mastery of linguistic harvesting.

Common Pronouns

all, another, any, anybody, anyone, anything, both, each, each other, either, everybody, everyone, everything, few, he, her, hers, him herself, his, I, it, its, itself, little, many, me, mine, more, most, much, my, myself, neither, no one, nobody, none, nothing, one, one another, other, others, our, ourselves, several, she, some, somebody, someone, something, that, their, them, themselves, these, they, this, those, us, we, what, whatever, which, whichever, who, whoever, whom, whomever, whose, you, your, yours, yourself, yourselves

Pacing and Leading

You've likely been exposed to information about mirroring body language or matching gestures in sales books or pop-psychology books. This module will expand your abilities for those techniques and show you methods that aren't common public knowledge.

Mirroring others' body language is a naturally occurring behavior in all humans and primates. When one person becomes familiar with and begins to like another, the person's body language and gestures naturally begin to match and mirror the other's. We automatically begin to copy and sync behaviors with those that we like and trust. The opposite of this natural occurrence is the natural human tendency to dislike or fear things that are different from us. While mirroring is a naturally occurring behavior within our species, we can use deliberate behaviors to subconsciously influence the thought patterns of subjects in the field. A vast majority of the training to come is very similar: we will take naturally programmed human behaviors and manipulate and engineer them into interactions that seem and feel natural.

We tend to like and trust people who are like us. Mirroring body language is simple to understand, and it requires a little bit of in-field practice to become unconsciously competent in its use. We can also mirror other parts of behavior: speech styles, vocal tones, speeds of speech, gestures, breathing, and even blinking.

This module has five sections:

* Mirroring Fundamentals
* Body Language
* Speech Styles
* Gestures
* Breathing and Blinking

Mirroring Fundamentals

Mirroring behavior is a naturally occurring human trait that you, as the operator, are going to deliberately control to shift the behaviors and emotional states of your subjects. Behavioral mirroring is not a gesture-for-gesture mimicry of subjects. Most of the gestures you will replicate follow a three- to four-second delay. Some gestures shouldn't be copied at all. Two concepts are at work when you mirror body language: the mirroring of body language and the matching of body language. Mirroring occurs when you are positioned opposite (or facing) subjects and replicate behaviors exactly. Matching occurs when you are next to subjects—that is, when you face a similar direction.

If you are positioned opposite to a subject who then crosses his or her left leg over the right, you would need to mirror the behavior by crossing your right leg over your left. This creates a mirror image of the body language display to the subject. Conversely, if you and the subject are standing or seated and facing a similar direction, you would match the subject's gesture instead of doing the mirror opposite; your left leg would be crossed over your right.

The shifts in body language should be subtle and appear natural. Drawing subjects' attention to unusual displays of your behavior will only activate their conscious defense systems (which we need to be offline to use the Ellipsis system). Never become obvious in your observations of their behavior before mirroring and matching. Beginner operators typically make the mistake of almost staring at subjects' movements before making their own movements—then they stare again to confirm they've done it right. This is hard to resist in the beginning phase of training. Your level of mastery will be directly proportional to the amount you exercise your skills in everyday life outside of operations.

Training Note:

The physical movements of our bodies influence our emotions and thoughts. Try this exercise: slouch your body and posture to the point where anyone who saw you in this position would believe you're having the worst day of your life. Make your facial expression match the feeling of having a horrible day as well.

While maintaining this posture, try to force yourself to feel happy and confident. It will become apparent that the movements of the body serve as sort of a gateway to feeling emotions.

Body Language

When mirroring body language and gestures, the best rule of thumb is to mirror or match three gestures and movements and ignore the fourth. This cycle should repeat until you have the ability to lead a subject's body language. Leading body language occurs when you've developed enough rapport within an interaction that the subject begins to unconsciously mirror or match *your* gestures. Once you've gained the ability to unconsciously influence behavior in this way, the brain becomes easily led. Leading the physical body creates a social context in which subjects' brains will follow you.

Since body language has so much influence on how we feel, imagine how easy it would be to modify people's moods simply by making them follow the body language signals you want them to. Typically, it takes about four minutes of mirroring and matching body language and gestures to cause subjects to follow your movements. After this point, the rule of thumb is to follow one of their movements every two minutes or so. While many experts have dedicated timelines to this process, conversations and interactions are so organic that any specifics applied to them would only degrade from an operator's capacity to influence subjects.

Regarding posture, some professionals use a physical-therapy tool to improve their clients' posture. This tool is a type of physical-therapy tape that is adhesive and stretchy. It can be applied to your back as a constant reminder to straighten your spine or lower your shoulders.

Speech Styles

When you listen to the way a person speaks, you can match the style of speech slightly. The mannerisms each person displays while speaking are varied, and the dynamics of which speech idiosyncrasies should be mirrored are complex. The table below displays the types of speech mannerisms you can mirror and how precise you should be in your behavioral matching.

Speech style	Mirror level	Description
Speech	Medium	Limited mirroring. Match speed to begin and slow down.
Rhythm	Medium	Match rhythm if fast and slow yours to create following.
Volume	Medium	Match only half of high-volume subjects.
Tone	High	Match tonality of subjects' voices until trance time.
Stutters	None	Never match uncertain or timid behaviors.
Uncertainties (uh, um, er)	None	Never match uncertain or timid behaviors.
Emotional tone	High	Keep current with positive emotional tones. Maintain neutrality and empathy with negative ones.

GESTURES

The gestures people use frequently can be mirrored. The time constraint in mirroring body language is not present with this skill. You are able to memorize gestural tendencies and feed them back later to highlight points that you want subjects to feel more agreement with. Subjects naturally use certain hand gestures and head movements more than others. When choosing the gestures, you want to use to activate psychological submission or control, memorize only the gestures they use when speaking of things associated with positive emotional content. For example, if a subject uses a baton gesture (Bg) while speaking negatively about a political candidate, eliminate this gesture from your mannerisms for the duration of the conversation. If subjects tilt their heads or make the shape of a ball with their fingers to illustrate positive points, immediately file that information away to be used for later phases of conversation.

BREATHING AND BLINKING

The rate of breathing will vary in subjects during the organic process of conversation. There is no need to pay attention to the per-minute rate of breathing during conversations. When you analyze breathing, the speed of breathing, whether slow or fast, is all you will need to mirror. In the first few minutes of conversation, you should match subjects' breathing and eventually slow it down when they begin to follow your shifts in body language. When speaking to their subconscious, as you will learn to do later, you can also match their breathing by speaking or starting to speak when they are exhaling and by pausing while they inhale.

The average blink rate of humans varies from about seventeen to twenty-five blinks per minute (BPM). As we become interested, curious, entertained, or otherwise focused on stimuli, our blink rates can slow significantly, to around seven to ten BPM. During stressful times and emotionally pressing events, our blink rates can soar up to about fifty BPM without us even realizing it.

How does this apply to real life?

As your subjects become more interested in you or your conversational topics, their blink rates will start to decline. This isn't a skill you have to practice much: within two days, you can likely become very proficient at observing this behavior.

What happens when you talk and subjects' blink rates start to get faster and more frequent? You're boring them, or the topic is causing emotional stress.

As a public speaker, you can single out a random sampling of an audience and monitor the room's average blink rate.

You can instantly determine how someone feels about you.

In a negotiation, the blink rates of the people in the room change as they become satisfied or feel threatened.

As a police officer, a suspect's increasing blink rate might imply coming violence.

CONFESSIONS

No person is socially attracted to absolute perfection in other people. Making small and sometimes humorous confessions of flaws will assist in bringing down the defenses of subjects and lowering resistance. Even something as small as an admission that you can't stop yourself from eating certain types of candy can open a subject up psychologically. Confessions that contain an element of truth are the best to use, because of the authenticity that will automatically show in your behavior when you make them. Small confessions that are also semiuniversal experiences can create more rapport as well because the person can relate to your imperfection when the confession is made. The following list can aid you in developing awareness of the technique and in creating a list of your own:

* Not being able to stop yourself from eating certain types of candy or sweets
* Worrying about an intruder in your bathroom while shampooing your hair
* Having an inability to control yourself from buying a product when you see it
* Wanting to examine the contents of cars of people you ride with
* Having a small thing you frequently procrastinate about

- Checking the time on your watch and then not being able to tell anyone what time it is
- Opening your phone to check something and getting distracted by other apps
- Saving greeting cards and not being able to throw them away
- Coming close to adopting or getting new puppies every time you see them for sale
- Having trouble making your schedule fit into your designated work hours
- Not keeping in touch with people you should call more often
- Talking trash to your GPS unit when you get lost
- Worrying too much about germs
- Having a secret career or hobby you wished that you pursued but never did
- Looking in your rearview mirror several times after passing a police officer

DELIBERATE SOCIAL ERRORS

Noticing a nonverbal display of timidity or defensiveness can affect your behavior in the field. Seeing a subject becoming defensive can influence your decisions and cause you to be more impulsive to alleviate the defensiveness you see in the subject. However, there are small but powerful techniques you can use to diffuse subjects' worry, to lower their barriers. Masterfully trained interrogators commonly employ these methods during their work to create the appearance of being slightly less than perfect, sloppy, or otherwise nonthreatening when they speak to subjects with high-barrier behaviors. Here is a list of common deliberate errors:

- Leaving a part of your shirt untucked
- Having a stain on your collar
- Having a small piece of food in your teeth
- Mispronouncing words deliberately

- Stuttering once or twice
- Tripping during the initial introduction phase
- Deliberately showing insecure gestures from the behavioral table of elements
- Using a small pencil to take notes on a tiny, cheap notepad instead of an interrogator's notebook
- Leaving a shoe untied
- Creating wrinkles in your shirt prior to the introduction
- Driving coffee grounds under fingernails to appear unkempt
- Having a childish ringtone installed and allowing a "planned" call to come through

When speaking to subjects, if you've placed them on the needs map and they need intelligence, your deliberate feigning an inability to use a certain feature on your phone or ignorance of the finer points of something you know they are proud to speak about can change their behaviors markedly. After you identify where people are on the needs map, they will require different, deliberate behavioral errors or shortcomings to feel contextually relevant or confident in your presence. Confidence is by no means the desired result with any subjects you work with, and to put them in a state of diminished capacity, where they lack self-esteem, requires you to use tactics to make them feel more comfortable.

CHANGING PERSONAL APPEARANCE

Your appearance can have tremendous influence on the outcome of an interaction in the field. When time permits, your appearance can be altered to conform to subjects' manner of dress, behaviors, and appearances. Some methods that physically change (with training) your body can increase likeability and trustworthiness.

Manner of Dress

The way you dress can make you seem similar in economic status to subjects, thereby increasing their trust of you. However, if authority is more important in the objective (as in an operation requiring more extreme levels of obedience), dressing in a way that inspires automatic trust or following behaviors may be more important to you than matching their manner of dress.

For instance, with an objective of having them believe that you are trustworthy and friendly, that you are someone they should want to be around, your matching their manner of dress will help you be more *like* them. On the other hand, if you need to recruit assets, need to use more coercive methods, or need outcomes that demand more direct obedience to suggestion, you want to dress for that as well. If you need your subjects to trust your opinion and to view you as an authority figure, you can modify the way you dress to suit the scenario.

Think for a moment about whom we trust to make important decisions. As a whole, our society tends to view people in sharp suits, doctors' uniforms, and law-enforcement uniforms as authority figures. You may recall reading about this earlier in this chapter, when we discussed the nature of human obedience. Something as small as having a stethoscope hanging from your bag can work the same way on people's unconscious minds as a full doctor's outfit. A medical-looking pager on your hip can serve the same purpose as well.

Small modifications in your appearance can go a long way toward getting the behaviors you want from your subjects. The appearance alone can do all of the heavy lifting in the initial phase of an interaction. Subjects react on an unconscious level to authority symbols like these.

Wearing glasses to build rapport is also very helpful if being seen as honest is more important to your outcome than being seen as authoritative. However, if subjects wear glasses, you can put yours on anytime during the interactions to increase rapport.

Physical Appearance

While there may not be a lot you can do to actually change your appearance, the following two methods, based on research findings, can help quite a bit in the rapid rapport-development process:

Studies have shown that people with shiny eyes are seen as more physically attractive and healthy (Patzer, 2006). Regardless of the sex of the person with whom you are dealing, increasing your level of attractiveness also increases your ability to develop rapport. Before an interaction, you can do two things to increase the physical appearance (shiny quality) of your eyes: carry an eye moisturizer or deliberately pull a few nose hairs out to cause your eyes to water immediately before the interaction begins. These can have lasting effects on the subject as you are creating a first impression that will stay in the subject's mind.

Having healthy-looking skin and hair can show the same qualities to a subject. Keeping your skin clear and your hair shiny and healthy looking can provide you with influence opportunities you would otherwise have to work hard to achieve.

Manipulating Subject Physiology

You read a moment ago that the movements of the physical body create internal experiences. When you can linguistically modify the physiology of subjects, you can open doors to the behavior-engineering methods that follow.

Think back to the last time you saw someone correct or adjust his or her posture while you were speaking with each other. This behavior causes immediate awareness of your own posture and likely made you want to adjust your own posture. As humans, we become aware of our bodies and behaviors when our attention is drawn in that direction. In a linguistic sense, all you have to do is speak about physiology or behavior to make subjects become aware of their bodies, encouraging them to feel that they need to adjust accordingly.

If you think about the physiology you want your subjects to exhibit, the physiology of comfort, interest, and trust most likely comes to mind. When you actually cause subjects to exhibit these physical behaviors, you are actually creating internal states in them that match the ones you create for their bodies. Your making them exhibit these behaviors requires nothing more than a short, easy linguistic technique. Consider the following physiological indicators of comfort, interest, and trust:

* Abdominal breathing
* Slowed breathing
* Shoulder relaxation
* Neck exposure
* Facial expressions of happiness
* Facial expressions of curiosity and interest
* Open and welcoming posture

All of these behaviors indicate rapport. They signal comfort, interest, and trust. Engineering these into subjects' behaviors is simple. Let's examine each behavior and how to control subjects' physiologies by using linguistics. Having the proper understanding will ensure that your messages and commands are heard more clearly and amenably, increasing the likelihood that subjects will be more receptive to everything that follows.

It's useful here to use a speech pattern that differs slightly from the one you've been using thus far in the conversation. Conspiratorial speech is most useful to enhance momentary focus here. Conspiratorial speech is simply speaking by lowering your voice and leaning in slightly toward subjects, as if you were sharing semisecrets with them.

Abdominal Breathing
Abdominal breathing is how we breathe in sleep—our most relaxed state. Knowing the power of language and its influence on behavior,

consider the numerous ways you could bring abdominal breathing into a conversation.

"I read the most interesting article last week about how successful people behave differently. They said when they watched all of these successful people, they actually breathe into their stomachs instead of their chests. They had that ability to just relax, I guess. It was interesting to read."

The simple mention of this is enough to draw awareness to it. Now that we have also associated this quality with successful people, the subject will most likely begin to mimic the suggested behavior.

Slowed Breathing
Simply mentioning the speed at which most people breathe is enough to focus subjects' awareness on their breathing. Doing this helps them to slow it down, which is the natural reaction to focusing on breathing, as no one consciously wants to breathe faster in social environments.

Shoulder Relaxation
The main reason for the rise of shoulders is fear, as you hopefully made notes of while studying the BToE. Most people, even in comfortable social environments, have a slight shoulder raise. Helping them to relax it is something that is as easily done as slowing their breathing down using linguistics. Your mentioning an article about how successful people have a lot of shoulder relaxation would work is an example of using linguistics. However, the physical motion of raising your shoulders for a second or two and making an obvious effort to lower them and express physical relaxation will cause subjects to follow suit, just like the adjustment of posture.

Neck Exposure
Using behavior, you can cause subjects to expose their necks in a few different ways. These are behaviors that are meant to make subjects tilt their heads or slightly lift their chins during conversations.

First, after using your body to match theirs (as you read about in the mirroring chapter), you can then perform the actions with your body that you wish for them to take. Tilt your head in the direction you'd like them to tilt theirs.

Second, using your hand while speaking in a natural way, raise your hand to where it is almost bladed to your face (holding your hand with your thumb toward you and making it almost flat, like a salute). When you raise your hand, it should be in the midline, where it's near your head and almost in front of your face. As you move your hand outward, exposing the palm a bit toward the subject and slightly to the ceiling, your head should tilt with the same motion of your hand. This movement should appear natural and is easily performed. It gives subjects more than one reason to copy the gestures you give their unconscious minds to follow.

The third method to get subjects to expose their necks is to use a hand gesture similar to the previous, except that you preface the gesture with a covert but natural hand movement that points at subjects' heads. This allows you to draw attention to their heads in a covert way before the gesture is performed. Taking no less than half of a second, this gestural point to subjects' heads should be casual and appear to have a natural place in the gestural harmony of your speech. This is much easier to accomplish than most people initially believe.

Facial Expressions of Happiness

You've thus far become familiar with the concept that human physiology and movements can trigger internal emotions. Conversationally forcing subjects to display a happy facial expression creates a feeling of wellness and enjoyment. The subjects should then, ideally, associate this with you. Simply asking subjects about times they immensely enjoyed themselves is a great way to get them to display happy facial expressions; however, you can prime their unconscious minds to make such facial expressions by feeding them information that causes them to think about the gesture. You'll soon learn the absolute importance of rehearsal in behavior engineering, and this method is a way that causes subjects to rehearse the mental process. The thoughts of the facial expression should naturally bring a small amount of awareness to their own facial expressions before you deploy conversational means of discussing the happy facial expression.

Facial Expressions of Curiosity and Interest

Triggering facial expressions in subjects can be done the same way that almost any other behavior is socially or behaviorally forced: using stories, mirroring, and eliciting information that causes the expression to come naturally. Facial expressions of curiosity are similar to the head-tilt force because they open the physiology up, therefore opening subjects up psychologically. This method simply uses a story about watching youngsters come downstairs on a Christmas morning. When you describe the scene (briefly), you must talk about a curious facial expression on the children and gesture with your hand to subjects' faces in a way that does not draw attention to your hand.

Open and Welcoming Posture

Causing subjects to open their physiology will inevitably open them mentally, making them more receptive to suggestion and influence. When subjects have crossed arms, are facing slightly away, or seem to exhibit closed behaviors, you can do one of these three methods to open their physiology:

First, cause them to physically alter their body posture by using objects. Handing them a pen, asking them to hold something, or asking them to look a certain direction at something—all are ways to create shifts that open their physiology.

Second, use mirroring: copy their bodily movements for a moment or two and open your own body language as you take in large breaths, as if it feels good. As you do this, you can comment on how awesome the place or weather is where you are or something else positive. Subjects, wanting to absorb positivity, will be more likely to follow the movement to soak up the feeling.

Third, discuss an article you read, one that describes how body language affects success and closed-off people are more likely to be underachievers. This mental need to be associated with success and to enhance self-identity can cause subjects to attend to their body posture. It is important to remember that the methods of this technique should be used without reference or gesture to subjects' body movements. Also, when you reach the part of the story about the article that describes the body language relating to openness, look away briefly and give the subject a judgment-free opportunity to shift their body language.

Profiling Strengths

Finding people's strengths isn't about discovering what they are good at; it's about finding what they want to be appreciated for. The power you have to profile behavior is already well above the top 10 percent on this planet. When you hear people speak, you must pay close attention to the themes and desires that are hidden within their language. Every conversation will reveal the speakers' hidden desires to be appreciated for something. Even if people's charisma isn't off the charts, when you see that they take pride in their ability to connect with others, you can deliver compliments that nourish their souls—that is, comment on their authenticity, sincerity, or magnetic personality.

Using these needs to deliver compliments is an incredible way to connect with people. Genuine and well-timed compliments are things we all remember for a long time. Use the following guidelines for delivering compliments:

* Spend your time looking for the positive aspects in everyone. Even the weaknesses and fears of your subjects can be positives if you keep yourself in the right mind-set.

- Pay attention to compliments you received from others in the past. The ones that stand out are probably the most genuine and probably addressed the traits you needed to be recognized for.
- Don't exaggerate compliments. Make them sincere and in the moment. "The best food in the world" actually sounds worse to most people than "amazing food."
- Use specificity about what you noticed that led you to giving the compliment. "I love how you told me that story. You're so open and sincere about everything. I love that."
- Compliments seem more genuine when they have follow-up questions after them. "You have this awesome ability to connect with certain people so well. Is that something you've had all your life?"
- Use an effect statement after compliments to make them real and impactful. "The way you stay so tuned in to people all the time makes me want to start working on that myself!"
- Pause after delivering compliments; give them room to breathe so they don't get lost in the conversation.

It's important to let subjects win small intellectual victories, in which they get to be right after you admit to being wrong. This serves the outcome. Being right and doing what gets results are very different things.

When subjects expose their palms, they are at the behavioral stage of appearing vulnerable, nonthreatening, and open. The best time to issue a compliment is immediately following a palm-exposure gesture.

ACTIVATING CONNECTION BEHAVIOR

We connect to others when we feel relaxed, liked, and open. To make someone feel this, it's as simple as discussing the topic of humility, connection, authenticity, and openness. This can come up naturally in almost any conversation. Even if subjects are talking about plumbing, it's easy to talk about a kind and authentic plumber you met and to conclude by commenting on how refreshing it is when people are open and genuine. This simple and small method can produce drastic behavior changes, even if no other methods are being used. Do not let its size fool you.

Eye contact is maintained while we speak. In America, the average time two people maintain eye contact is seven seconds. If eye contact is avoided for a few moments then reactivated during a passionate part of a story when your eyes light up, it can cause strong connections. When meeting a person, say that you already find him or her familiar; then use the phrase "that feeling of connection." This is the point where you should reestablish eye contact, before you go on to describe further your sense of connection.

Sincerity can be communicated by tilting your head slightly while speaking and simultaneously placing your hand on your chest.

CONCLUSION

Developing rapid rapport is easy if you follow the patterns you've learned thus far in this book. Having rapport with subjects makes them exponentially more likely to follow your lead and to become increasingly susceptible to commands and suggestions. Here's a bulleted list of the basics of rapid rapport:

* No one likes perfect people.
* Authenticity is one of the most socially attractive behaviors you can exhibit.
* Making others feel interesting creates automatic rapport.
* Listening and commenting on what you hear from subjects shows you're paying attention.
* When you are nervous or insecure, your "chords" are vibrating (activating) at the same frequencies in your subjects.
* The only information subjects can use to judge you is what you provide. Your authority and authenticity are limited only by your display of the techniques.

* Tilting your head while listening to detailed parts of subjects' stories will help to convey interest and curiosity.
* If subjects show signs of timidity or insecurity, remove such trepidation by asking them questions about topics they are confident about, and get them back into their mental comfort zone until they no longer show nonverbal signs of timidity.
* Never criticize or complain. Your efforts to create rapport may be tremendous, but as a master, you must never show that anything has challenged you. You must make it all look easy.
* If you're wrong or have made a mistake, admit it immediately and openly, without attempting to justify your error.

Cold Reading

• • •

COLD READING CAN PRODUCE A profound feeling of connection and warmth with subjects. Cold reading typically refers to the practice of making slightly educated guesses about a person, and it is somewhat based on the Barnum effect and Forer effect. The Forer effect is based on a demonstration that Professor B. R. Forer presented to his students that made the majority of them believe he could ascertain private aspects of their lives and personalities. The following is the script Professor Forer gave to his students, presented as an analysis of the students' personalities (Forer, 1949, p. 118–123):

- You have a great need for other people to like and admire you.
- You have a tendency to be critical of yourself.
- You have a great deal of unused capacity that you have not turned to your advantage.
- While you have some personality weaknesses, you are generally able to compensate for them.
- Your sexual adjustment has presented problems for you.
- Disciplined and self-controlled outside, you tend to be worrisome and insecure inside.
- At times you have serious doubts as to whether you have made the right decision or done the right thing.
- You prefer a certain amount of change and variety and become dissatisfied when hemmed in by restrictions and limitations.

- You pride yourself as an independent thinker and do not accept others' statements without satisfactory proof.
- You have found it unwise to be too frank in revealing yourself to others.
- At times you are extroverted, affable, and sociable, while at other times you are introverted, wary, and reserved.
- Some of your aspirations tend to be pretty unrealistic.
- Security is one of your major goals in life.

These words, like many horoscopes and psychic readings, resonated with so many students that they mostly believed that the professor had accurately read their personalities. When this happens in conversations and when it's presented in a way that makes it sound like an in-the-moment observation, it creates increased transparency in subjects and often opens several doors for them to discuss very personal information.

Some of the above traits are common to almost everyone. Since the journal article referenced here was published, in 1949, there have been inadvertent advances in cold readings. With the proper application of the behavior training you've learned thus far, any kind of reading you do will no longer be a cold read but one that's quite warm.

For *The Ellipsis Manual*, an effective list that is up to date and applicable in social conversations was compiled; it was based on social trends, online surveys, and common questions on social networks. Here is the list:

- "You're very sensitive to rejection and hesitate to speak your mind sometimes."
- "You desire attention. You sometimes do things that might be rash to get attention from others."
- "You dwell on the past too much. You continually relive moments that were negative rather than remember positive moments."
- "You worry about taking better care of yourself. You're not lazy, but you just can't make the sustained effort."

* "You compare yourself to others in terms of property, success, and social status."
* "You eat when you're not hungry. Sometimes you don't even notice you're doing it."
* "You feel like you're fooling the world sometimes. You wonder whether you really deserve it and worry about being found out, even if you're at the top of your food chain."
* "You worry about being overly controlled. You have thoughts about the negative things that would happen if too many regulations were imposed on you."
* "You fear that important things will be taken away from you. You fear the important people will leave you and valuable items will be lost." (This is common in subjects with several siblings.)
* "You don't do the real things that would genuinely make you happy. Even though you know they would, the things that would truly make you happy are far away from your priorities."
* "Compliments make you uncomfortable sometimes. When someone compliments you, you may feel good, but compliments create discomfort in general, so you change the subject often."
* "You take joy in hearing the confessions and secrets of others."
* "You sometimes secretly enjoy being angry. The feeling of anger makes you feel stronger, but your habitual response doesn't make sense."
* "You can feel alone even when you're around friends and co-workers. Even in a crowded room, it's easy to feel alone and disconnected."

This list can serve several purposes. You can use the items to make personal confessions, knowing that most subjects will identify with them. This creates a bond without the risk that speculation will cause resistance in subjects. Secondly, the list's items can be used to pace subjects' states. If you mention that most people possess a similar trait and follow up with suggestions to lead subjects' trains of thought, you can covertly pace these subjects' internal beliefs without overtly pacing situations or thought lines.

For cold reading, it's best to present the above items as interesting things you've noticed about your subjects. It's best to start with something positive they are not likely to have heard before. For instance, the phrase "I've noticed you seem to have an amazing ability to..." can be used to initiate a positive cold read. This serves to compliment subjects and let them know they possess a trait or traits that others are also likely to notice. By no means should this be presented as a profiling skill or a psychic ability. It's simply presented as something you offhandedly noticed about each subject during the relevant conversations.

This method should be used no more than two times in any interaction. Make your observations positive, and reframe any observation you make in a positive light. The following examples of cold reading can be used to begin the process to open subjects up to talking about themselves:

* "I can tell that..."
* "The way you spoke about..."
* "Just be seeing your face light up about..."
* "It's clear you have the ability..."
* "There's something about you. I'll bet you..."
* "I can see that you..."
* "You have such a passion for..."
* "There's something different about you..."
* "I'll bet you..."
* "You truly have that natural ability to..."

Keep in mind that the traits you compliment subjects on should be aligned with the goals you have for changing their behaviors. For instance, you would not want to compliment someone's ability for skepticism or an ability to take control of social situations. The initial parts of cold readings should be positive and should involve one of the following traits:

* Ability to connect well with others
* Passion for something important to them
* Drive and motivation
* Leadership
* Their abilities to focus
* Having positive influence
* Being a good friend
* Being open minded and smart
* The ability to let things go and just be totally in the moment

Authenticity

This should be something you practice and get an intuitive feel for before you begin using this skill in the field. When you perform this simple technique on subjects, the reactions you see will shock you. Subjects will open up completely and begin spilling information and secrets, handing you the keys to their unconscious minds.

Priming

• • •

OUR BRAINS HAVE A SPECIAL wiring system that allows us to adapt quickly to new incoming information. It is a mechanism that recognizes familiar or known concepts and begins to search for and prepare the brain for similar concepts. For instance, if you were shown the word *wheel* before being exposed to a small group of words containing the word *tire* in it, *tire* would stand out more than the other words, and you would likely see it first.

Priming can occur through various stimuli. If you were shown a small list of words containing the word *start* and were later asked to think of a word starting with the letters *s-t-a*, your response would likely be *start*.

Emotional priming can work in very similar ways. If you feel extremely motivated and energetic, you are far more likely to want to make positive decisions. If you feel helplessness and despair, your actions will seek out information to confirm your feelings and possibly deepen them as well.

Imagine you were in a pet store and took some time to look at tiny puppies. Afterward, if you left the pet store and encountered a lost dog on the road, you would be far more likely to pull over and help him or call the owner than if you hadn't visited the pet store at all. Conversely, if you encounter the exact same dog as before after leaving the emergency room because a stray dog had attacked your child, what are the chances you'll stop and help?

Imagine a small child playing with a toy shaped like a large ball that has various holes designed to fit variously shaped pieces into them. Some are shaped like stars, triangles, circles, and so on. Sometimes you can force a piece into a hole it wasn't designed for, but they pretty much fit into their respective holes and fall into the ball.

Keeping this visualization of the toy in mind, imagine your brain as this large, round toy. Several shaped holes cover the surface, but these holes change their shapes based on what you are exposed to. If anger, for instance, is a square, when you become angry, many of the other holes automatically change into being able to receive only square-shaped pieces. When you are extremely excited, for instance, all of the holes change themselves to receive the shapes that are associated with excitement. When we experience emotions and feelings, we are primed to receive more of the same.

If you speak to subjects for a while about skepticism and doubt, how would their brains receive new information they aren't familiar with? If you try to present subjects with something new after having primed them for skepticism (even if it was several minutes before), they will be far less likely to accept the new ideas or suggestions. When you get subjects to shift their moods, thoughts, feelings, or beliefs, you are essentially changing the shapes of the holes in their brains and modifying them to receive different types of information and suggestions. After bypassing their autopilots, developing rapport, and establishing conversational authority, you gain the ability to manipulate the directions in which their thoughts will naturally travel. In a sense, you can give subjects thoughts, at this point. This concept will continually come up throughout this volume, but it is important that you develop an understanding of the idea of priming and how powerfully it affects subjects' unconscious minds.

A subject can be primed physically, visually, or linguistically. Physical priming, which is not covered in this volume, involves the use of actors and environmental manipulations to achieve desired mental states in subjects. Visual priming involves strategically placing words and images within view of subjects' to steer their unconscious thoughts along desired directions. This will be covered briefly below and is outlined in detail in a separate volume.

Think of the last time you purchased a new car. It's very likely you immediately began to notice every car on the road that was the same make and model as yours. When you get a new gadget, you're more likely to notice people with the same gadget as well. This syndrome occurs in all of us because of the importance our unconscious minds place on these new items. When the unconscious deems something is important or relevant, it causes the conscious mind to seek it out and identify it. This is likely an evolutionary trigger that helped our ancestors identify predators after having encountered them in the wild. Our using priming techniques is one way we can directly communicate to subjects' unconscious minds that something is important. Doing this helps them to make decisions and shifts their minds into the shapes we want them to be in later, for future parts of the interactions.

Attention is the most important ingredient in all of your interactions. Without attention, nothing exists.

A principle associated with priming is the access-state principle. As much as the name sounds scientific, it simply means that people in certain moods or mind-sets will require those mind-sets again to produce the same results. There's a joke about the old drunk who tried to walk home one day and couldn't find his house because he'd never tried to do so while sober.

Knowing that subjects naturally want to follow your lead, it becomes easier to use authority to prepare their brains to receive the ideas you want to give them. More on priming will be covered in the hypnotic-control chapters to follow. By now, application of the skills you've learned should enable you to control several social situations. The linguistic methods that follow are exponentially more sophisticated and can be applied elegantly to what lies ahead in your training.

SENSORY PRIMING

All of us are extremely susceptible to priming methods, regardless of the method of delivery. Within your work as an operator, there will be several instances where priming subjects by using sensory input will drastically change their behavior. For instance, an operation requiring subjects to be in a carefree, adolescent, or otherwise happy mood can contain numerous priming methods. The smell of sunscreen is almost universally associated with fun, carefree enjoyment. Operators would strategically use this method by applying sunscreen to themselves before the relevant operations, and they might even carry the bottle of sunscreen into the field, which could be disposed.

Let's examine the other situations that can benefit from sensory priming methods. Activating generosity in subjects can prove to be beneficial in the field for a number of reasons. While you'll learn later to manipulate outcomes to create employees and subjects who will offer money or free products, there are many more applications for activating generosity and a feeling of giving. Without reading further into the volume, what can you think of now that could make someone feel generous? Within the sensory realm, there are no universally recognized smells that can cause people to recall times when they were generous. Their visual fields are still a valuable sense to use in this context. Something as small as a Band-Aid on your hand, a physical limp, or a seemingly genuine appearance of being intimidated can make people activate their own caretaker needs.

Using small indicators of thriftiness goes a long way to enhance trustworthiness in tight spots. Something as small as a piece of tape on the corner of your glasses or a wrap of tape around the band of your watch can trigger trust in subjects.

When doing regression work with Ellipsis methods, you can strategically let loose the smell of mothballs during conversations about people's memories of their grandparents' homes or their childhood memories of other people who always spoiled them. Ellipsis research has proved this to be about 70 percent effective in activating stronger and more emotional memories in subjects. Operators can carry a small sandwich bag in the field to open it inside of a pocket, during regressive conversational work.

If you are operating in an environment where you need a subject to experience anger or frustration with something, squeezing a fist (especially after you've developed mirroring with the subject) can cause the subject to do the same or at least to activate the muscles that make a fist, thereby signaling frustration or anger in the subject's mind. You can apply this method by using the gestural, hemispheric tendency profile you've created for the subject, moving to the subject's negative-reference hemisphere to employ the technique.

Establishing a profile of your subjects can provide valuable data for your operations. This simple step can make the difference between disaster and success. Imagine using an old-fashioned cologne with the intention of making subjects recall the times they were taken care of or were with their father figures. If subjects were abused by someone with the same-smelling product, the reaction could be disastrous.

The smell of rubbing alcohol can trigger feelings from all corners of subjects' minds. For example, a subject might have a memory of hand sanitizers in a doctor's office, in which the subject remembers the horrible pain from pouring the sanitizer into an open wound. If you use medical metaphors within conversations to modify subjects' beliefs or thoughts, you will need to reinforce those impressions before the pertinent smells are exposed to the subjects.

The smell of pine trees (Christmas trees) can also trigger memories of childhood curiosity and joy. This priming method is dependent on subjects because some adults may react negatively because of the financial and social stress of the memories of holiday times. Without research, this method isn't employable and can cause a reaction that produces results contrary to your desired outcomes.

You will, indubitably, have countless opportunities to exploit sensory-priming methods with subjects. The applications are limited but have far-reaching mental effects on subjects. You may eventually come up with other methods for uses of sensory priming in the field. You are encouraged to ensure that subjects are profiled to the point in which you are certain of success in using the priming method.

EMOTIONAL PRIMING

Behavior in the field can take many forms; you are not only modifying and deliberately creating your own behavior to activate parts of subjects' thought processes, but also using methods of behavior that literally make changes within your subjects on a physiological level.

The emotions you will learn to activate in the field are innumerable. However, you will, indubitably, eventually be able to control emotions quickly without the use of nonbehavioral methods. Trust, respect, and interest are the most effective states you can activate on an emotional level in subjects.

Creating trust is a fundamental part of hypnotic work, whether you run a private practice or run a black-site interrogation laboratory. In the field, however, methods of creating trust rely much more on the covert application of subjective experience. For instance, imagine being within earshot of a subject and having a phone conversation in which you are speaking to someone about a wallet you found that morning and decided to turn in to the front desk. As you speak, you ask questions about the wallet to determine whether anyone was able to claim it. You end the brief phone call by expressing concern for the person who lost it and hoping that person is able to get all of the cash and cards back soon.

As the subject hears that conversation, even if only for a moment, the subject will begin to see you as a trustworthy person. You have demonstrated this not by telling the subject you are trustworthy but by having a private conversation with another person, within the subject's presence. Thus, the subject becomes much less likely to have any doubts, concerns, or incredulity regarding your trustworthiness, because the subject had no opportunity to screen the information.

Small acts like this one frequently bypass dozens of mental doors that would otherwise stand in the way of creating emotions within your subjects.

Imagine sitting in a café. As you extend a ten-dollar bill to people at the next table and ask whether any of them dropped it, they say they have not. You hand it to the cashier, saying how someone dropped it and that individual might later come back to claim it. As you sit back in your seat, starting a conversation with built-in trust becomes exponentially easier and gives you the ability to bypass several minutes of conversational work to establish the trust.

The options you have for developing trust are limitless, and these options will present themselves differently in different environments. Establishing respect is much the same, and you can use methods similar to the above methods.

Respect and interest can serve the same purpose and can also be created in tandem, often by a very small act. Interest can be established in environments where you need to control the focus of your subjects, where you have a goal of eventually compromising subjects' decision processes. Your having a stethoscope hang from a bag, your speaking in a foreign language over the phone before interacting with a subject, your showing up to a meeting with the day's crossword that's already been filled in, or your having a puppy or baby animal (depending on the environment)—such premeditated actions can go a very long way to establishing the initial interest needed to control subjects in the ways you need them to move.

Making deliberate social errors, as described earlier, can lower subjects' defenses as they speak with you. Where subjects would otherwise have reservations about letting go in your presence, because of their increased withholding behavior, your appearance of being an imperfect operator can benefit certain subjects who need help opening up. The following methods are ways of appearing more approachable and flawed in the eyes of subjects:

Keeping your eyebrows or shoulders raised slightly above normal levels implies a slight amount of social fear, upon initial contact, to subjects who might otherwise be confrontational because of their insecurity or their feeling the need to be more dominant than the people they deal with.

In the beginning of interactions with new subjects, a single arm wrapped around your torso can show them your insecurity, if doing so is needed.

During the initial stages of interactions, tilting your head to your left while subjects speak indicates curiosity, keeping them in an emotional state of satisfaction as they speak. They will usually continue to speak. While employing this movement, keep eye contact and nod after your subjects have stopped speaking to cause them to speak even more. This will often provide you with information they would have otherwise withheld. This need to continue speaking often results in this phenomenon because of the increased desire to fill an otherwise empty conversational space. When this happens, subjects are highly likely to simply say what is already within their minds, rather than make up things, thus saving mental energy and appearing more comfortable in the interaction.

Eliciting Desired States to Prime Subjects

The simple act of describing a scenario to subjects or asking them to describe something to you creates a mandatory human experience they have to go through: imagining. Even the act of reading about rain hitting a roof creates a space where you have to imagine it happening to make sense of it while you read a book.

Using this principle, you can directly control the imaginative experiences of the subjects you encounter by deliberately asking questions that will lead to certain imaginings or to speaking about the same.

Speaking about an event causes subjects to go through the event in their minds to make sense of it. If you discuss a feeling, subjects, even if only temporarily, must experience this feeling to follow the story.

The books and movies that we read have this power to capture our focus and imagination. The book or movie then moves along a path—the path it wants you to follow. The art of eliciting states in your subjects is based on this fundamental principle.

When we speak about the theme of imagination, it's easy to capture someone's imagination. It can take less than ten seconds of speaking with the right tonality and skill to establish a powerful amount of focus in subjects. A problem arises when you attempt to tell them what to think. If you speak to them in a noncovert way and discuss the process of enjoying a vacation, it quickly becomes obvious that there is motive behind your speech. With this caution, think about how subtly and covertly you would be able to discuss a friend's vacation. By implying the information came from a separate and third party, you bypass the part of subjects' minds that screens, criticizes, and filters information to test whether the information is viable and actionable.

Along this same thread, if you were to discuss a program you saw on television that spoke about how people focus differently and have different experiences when they enjoy themselves, the critical mental-gate guards would not be alerted to screen the content of the language.

Speaking directly about your own experiences can produce results but has a higher likelihood of activating the critical factor. Listening to a story about the person you are speaking with engenders a feeling of criticality because the source of the information is right in front of the listener. Unconsciously, the person will still go through the process of having to imagine and participate (mentally) in the story you are sharing, but it is more difficult to lull this same person's mental-screening process to sleep if the stories are strictly about you.

FOCUSED PRIMING

In focused priming methods, subjects are given a survey or questionnaire that is loaded with priming words and phrases. For instance, a cult-recruiting questionnaire would ask subjects to rate, on a scale from one to five, the degree to which they desired help in their lives, they felt out of control, they felt as if they had no connection to others, and they wanted to become new people or attain new lifestyles. Simple questions like these can affect subjects even if they aren't taking a survey. In such cases, operators are causing electricity to connect in subjects' brains, in the particular areas where they want it to.

Establishing Initial Control of Subjects

● ● ●

WHEN A SUBJECT BECOMES FOCUSED on a conversation, the slight shifts in your behavior allow further building of advanced compliance and assist in the achievement of your outcome.

The first phase of gaining advanced control is to use leading body language. After having developed subjects' desires to match your body language, you can move in certain ways that cause them to begin allowing you more and more control of their physical movements, which lead their emotional states and beliefs about you.

As you learned in the pacing and leading section, small changes in your body language cause subjects to change their body language to match yours. The following methods are available in this phase of the conversation to encourage subjects' physically copying you:

Take a step back to cause subjects to feel a need to step forward to fill the physical void you created.

Look away from the interactions to test your ability to have subjects follow your cue. These are called gaze-cue behaviors.

Point and make them look in the directions you point, and reward them for complying with your movements by giving them your attention.

Take a deep breath to test compliance, and visually check to see whether subjects follow your lead.

Straighten your posture to visually check whether subjects are following you. (This shift in posture is a hygienic gesture and is far more likely to be performed when you are *not* making eye contact with, or looking directly at, your subjects. They feel more able to shift their posture after you do if you look away briefly.)

Take sips of your drink (if drinking) and count the seconds until subjects do the same. (Seven seconds or less is considered to be the rule of thumb for Ellipsis operators.)

SUBMISSION AND FOCUS PHYSIOLOGY CREATION

Make suggestions or observations on abdominal breathing. As you've learned already, physiology can inwardly affect the emotional states of subjects. Controlling or modifying the states through conversational suggestions can create the emotionally relaxed state you need to do Ellipsis work in the field.

Speaking in a hushed tone (a conspiratorial tone), as if you were sharing a secret, can inspire rapt focus in quiet environments.

FOCUS, INTEREST, AND CURIOSITY

These three states, when felt by your subjects, are the building blocks of every part of your operations. Regarding the ability to influence subjects' behaviors, having the ability to develop these states in your subjects can almost stand on its own power.

Focus should be the first state you engender in subjects during your encounters. Using the methods about the autopilot and the methods you will learn in the coming chapters, you will develop the ability to establish focus quickly and efficiently. For you to be a highly skilled operator, the ability to develop focus should be the cornerstone of your initial training. Focus, interest, and curiosity can be developed for maximum effectiveness, leading to the ability for you to psychologically engineer outcomes. Once you've developed focus in your subjects, their interest becomes easier to manufacture, which naturally leads to curiosity. Let's explore these terms—focus, interest, and curiosity—in depth and what they mean to subjects.

Focus

Focus is the gathering of attention resources and directing them to concentrate the mind's efforts onto a single task. When subjects become conversationally focused, things they would have otherwise paid attention to begin to fade away. All of their attention and mental resources become like a spotlight instead of a floodlight. This happens to all of us almost daily. Something gets our attention, and our minds decide whether it is interesting, relevant, or valuable. Once this short decision process is complete, our mental resources are directed to the point of focus. Think of the last time you found yourself absorbed in a fascinating book or a great movie. Even the visual areas around the book or the screen became blurry and stopped being significant. When we experience focus, it is usually brief unless we then become interested in the relevant stimuli. It's important to note what lies behind you when bringing subjects into focus. Ensure your background isn't going to be excessively distracting. Televisions, crowds, and large rooms tend to draw attention away from the operators. In this initial phase, keep subjects' focus until they become accustomed to your voice and behavior.

Interest

Interest follows focus, and more focus follows interest. When subjects become interested in someone or something, their attention is directed with enhanced motivation to gather more information. The psychological amounts of involvement increase markedly, and the subjects become more connected to pertinent information when focus and interest are present.

Curiosity

Once subjects have focus and interest, curiosity naturally follows, giving them a much stronger desire to learn more or to listen more closely. They will ask more questions, be more attentive, and become less aware of their surroundings at the opportunity to learn and hear more from you as you speak.

Recognizing Trance Behavior

● ● ●

IF YOU ARE UNABLE TO identify trance signals in subjects, you may expend more effort than necessary. As you've come to know, even the smallest signal can transmit a vast amount of data to the trained operator. Before we begin the discussion of trance-behavior signals, it's important that we cover the methods to train your mind to recognize them. Our being in social situations provides us with so many stimuli that it's often difficult to drill our focus down to a single thing. The trick to spotting behavior while in conversations is to relax and have confidence in your ability to spot the signals. Simply acknowledging that you're well trained and competent will relax your mind and sharpen your focus on signals. This confidence in your ability is a tremendous resource, and I cannot overstate its importance. Remind yourself at every opportunity of your above-normal abilities and what training you have. Simply having this manual gives you access to more information than 99 percent of the world. Know you are good, and you will be good.

Trance behavior is exhibited in slightly different ways in each person. We all show behavior differently, based on many factors. For this reason, we have separated the list of trance behaviors into two sections: clear and subtle.

Clear indicators of trance behavior:

* Decrease in breathing rate
* Shifting from chest to abdominal breathing

* Relaxation of facial muscles
* Eye fixation on operator
* Limited hand and arm movement while speaking in dialogue
* Subtle indicators of trance behavior:
* Jaw lowering while listening (lips may be closed, but teeth are parted)
* Decrease in eye-blink shutter speed
* Decrease in blink rate
* Decrease in swallowing rate
* Slowed rate of speech
* Limited movement of feet
* Relaxation or lowering of shoulders

The lists of trance behaviors are well worth continued study and analysis. Developing your skill to spot these signals can save you valuable time in the field.

When you recognize trance behavior in subjects, continue with your progress and limit the number of times you use their names while speaking and making physical contact. If you haven't begun already, begin exhalation-based speaking and speak as they exhale.

Linguistics

● ● ●

INDUCING TRANCES IN YOUR FIRST few subjects will be an incredible experience. Words have tremendous power, but much like electricity, if they are not harnessed and issued to an audience in the right way, they become nothing but a means to deliver information to another person.

Covert trances are more difficult to recognize, but creating them is much easier than most students assume. There are several ways to create this state in subjects, and the chapters that follow all have hypnotic elements in them. The study of neurolinguistic programming has swept the nation and has reached a lull in the last decade or so. Neurolinguistic programming (NLP) was originally created (discovered) by Richard Bandler and John Grinder in California in 1973. Both men were pioneers and contributed significant steps forward in the field of influence and therapy. More importantly, they created a system that caused more questions to be asked about the efficacy of traditional therapy models. The tenets of the system state that there is a direct link between the auditory language we hear and the neurological functions in the brain. It has since been effectively applied in psychotherapy, hypnosis, and several cognitive behavioral therapy practices around the world. While NLP receives scientific criticism for what seems to be a lack of empirical validity and misappropriations of terms, it is a system designed for organic interactions and cannot be fully measured in a laboratory (Witkowski, 2010; Bandler, 1975, p. 6).

Much of NLP is based on the astounding work of a masterful practitioner named Milton H. Erickson, who was a psychiatrist and hypnotherapist specializing in family therapy and was the founding president of the American Society for Clinical Hypnosis. Erickson firmly believed that the unconscious mind is always listening and that even if a subject is not in a trance, suggestions can be effectively delivered when linguistically made to have some resonance at the unconscious level.

All language has an effect on the brain. Our neurochemistry is being changed every single moment we are in conversation. The landscapes of those neurochemicals can drastically change in the blink of an eye if stimuli create a platform for them to do so.

Given the vast amount of information on linguistic behavior-modification techniques, there is no perfect starting point from which to begin training. The topics that follow are in an order that is best suited for rapid absorption, and they have no contextual relevance to the chronology of events within the Ellipsis progression.

There are several chemical and physiological components that work in tandem to create our experiences and our experiences of language. If someone were to tell you not to think of a bright-red cat, your first response would be to think of a bright-red cat. To process information, our brains absolutely must bring it into our experiential awareness before we can consciously delete it or decide not to think of it. When you tell a story to a subject about a happy event, the subject must (even if to a small degree) internally process the emotions and feelings within the story to make sense of it. Any communication involves the internal processes of the listener. A compelling or interesting movie has this ability to put you in the characters' states of mind, causing you to experience the levels of emotion, arousal, and excitement that are on the screen. Any well-told stories involve listeners to the extent that they become involved and process the emotions alongside the characters in the stories.

Within an organic conversational framework, there are several ways to influence the emotions and thoughts of your subjects. The first skill set you will need to develop is linguistics. The words you use can form vast landscapes in subjects' minds; the way you use that language dictates the beauty, color, and context of that landscape.

TONALITY

Tonality is the foundation upon which all of your linguistic prowess will stand. With nonverbal communication composing over 80 percent of communication, tonality is extremely important in communicating the right message. Consider how the following phrase sounds with the emphasis put on different words:

* *I* didn't say that we were going to steal the car.
* I *didn't* say that we were going to steal the car.
* I didn't *say* that we were going to steal the car.
* I didn't say that *we* were going to steal the car.
* I didn't say that we *were* going to steal the car.
* I didn't say that we were *going* to steal the car.
* I didn't say that we were going to *steal* the car.
* I didn't say that we were going to steal the *car.*

There is a subtle communication taking place, indicating a different meaning in each sentence.

The tone of voice you use to communicate and the emphasis in your voice will have a tremendous influence over the conscious and subconscious minds of your subjects. Authority is communicated in a downward tone. Ending a statement with an upward inflection implies uncertainty and a need for the subject to confirm your thoughts to you. Your tonality will be emphasized in almost all of the coming lessons and chapters. It is the ammunition that fits in every weapon you use. When speaking with hypnotic tonality, the ideal scenario involves the subject becoming compliant and relaxed. A high-pitched tone does not accomplish this. A hypnotic tone of voice in any scenario should be low in tone and high in vibrational resonance.

If you place your hand on your lower chest and say "ninety-nine," you should be able to feel a vibration when your hypnotic tone is present. Of course, not all your communication will use this tone. This specific tone is what you will use to plant hidden messages in conversations, give suggestions, and issue hypnotic commands.

SPEED

People's speaking rates vary depending on the contextual framework of the environment. Excited people tend to speak faster, and relaxed, calm people tend to speak much slower. Using the speed of speech and matching the speeds of your subjects, you can gradually slow down the rate of speech to physically induce relaxation. Subjects' rates of speech will likely slow with yours, even if minimal rapport has been established.

As a general rule, your objective in the introduction should be to match subjects' rates of speech, unless you're deliberately speaking more slowly to gain attention or establish social authority.

As you begin to employ hypnotic methods of persuasion, you will naturally develop the ability to use natural rhythms in your speech. This skill is something that takes practice—only through substantial practice can you learn to fully calibrate your speech to subjects'. When using hypnotic methods, your speech should be paced as if you were reading a poem.

EYE CONTACT

Using eye contact strategically can change subjects' responses to linguistic methods. Many students initially assume that there is a high degree of solid eye contact during the control and suggestion phases of Ellipsis. While this is sometimes correct, eye contact can be interpreted and processed differently by every subject. Your use of eye-contact methods will vary based on your sharpened abilities to read subjects and calibrate your reactions to their nonverbal behaviors. For example, when you are speaking to women who are in trances, eye contact may make them feel self-conscious or keep their conscious minds activated to maintain eye contact with you. In such cases, put your head down a bit and continue to speak as if you were talking to the floor. The need for subjects to be conforming while they are being watched is alleviated. The lack of eye contact gives them an opportunity to draw upon more of their attentional resources and to go deeper into their trances.

While you may read some books that encourage powerful eye contact in conversations, it doesn't help to overdo it while using Ellipsis techniques. The increased level of tension created by prolonged eye contact can cause people to focus more inwardly (sometimes as a stress response), but it also occupies people's attention in unknown locations. Their minds may focus more on their discomfort than on your linguistic techniques.

The average eye-contact duration in conversations is about seven seconds. When this time is up, most people naturally look away, cough, check something, or perform any other number of actions to unconsciously avert their gazes. However, there are times you would want to prolong eye contact. When you are in the latter phases of the operation and when subjects are sharing personal details, they feel strongly about or are very proud of, prolonged eye contact helps them open up more and keep talking, allowing you to profile their language, direct their moods, and control the direction of the conversation.

USING PAUSES

As you will learn in the coming chapters, using pauses before and after key phrases and commands will enhance your command's power and give you the opportunity to implant subconscious messages within your speech. Your pauses can be used to accentuate commands to unconscious minds or can be made during the respiratory cycle once you've matched your breathing to subject's. In the following pages, pauses within written dialogue or speech are indicated by ellipses.

Hypnotic Language

Though we may be using the term hypnosis, all communication that is persuasive and controls the imagination and emotions of a subject can be said to be hypnotic in nature. As you progress through this chapter, the phrases presented as examples can be used almost anywhere. The examples and phrasing techniques will be applied to the next lessons, and they will continue to have a compounding effect. The examples of scripted language and phrases will continue to become larger and more focused on outcomes.

Words direct the attention of the conscious and the unconscious. Most people use language in a way that feels comfortable to them, a way that does not require time. To attain mastery, you must use words so that the words are selected, sharpened, and deliberately used to change the direction of thoughts.

When you remember a past event, your thoughts drift to the emotional content of the event you are remembering. When you listen to a story about an emotional event experienced by someone else, your thoughts and emotions drift in much the same way as if you were remembering your own experiences. This principle accounts for about half of the influence tactics you will employ as an operator.

If you want subjects to begin feeling curiosity, for example, here are three options you have to capture their attention and to lead their imaginations in the required directions. Consider the following options:

Ask subjects a question to cause them to remember times they were curious.

Tell subjects about a time you were curious.

Explain how you read an article about how people become curious differently, and ask them for a response.

There are hundreds of possibilities within each of the examples above. These are some of the techniques you will learn first. Asking simple questions is an easy task, but asking them with advanced linguistics and goal-focused language will exponentially change the outcomes you get in subjects.

THE POWER OF METAPHOR

A story is a vehicle. Most people use stories to simply deliver the stories themselves. However, stories are basically metaphors that can contain hundreds of hidden messages in the form of commands, suggestions, and other forms of language. While the conscious mind is focusing its attention on the story, the hidden messages you place into the story are being absorbed much more easily by the unconscious. This is a common practice used by advertisers and marketing campaigns. Once you understand the details, you will see commercials in a very different light.

Try this exercise: Talk about the last time you went to the doctor's office, and see how many times you can use the phrase "you're absolutely fine." This is a phrase someone would commonly hear while speaking to a physician. As you tell the story in a conversation, the way you say the phrase determines the level of attention the unconscious will place on it.

When you tell stories that captivate subjects' imaginations or focus, you have the ability to deliver messages to them, messages that bypass their abilities to criticize the messages and their abilities to resist absorbing the messages. Despite what some books may say, there is no way to become proficient at this without practice and study; there's no magic pill.

Try this exercise: Discuss (preferably out loud) the last time you learned a new skill and someone helped you learn it. In your story's telling, see how many times can you use phrases that resemble "you have to let go," "the only way to be good is to surrender," and "the harder you try to fight yourself, the worse it gets."

Speaking about learning something, especially sports, lends itself to the inherent ability to insert hundreds of commands for the surrender phase of the Ellipsis progression.

Try this one last exercise: Recall the last time you read a great book. While describing how you liked the book, see how many times can you use phrases like "become so focused," "everything outside fades away," "become so fascinated with this," and "can't think about anything else."

You'll soon be able to control how these phrases come out and how to "weaponize" a simple story and fill it with powerful hit phrases.

THIRD-PARTY METAPHORS

Using metaphors about your own stories works, but talking about your subjects' stories bypasses the critical factor of your subjects even more. For example, discussing an article you read about how people learn to connect with others is removed from the immediate interaction and is therefore less scrutinized by the subjects' conscious filters. Mentioning a news article, television show, or the story of a friend can become a vehicle for whatever metaphor you'd like to deliver.

Here are several examples:

* "I saw this amazing show on television last week. This guy was describing how we all have this ability to…"
* "I remember seeing this documentary about how we all fall in love in one of three ways…"
* "My friend said he took lessons once, and they told him…"
* "There was a really interesting article about that, which I just read. They said…"

* "I remember something our gym coach told us when I was a kid: he said that when we..."
* "My sister told me about this awesome experience she had. There was apparently..."

You'll see many examples of these in the coming chapters.

THIRD-PARTY AUTHORITY

Thinking about the previous lesson of metaphors, consider whether you have a particular point you'd like to keep your subject from questioning. Using the authority principle of human behavior and obedience, you can directly quote an authority on the relevant topic while using a third-party metaphor.

Here are several examples:

* "I was watching Dr. Oz last week, and he had a show about how resistance causes depression..."
* "I remember reading this quote from a Nobel Peace Prize winner about how we all..."
* "When this champion surfer came on TV, he said the most amazing thing..."
* "The Dalai Lama always says that..."
* "This thirty-year trial lawyer said the most important thing about..."
* "I saw the head of that organization on an interview last week; he was saying..."
* "After I saw [insert celebrity] speak about human connection, I was so moved. He said..."

By using the figures your subjects are likely to associate with authority, you can insert beliefs and cause idea chains to start forming in the direction of the outcomes you'd like.

The Alliterated Friend

Alliteration simply means that two words that are adjacent or closely connected start with the same letter or sound. When your name starts with the same letter as someone else's, you're statistically more likely to like and identify with that person.

Several bodies of research have identified a strong link between life choices, rapport, and the first letters of our first names (Science, 2011).

Some cults use this in their recruiting practices by having recruiters ask what prospects' names are, then using the first letters of their names to make up names for themselves on the spot. For instance, if you were recruiting for this cult and you met a young prospect named Mark, you'd introduce yourself as Matt.

This phenomenon doesn't apply just to cult recruiting. We tend to identify more with people who share the first letters of our first names and have a much higher chance of developing rapport with them. Not only does this work in social settings, but the first letter of your first name also dictates what products you're most likely going to be loyal to and which celebrities you tend to identify with.

When you're telling a story about a friend of yours who did something, you can insert a name that starts with the same first letter as your subject's first name. When you are describing a positive experience, the subject will identify with your friend much more easily and be more absorbed in the metaphor you're providing. If you meet someone named Hannah, you can tell her about your friend Heather, who learned an important lesson or experienced something amazing.

Shifting Metaphoric Pronouns

When you tell or hear a story, the pronouns fly by your awareness for the most part. As the pronouns shift around as you listen to a short story, they go unnoticed. When telling stories and describing experiences you'd like someone to internalize, you can start by using nouns such as "people" and switch to the pronoun "you" in the middle of your statement. Being aware of this, notice the shift in the following story: "I remember going to the beach there as a kid. It was so easy to just let yourself relax. You would walk down the beach, and it was like that was the only thing happening in the world."

As you read that, I'm sure you could notice the pronoun shift. We shifted from a story about the operator to speaking directly about the subject by using the word "you."

Here's another example: "It's so interesting when people actually feel connected. When you start to have that sense of connection, you have already developed so much trust in someone."

You will do a lot of storytelling and story elicitation in your practice. The ability to shift pronouns can shift the power structure in your conversations and allow you to literally plug any thoughts or ideas that you'd like into subjects' heads.

This should be something you practice regularly until it becomes second nature. As you progress in your training, do not forget the importance of your journals and notebooks. They are invaluable. A lot of students fail because they don't practice. This is a complex system to turn you into a human weapon; if you were learning surgery, simply reading a book and visualizing your practice wouldn't make you a skilled surgeon.

PRESUPPOSITIONS

A presupposition is a statement that implies or tacitly assumes that something is true or absolute. For a statement to initially make sense, the presuppositions it contains must be assumed to be true. The words leave out the important details of what is being spoken about. These are some of the hardest linguistic structures to spot when they are being used. They are a powerful resource when combined with the methods you will learn shortly. While the following examples will break down several types of linguistic presuppositions, it is in no way necessary to memorize the different types. You will eventually develop skill in their use and recognition as you progress, and you will see them used many times in the example conversations that the following chapters will display. Make notes of the ones you've been able to identify previously and the ones you may have heard but didn't notice when they were spoken.

Construct your own examples and see how many you can make for your outcomes. The way to structure them is to simply have a goal in mind and decide what has to be assumed for a subject to possess a desire to achieve that particular outcome.

The phrases typically function as a statement or question that implies the existence of something or someone, as the following examples show:

* "He came into the house." Implies that there is a male and a house and that you should automatically understand which male and which house.
* "Who is your informant?" Implies the presence of an informant.
* "All of the rich people were at the party." Implies that there is the presence of rich people, that there is a group of people called "rich people," and that there is a party you should know about already.
* "Whom would you like to speak with today?" Implies you want to speak with someone.
* "When you go to the gym, which car will you take?" Implies you will go to the gym and that you have more than one car.
* "As you begin your graduation process, what do you all have to buy?" implies you will begin a graduation process and that you have to buy something.
* "Did you notice the lights become dimmer?" Implies the lights became dimmer, asking only whether you *noticed*.

- "When you start to feel a sense of trust with someone, what does it feel like?" Assumes you know this feeling.
- "Your next source will surely provide you with more information." Implies the end of the relationship.
- "When you do that again, you will notice more openings happening for you." Implies you've done it before and that you will do it again.
- "When you come back, there will be more opportunities." Implies you are leaving and you will return.
- "It's really amazing how you can become so strongly focused on something that matters." Implies you have the ability to focus strongly and that the person has seen you do it before.
- "Your breathing has slowed down significantly. Have you gone into trance?" Implies one thing equals another and that the first is true.
- "They don't typically talk about you." Implies they talk about you sometimes.
- "The last time you did that, it must have been amazing." Assumes you've done that before and that you enjoyed it.

Using presuppositions in language can completely bypass the critical factor (gate guard) of the mind. The words alone are unconsciously processed when associated with a normal conversation. These can be combined to form irresistible language packages that can be delivered directly to the unconscious. Imagine, for a moment, pairing the profiling skills you've learned and reading no further than this. You will already have surpassed many of the hypnotists, interrogators, and behavioral profilers in the country in the depth of information you have and the level of simplicity that the subject matter is presented here. As you continue your training, make notes and recordings of your own voice using these methods. Even if you read through the examples, get used to hearing yourself speak comfortably in this fashion. The one time you need these skills in the field for the "big game," you'll want to be well rehearsed.

Presuppositions are the foundation of hypnotic language. You will see in the next chapter that they bleed into every aspect of influence and covert-behavior engineering.

Double Binds

● ● ●

PARENTS AROUND THE WORLD ARE familiar with this concept. Asking their children whether they want to brush their teeth before or after they take a shower implies the shower will take place. No matter what choice the children make, they are agreeing to take a shower. The double-bind technique has the potential to be much more elegant and sophisticated, however.

Double binds create a conversational illusion of choice. When creating and using double binds in speech, you present two outcomes or options to subjects, both leading to the results or choices you want. Either decision they make will have the same result. There are a few basic types of double binds you can create and use.

1. Do you feel more _____ when you _____ or when you _____?
2. When you _____, do you feel more _____ or _____?
3. While you're _____, would you rather _____ or _____?
4. Do you feel more _____ or more _____?
5. So when you feel _____ and that starts to grow, do you _____ or _____?
6. Would you rather _____, or is it better to just _____?

7. As you _____, a person can either _____ or _____.
8. When it feels amazing like this, does it start in your _____ or your _____?

Using these language tactics during training can make you feel that you will be caught using them. But you will be surprised to find out that no one will ever notice. Let's unpack some of these tactics to give you a few examples to work with. As you develop your own and use them in the field, they will begin to come very naturally to you after you use them only a short time.

DO YOU FEEL MORE __ WHEN YOU ___ OR WHEN YOU __?
This double bind is great because it implies a mood, makes subjects process the first blank, and then leads them into making a choice of feeling one of two choices, both of which will enhance their states. Consider the following double-bind questions:

Do you feel more focused when you tune everything out around you or when you just completely collect all of your attention in one place?

Do you feel more curious when someone says he or she has a surprise for you or when you have to stare at a wrapped present in front of you?

Do you start to feel more interested in something when you become extremely curious or when something seems too irresistible to ignore?

Do you feel more in tune with someone when you first get to know him or her or when you let go of judgment?

Do you feel more confident when you are in a great environment or when you're with someone whom you trust and like a lot?

WHEN YOU ___, DO YOU FEEL MORE ____ OR ____?
As you are likely noticing, these double-bind statements provide a perfect platform for using embedded language and choosing which states the subjects feel. This platform includes much of the same language as before, with the only difference being that the structure is modified.

This gives you more flexibility in the field to make choices of which ones you will use.

When you become focused on someone, do you feel more interest or curiosity?

When you feel that amazing, do you feel more lost in the enjoyment or as if you've just let go of thoughts altogether?

When you relax, do you feel more unwound or just completely in the moment?

When you feel like this, does it transition into...

You can also add the phrase "before you" at the end of this double bind:

When you meet someone, do you feel more of an initial attraction or a building curiosity before you start to feel addicted to him or her?

When you get this curious about someone, do you feel more interested in what he or she says or focused on how you feel before you start to become attracted?

WHILE YOU'RE __, WOULD YOU RATHER ___ OR ___?

While you're focused on something, would you rather just relax and listen, or concentrate and let everything else fade away?

While you're feeling that way, would you rather completely enjoy something or make the decision to shut off all of your thoughts for a while?

DO YOU FEEL MORE __ OR MORE ___?

Do you feel more interested or more focused when you...

Do you feel more curious or more aroused?

Do you feel more focused or more able to shut off the outside world?

SO WHEN YOU FEEL ____ AND IT STARTS TO GROW, DO YOU __ OR___?

So when you feel completely focused on something and it starts to grow, do you shut out the outside world, or does it just drift away without you even noticing?

So when you feel curious and it starts to get stronger, do you become more curious or does it turn into something you can't let go of?

So when you feel that good and it starts to grow, do you become completely focused on the experience or do you just relax into the moment and let your mind focus?

WOULD YOU RATHER ____ OR IS IT BETTER TO JUST ___?

Would you rather feel good about something new or is it better to just know that you like something and see what happens?

Would you rather let the world just fade out while you're having fun or is it better to just let go and let your focus shut everything off for you?

Would you rather become completely curious about something or is it better to just let it build naturally?

AS YOU ___, A PERSON CAN EITHER ____ OR ____.

In this type of double bind, as in others, you simply state a feeling the subject has experienced in the conversation or a feeling you believe the subject is currently experiencing. This method allows you to lead the subject's thought process into the double bind and to attach an outcome or meaning to that feeling. The words "a person can" take the pressure off the subject by not suggesting he or she directly experiences what you say. However, your skill level now allows you to know that a subject's thoughts are led by words and descriptions, whether or not they directly imply the involvement of the subject.

As you become focused, a person can either shut out the outside world or let it fade away naturally.

As you first get to know someone, a person can either enjoy the conversation or become completely open.

WHEN IT FEELS AMAZING LIKE THIS, DOES IT START IN YOUR ___ OR YOUR ___?

This method should be used when you are aware of subjects' experiencing positive states that are in the direction of the outcomes you want them to have. The positive states they have are then tied to both ends of the double bind, giving them a choice to amplify their states by using one of the two choices you've provided.

When it feels amazing like this, does it start in your stomach, or is it a full-body experience?

When this kind of intense excitement happens, do you feel it in your body first or do you seem to attach it to someone you are with?

When you get that feeling of trust and connection with someone, does it start with a feeling of connectedness or do you just feel like you know this person is different and you can let go?

Using double binds in conversations becomes second nature quickly. Most operators discover that they either use them intuitively right away or apply them so often that they become part of their everyday language. The double binds can be used in many ways. They can be linked linguistically to what subjects say, emotions they have, or experiences they discuss. Double binds can be used before you become emotionally invested in subjects or after you've created the states you want them to be in.

Fabricated Sage Wisdom

As a species, we respond very readily to quotes from famous or noble people. Books are littered with such quotes, and they seem to hold special power in society. Of course, our question is, how can we exploit this loophole in our society's logic?

After learning how people naturally tend to believe advice, quotes, and wisdom when the information is attached to a famous, noteworthy, leader-like, or honorable person, we can use this cultural tendency to create ideas where they would otherwise not exist. Simply speaking a random quote and attributing an author isn't enough, however. To bypass the critical factor, we need to use the same power that makes a story effective: third-party discussion. By discussing a third party or event, we turn down the critical factor. When a person hears a story along with a quote, the story further removes the quote from the present situation, and the brain feels less of a need to criticize and screen the information coming in. Consider the difference between the following two fabricated statements:

* "Yeah, I heard Eckhart Tolle say, 'Surrender to what is. Say yes to life—and see how life suddenly starts working for you rather than against you.' "
* "I was reading a magazine last week and saw the most amazing thing that made so much sense. There's an author named Eckhart Tolle, and when I read this, I had to write it down: 'Surrender to what is. Say yes to life—and see how life suddenly starts working for you rather than against you.' "

The same quote is delivered each time, but the second example illustrates the quote being embedded into a small story to remove it from the current conversation. While this is an actual quote from Eckhart Tolle, almost anything can be said that needs to be absorbed by your subjects. While you're not in the business of fabricating quotes, modifying them on accident to suit what you need is probably okay. If you need trust, describe a quote about trust and how it leads to genuine happiness, or describe how being mistrustful leads to depression and sadness in life.

Let's look at a few more examples:

* "I was traveling through the country once, and I was at a gas station. When I asked whether my unlocked car was safe while I went to the bathroom, a person told me the most amazing thing I've ever heard. He said, 'As long as you don't trust the world, it'll keep on proving you right.' "
* "I listened to a [insert famous person who you think the subject would trust or admire] speech a few days ago online, and I heard something I had to write down. He said, 'As long as you are alive,

you are either going to let go and do what feels good, or you are living in fear of something.' "

* "When I read his last book, I had to take a photo of one of the pages. He had a quote in there that said, 'Nothing is precious until you focus, let go, and follow it back to you.' "

In the above examples, the quotes are delivered in a particular way: they serve as vehicles for the information to be injected into subjects' minds. The story around the quotes distances the delivery from the subjects.

SOCIAL-PROOF LANGUAGE

Thus far, you've spent a lot of your time learning to bypass the criticality of the human mind. This bypass helps to deliver your message so that it's accepted without too much judgment and scrutiny. Social-proof language performs the same action while using a different method to bypass the castle guards of the brain.

The term *social proof*, also known as informational social influence, refers to a behavioral phenomenon in which humans behave like others around them in an attempt to display the correct behavior in specific conditions. This phenomenon tends to become the most powerful when people are in conditions that are socially ambiguous in terms of commonly accepted or expected behavior. The behavior in these conditions is compelled by an unconscious assumption that the group as a whole possesses more knowledge and understanding about the social situation and the proper behavior to exhibit.

The infomercials you see that talk about how they've sold thousands of products and the statistics you read help to shape your beliefs without you knowing what is happening. Both of them work on the same principle: once something is socially accepted by others who are somehow similar to you, it becomes much easier for you to decide that it might be right for you as well. In the first example, companies talk about how many hundreds of people have already bought this product, in an attempt to normalize buying behavior for the viewers. In the second example, when we read statistics (true or false), we tend to normalize our thoughts toward the socially accepted norm once we see that people like us tend to vote, think, or behave a certain way.

As you develop mastery of the skills here and your linguistic acumen improves, social-proof language will creep more and more into your everyday use. Exploiting behavioral phenomena is something you'll learn to do in thousands of ways, but this technique seems to produce the most profound surprise in new students when they use it properly.

In short, the method is to tie a desired behavior to a massive group of people similar to your subject. For example, you could mention that you saw a statistic that 89 percent of the top CEOs were able to completely tune in when they listened to people.

This method can be used in so many ways, and it will eventually become one of your go-to tools for getting quick change. Here are several examples that illustrate how this can be applied:

- "I saw this research that seventy-five percent of people have expressed regret about not taking action and just sticking to their routines instead of just doing what they want."
- "Everyone I've met since getting into business says that developing the ability to trust your unconscious is the key to becoming successful."
- "I remember seeing that about seventy-five percent of people who are under thirty admitted secretly that they felt held back and shameful about letting go and just living their lives."
- "It's interesting how almost everyone secretly thinks about breaking rules all day and how most never get to really act on their impulses."
- "Looking at everyone as a whole, it's so easy to see that we all have these desires to just let go. I think it takes the ones with courage to fulfill it. You know, those people who just have the

perfect life because they have no resistance and don't feel guilty for tuning in and doing exactly what they feel."

* "Speaking of widgets, when I was talking to the CEO of that big widget company last week, he mentioned that there are only three main critical points, and as we are the only company that hits all of those, I think we should…"

* "Everyone I've met here says that the men who live here all seem to have some kind of childish demeanor and haven't grown up."

NEGATIVE-DISSOCIATION TECHNIQUES

When interacting with subjects, you may want to eliminate one or two of their negative traits. Your seeing them exhibit such traits or preemptively deciding to ensure that subjects' don't display them are reasons to use negative-dissociation techniques. These techniques are powerful with or without having the subjects in trances, as all linguistic methods are. There is a very simple and easy-to-use formula for giving statements that create negative dissociation:

1. Pick a topic or a group of people your current subject has negative views about.

2. Use a presumptive statement or observation about those things or groups.

3. Attach the negative thing to whatever quality you want the subject to either not possess or completely suppress in your presence.

This may sound complicated, so let's unpack this formula. It's simple and powerful once you've done it only a few times. It becomes second nature rather quickly.

Let's assume your current subject doesn't like lazy people and that you learned this through a passing comment the subject made, regarding how a strong work ethic is what keeps businesses running well today. Understanding that the subject values a strong work ethic, it is safe to assume the subject possesses negative beliefs (to some extent) about lazy people. In this conversation, let's assume you want the subject to completely focus on your words and actions and to tune out the outside world while you speak. Here is an example of what a basic negative-dissociation statement would look like: "And it's so amazing that every time I had lazy people working for me, they all had the same basic traits in common: they weren't able to focus on something important—to tune everything out and completely focus on one thing."

In the above comment, you can see how you have taken the subject's negative beliefs about laziness and tied them to something you don't want the subject to have or do. Let's look at a few more examples:

A subject has expressed a hatred of horrible drivers on the road, how careless and inconsiderate they are. The subject used those specific words to describe them, so the automatic linguistic-profiling system you've built into your head identifies the words and prepares them for future use.

Your operational goal with this subject is to create trust to get him or her to reveal a secret or a password. The next step is to identify what qualities you do not want the subject to have. This, in turn, will amplify the opposite of those qualities, which you *do* want the subject to have.

You want the subject to show trust and openness and to let his or her guard down. You have the ingredients to make the negative-dissociation statement now. Here's an example of what a simplified negative-dissociation statement would look like: "And I completely agree. So many people being so inconsiderate. It's almost as if carelessness is the norm now. Every time I see that on the road, I'm infuriated. Every time I meet people like that, they all seem to be the most closed-off and untrusting people. They don't trust anyone because they feel as if no one should trust them. They are just closed up and don't ever let their guard down—not very authentic."

In this example, you can see how you have taken the subject's words and used them to remove an unwanted quality.

The next example shows how you can begin using compliance techniques in the statements. Compliance suggestions can be woven into any linguistic method you learn.

The subject has expressed a love for reading books. The subject also made a passing comment a few moments ago about how illiterate our culture is becoming.

The operational goals with this subject are compliance and obedience. You may need to recruit the subject to provide information or simply keep the subject as an obedient resource to use in the future, should you need something.

You want this subject to be compliant and obedient and to see your suggestions as commands instead of something the subject would normally have the option of turning down. Here is what you might say in this scenario: "It's extremely shameful. So much media breaking down the desire for people to read and become educated. Every time I meet people who brag about how little they read, they always come off as so selfish and unwilling to let go and just take in the information that is important. Those types of people always seem so unwilling to listen to a conversation for more than a minute, much less do what's asked of them."

In that example, you used the subject's words again and changed their perception of how helpful he or she might be in the future toward you. This utilizes the priming effect if it's done in the beginning of an interaction.

Talking negatively about any state you do not want subjects to experience is a form of negative dissociation. Even if you haven't heard subjects speak negatively or positively about any subjects, you can preempt their behavior by using negative dissociations early, later adding in qualities you do not want displayed during the interaction.

POSITIVE-ASSOCIATION TECHNIQUES

The positive-association method works very similarly to the negative-dissociation method. In the positive-association technique, you simply take qualities that subjects value or a group of people they admire and attach the disliked items linguistically to qualities you want them to display. The formula is similar to negative dissociation:

1. Pick a quality a subject likes, a group the subject admires, or a trait the subject thinks is important.
2. Use a presumptive statement about what you've picked.
3. Attach the positive feeling to a feeling or condition you want the subject to have or be in.

Example:
Let's assume your subject describes a personal love or deep appreciation for art.

Your goal with this person in the initial phase of interaction is to establish focus to develop a trance.

Your choice of feeling here could be focus, intensity, curiosity, and attention: "That's incredible! I know so few people who can appreciate art. I've noticed that all of them seem to be so much more genuine and able to focus on the people around them."

In this example, you used the word *genuine*. Since nearly all people in the world would say they themselves were genuine, you are using this to tie in more than just your current subject's love of art. As soon as the subject accepts the appreciation of art and agrees with you about being genuine (in his or her mind), the subject will naturally and automatically follow whatever positive quality you happen to staple onto the end of the statement. The method using this behavior-prediction technique is covered in detail later. It is presented early in this chapter to illustrate its interchangeability within the linguistic structure.

Example:
Your subject, wearing an expensive watch and new shoes, makes effort to talk about a new car recently purchased.

You can reasonably assume that the subject "appreciates the finer things." Whether the subject is disgustingly superficial or has come from poverty is irrelevant—the way the subject views his or her choices is the only relevant issue in influence.

Your goal with this subject is to develop trust and openness. Say something similar to the following comments: "I agree. It's so refreshing to see someone who appreciates the finer things—people who are just completely open and don't put up barriers to the world."

In this example, you have tied one of the subject's "identity statements" to the quality you want the subject to have with you. It should also be noted that you have added a small reference away from a negative at the end to solidify an otherwise partially effective statement.

Example:

A subject is known to volunteer at homeless shelters and frequently gives money and time to local children's hospitals and shelters.

Without an overt verbal indicator, we can assume the subject considers himself or herself to be bighearted and caring. A verbal confirmation isn't always necessary.

Goals with this subject are to develop trust and an interpersonal connection. Say something like "what an amazing story. You know, there are so few people with the kind of heart you have. Every time I meet people who are just caring and so selfless, it's so amazing how connected they are with people—just so trusting and genuine."

Again, you used the word *genuine*. Doing so tied the desired action to the self-belief already held by the subject.

EMBEDDED COMMANDS

Embedded commands are phrases that are hidden within normal language, designed to be absorbed directly by the conscious and completely bypass the critical part of the conscious altogether. Through strategically placed words, small changes in tone and volume, pauses, and gestural references, embedded commands can be woven into the innermost parts of conversation without any conscious awareness on subjects' part. This chapter will use and incorporate other Ellipsis techniques to make embedded commands even more powerful.

The science of embedded commands goes back centuries. However, the most recent developments were made by Milton Erickson and later codified and made into a replicable system by Richard Bandler (founder of neurolinguistic programming). This method used to be shrouded in secrecy. Anyone wishing to learn the use of embedded commands had to have a PhD just to attend the training. The medical representatives around the nation believed these methods were so powerful that only practitioners within the medical community should be allowed to learn them. Here's an example of a simple embedded command:

A person can feel completely focused.

The first part of the embedded command is simply a vehicle to deliver the command. The phrase that precedes an embedded command is typically a permissive one but can contain almost any language you deem necessary for the outcome to be accomplished.

Constructing Embedded Commands for Covert Use

Embedded commands have three main parts:

1. The vehicle
2. The command
3. The continuum

The Vehicle

The vehicles are the phrases that lead into the embedded commands. They set up subjects to begin following your train of thought and make the embedded commands seem much less like actual commands. The following are examples of vehicles that can be used in conversations to embed commands into language. Keep in mind that any story, thought, response, or comment can contain opportunities for embedded commands. The following list is by no means an exhaustive or all-inclusive one:

You probably already know…
I wouldn't tell you to _____, because…
You may _____.
Some people…
…said, "_____."
…and they said the best way to _____ was to…
One might, you know, _____.
A person may not know if _____.
When you just _____, it's something so powerful.
I'm wondering if you'll _____ or not.
I could tell you that…but…
Maybe you haven't _____ yet.
The doctor told me to always _____.
It's easy to _____, is it not?
Sooner or later…
You may not know if ___.
Maybe you'll ___.
You don't have to ___.
You might notice how good _____ feels when you _____.
Will you _____ now, or will you ____?
You might notice the sensations in _____ while you…
You could _____.
You might notice it feels _____ as you _____.
Eventually, _____.
You can ____, because _____.
Can you imagine _____?
Can you really enjoy _____?

How would it feel if you _____?
People can, you know, ____.
People don't have to _____.
Try to resist when you _____.
A person is able to ____.
A person might _____.
You might _____.
...once told me, "_____."
One could _____ because...
You might not have noticed...
A person could _____.
One may _____.
You can ____, can you not?
I don't know if ____.
If you ___, then...
What happens when you ____?
A person may ___, because...
When you ___, then...
You are able to ____.
Sometimes...
You may or may not ____.
I'm wondering if you...
Will you ____ or ____ or ____.
You might want to ____ now.
One can ____.
One doesn't have to ____.
Don't ____ too quickly.
My friend said it's so easy to _____.
When you _____.
The feeling that makes you want to _____.
And it's so natural to just _____.
Nothing really feels as good as when someone is able to _____.
Most people don't notice when they _____.

How do you feel when you _____?
I'll bet that feels _____.
And you can really _____.
No one has to _____.
Everyone knows how to _____.
Having the ability to _____.
All of these are small bits of speech that fit naturally into conversations.

THE EMBEDDED COMMAND

Delivering the command and structuring it in your mind before delivery is an easy process: simply choose a command you'd like to give a subject, such as "feel completely focused," and insert it into the conversation using a vehicle.

When delivering embedded commands, you can mark the command with more emphasis on the command words. This can be done using tone and volume. The shifts in volume and tone of voice are small signals that tell the unconscious parts of subjects' minds that there is more relevance in those words. While the conscious can hear the difference, it is almost always ignored. In the examples that follow, the italicized words are to be marked by volume or pitch in voice:

- "A person can *feel completely focused* when he or she finds something interesting."
- "It's easy to *become curious* when something really piques your interest."

These examples show how the increases in tone and volume can become significant to the unconscious by their differences alone. This small raise in volume creates a slightly higher level of attention and absorption, much the same way a normal conversation would involve people speaking in different volume levels as they move in and out of what they see as the key points.

Marking the embedded command by using volume and tone is the first way of bringing unconscious attention to the command. The second method of marking the command is the use of tactical pauses, or small pauses before and after the command to make it stand out in time, as well as in the sensory department of subjects' minds. Take a look at the examples you just read over again with the small pauses inserted into the speech:

* "A person can...*feel completely focused*...when he or she finds something interesting."
* "It's easy to...*become curious*...when something really piques your interest."

In these examples, you can see small pauses that insulate the embedded command from the rest of the syntax. While there are formulas that contain pause-length calculations, simply pausing and becoming proficient in the use of implementing volume, tone, and pause markings will create an automatic timer within your mind when you speak. Having the other behavior-analysis information and keeping track of subjects all the way down to their breathing and blinking are already enough to keep your mind busy during training and operations.

Embedded commands should almost always end in a downward vocal tone. In most countries, when people ask questions, regardless of the language being spoken, the tones of their voices rise. When giving commands, a downward tone labels it as a command and helps the unconscious determine what it is supposed to do with the information.

Regarding the development of embedded commands, they should just be actual commands that are inside of the sentence. The following examples are commands that can be placed within a conversation:

1. Feel excited
2. Become comfortable

3. Get curious
4. Completely surrender
5. Let go completely
6. Focus
7. Listen so closely
8. Feel interest growing
9. Get excited about this
10. Trust in this person
11. Be comfortable with this person
12. Watch closely
13. Get completely curious about something
14. Start to want something
15. Begin to get focused on this
16. Surrender to something
17. Let go of the need to control
18. Allow yourself to become curious
19. Desire something
20. Become obsessed with something
21. Have desires that grow
22. Become fascinated
23. Let your attention sharpen
24. Feel the need to please
25. Feel the need to open up
26. Become more open and receptive
27. Give yourself permission to feel amazing
28. Feel awesome
29. Notice how this feeling grows
30. Feel attraction
31. Become infatuated
32. Combine all the feelings of attraction and curiosity
33. Start to act on your desires
34. Let your whole body just focus on this

These embedded commands make up less than 1 percent of what you can and should be able to use in the field. Regardless of the desired outcomes, the embedded commands listed above can create strong states in subjects and cause complete surrender by themselves if needed.

During most social interactions with new people, we don't intentionally make foot-to-foot contact under a table. Making deliberate contact with a person's foot under a table or otherwise creates a tiny spike of discomfort. When the action is done to look accidental, it can be excused. This spike of discomfort can be exploited by making the contact at the same time you speak about something you want to linguistically frame as being negative or bad. While the linguistics work on their own, the compound effect of adding discomfort helps the subject along to associating the topic with discomfort.

Using embedded commands in language will pay the fastest dividends for the amount of time invested in studying. Sometimes, to cause subjects to avoid unwanted thoughts or behaviors, it may be necessary to use embedded commands that associate negative feelings with the behaviors you want your subjects to avoid. Here are some examples:

* "And it's one of those times where you know as soon as you start wondering about _____, the headache comes almost immediately. Just building at first, but you know it's going to be big."
* "It's easy to see how quickly you can start to feel sick, nauseous, and uncomfortable for no reason, and the more you try to pinpoint the cause of something like this, the more it just grows and grows."
* "Every time people try to focus on analyzing everything, it seems to lead to headaches. Have you ever had a time where you just got a headache all of a sudden, like where it builds and grows and all you want to do is avoid it, just to let go when it comes?"

Using embedded commands within stories is a very powerful way to deliver messages. While the following example contains implied uses of other various persuasion techniques, consider how embedded commands can be used to get out of a speeding ticket: "Apologies, Officer. My son's been sick, and I've gone around and around trying to find something to give him. I thought about Nyquil, and the pharmacist said don't give him anything, he just needs to carry on, let him go, and he'll just get better on his own. No one seems to have any advice that matches the other one."

In this overly simplified example, small commands have been inserted into something someone might normally say. A situation such as this would require a hurried speaking pace, indicating confusion and honesty. Speaking to an officer about such matters in a relaxed tone would, no doubt, raise flags. However, police officers are used to nervous and confused citizens in their autopilot roles as officers, assuming the confused, hurried speaking pace matches the tone of the language being spoken.

Functioning Ambiguities

Using ambiguities in punctuation provides a window into which you can follow a command with a phrase to take action. The ambiguity makes the follow-on statement seem as if it's the beginning of the following sentence.

Consider the following sentence: "Knowing information like that can really help you to fully let go...now with me...I think that's the only way to live."

The words "now with me" are spoken so that they sound like the beginning of the next sentence, but you are still marking out the embedded command phrase. The whole embedded command is now "let go now with me." In conversation, it blends directly into the flow of speech, allowing the speaker to boost the power of the embedded commands. Delivering ambiguity following an embedded command should be done no more than a few times within a single covert-influence operation. If you take advantage of the ability to give an embedded command as an action command, you will double its power. For this reason, you should use this technology only on the most important embedded commands. Let's examine a few more examples and dissect each one so that you're able to use them today:

- "The possibilities are endless when someone starts to <u>feel completely connected. Now, with me,</u> I think that discovering a connection is a rare thing."
- "Being a professor is challenging. I can imagine you have a lot of college students who <u>start to become dependent. Now, here,</u> this is where I went to college, and we had amazing professors the whole time I was there."
- "Making a decision like that must be difficult. All of this stuff going on and finally having to just <u>stop and let go—just surrender. Now, to me,</u> the decision process always becomes…"
- "We just saw that movie last week. It was absolutely amazing. You just sit [or stand] here watching, and <u>you can't take your attention away. It's right here, now,</u> the theater we went to is very close by."
- "I remember the first time I did that. Everything seemed so chaotic, and finally, I just let my shoulders fall and surrendered. My friends said, "It gets better the more you're able to just <u>relax and keep an open mind." With me,</u> I've started doing that, and life's been increasingly easy to manage."
- "I think a lot of those people <u>keep an open mind.</u> When you <u>have a great outlook on life,</u> it's easy to <u>become joyful and let things happen for your own good. Right now,</u> I think that company is going to succeed because of that single philosophy."

When ambiguity statements are used like this, it's easy to see how the power and effectiveness are almost doubled on the unconscious level.

You'll see these examples in the coming chapters, as the skills you are learning start to build on each other.

Situational Pacing for Agreement

Pacing is a neurolinguistic programming technique that has been described in many books (but the earliest citation could not be found). It's a simple concept that entails listing a few small facts that subjects know to be true and following these up with statements that you want subjects to agree with. For example, in a conversation, you could list the place you are at, the weather, and the sounds in the room, followed by a statement you want your subject to completely accept. This example is elementary and should not be used. As an Ellipsis operator, you are expected to be much more sophisticated and well trained than a common persuasion expert. Consider the following examples and write your own as well:

- "We're in the middle of the city, so many sounds coming at you at one time, these people all having their own boring lives to live, and you...sitting here with the ability to step above it all."
- "So you came from Detroit, went to Dartmouth, and started working, and you've finally reached the point where you know what you want, even if it's hard to describe."
- "Sitting there, listening, breathing, it becomes so obvious when you see people that they hide their suffering from the rest of the world, and you have that ability now that you can see that little people don't seem to take action and focus when they talk." (This is deliberately confusing.)
- "You know, so many people come in here, sit down, have coffee, read the paper, and wind up discovering something they wouldn't have otherwise."

* "You're twenty-two years old, graduating from college soon, considering all these options…and you can start thinking about opening up to new ideas in all directions."

* "You've been working here for seven years, did a great job so far, and everyone likes you, and it's absolutely relaxing to think about where you are right now."

* "It's eleven o'clock, thousands of people still wondering what to do, hundreds driving drunk right now, but you're getting ready to take action."

Using Confusion as a Weapon

• • •

CONFUSION IS A FREQUENTLY OCCURRING state in conversations between two people. The feeling of being confused seems to create desperation within all of us. As we become confused, our need to understand is made more powerful by our need for something certain that makes sense. When a person becomes confused, these feelings tend to overtake anything else that might have already been in his or her thoughts. Within the structure of conversation, you can use confusion to induce a higher state of suggestibility in your subjects. This state can also induce an immediate trance, and you can take advantage of this with the knowledge of what steps you need to take immediately following the deployment of confusion methods.

Confusion can and should be your go-to weapon when you need quick results or need to correct problems within conversations.

The use of confusion for influence relies upon a simple principle: people feeling as if they were drowning reach to grasp whatever solid object is presented to them. Confusion, being the drowning, produces a state of unease and uncertainty. Following confusion methods with easily understood suggestions creates perfect "solid objects" for subjects' minds to grasp. The suggestions and statements you can provide after confusing someone will be more readily accepted and don't tend to be processed by the critical parts of the brain, because subjects accept such suggestions out of a need to relieve discomfort.

Many hypnosis practitioners use confusion in traditional hypnosis methods. Using it in conversation produces the same results but requires a much different procedure. The procedure to use confusion in conversational work is as follows:

1. Speak the confusion statements with sincerity, certainty, and gravity.
2. Give suggestions that offer subjects certainty that can move them in the desired directions of mental travel.
3. Return to the conversations.

Consider the following comment: "And most people don't realize that what isn't here still has an impact on what isn't noticed." Consider the following comment as if it had been spoken with conviction: "Nobody knows what's going to happen a week ago isn't even the right place to start."

Some confusion statements can blend time, senses, interruption, and confusion. Identify them in the following comment: "And Jason [after your touching his arm], some people aren't even aware of what they aren't noticing until a week a-goes [mixing "a week ago" and "a week goes"] by the way you *see* things can feel perfect and quiet for a moment."

If spoken in a way that sounds as if the speaker believes and understands it, the statement creates a natural expectation that the subject understands it as well. However, not being able to make sense of the comment, the subject experiences confusion and slight mental discomfort for a brief moment of time. Go back and try to read that statement as if it were the most important, interesting, and true thing you've ever said.

Try this one now: "And it's easy to completely separate the part listening closely, and not actually doing than the part that isn't not completely focused."

This confusion statement has implications within it that also suggest listening closely and "not doing" that can work themselves into the confusion state before you even deliver a suggestion.

Structuring a confusion statement is easy, but it is recommended that you keep several saved in your memory, so they can be used when you need them during your conversations. If a moment occurs that creates discomfort while you are operating, the ability to manufacture a well-crafted confusion statement on the fly is going to be hindered significantly. Having a few well-written confusion statements can assist you in times of need. There are only a few things that make up a confusion statement. The following rules will help you create your own:

The statements or questions should be worded so that they sound as if they made logical sense, even though they will not.

The use of double negatives is a confusing linguistic tool that can be used in almost any confusion structure.

Using the blending of senses, time, and awareness should be the central part of each statement.

Consider the following examples, and try to find the parts of each statement that involve the rules you just reviewed:

- "How different would it be if the same things started looking now like it wouldn't change if nothing else really did?"
- "What is the difference between not thinking and realizing what you aren't thinking about?"
- "Next week looks just as warm as the week before it wasn't like it is now."
- "How often would it feel like nothing isn't really changing?"
- "Even trying to remember what happened in so many days ago, not noticing what didn't happen becomes harder, even thinking back to next week."
- "Half of all of that isn't the same for everyone, even if they paid attention."

* "You can't depend on your eyes when your imagination is out of focus" (Mark Twain).
* "How many times will this power surge happen like it's still going on tomorrow?"
* "Nothing can explain the seed never seeing the flower, and it can't."
* "And just like the absence of our awareness of what lies beneath the surface of the ocean, so much of what we don't know is there is something we don't see the detail of until we...focus."
* "It's such a good feeling to just lose yourself into what captures all of your focus when nothing can become what you aren't noticing."
* "After today, nothing can move forward into last month's events right now."
* "I wonder what it would be like when we were there" (Jones, 2008).

Building on Confusion

When a statement designed for confusion is used, the outcome should be to direct the subject's attention or focus in a predetermined direction. In most cases, you will use confusion to refocus subjects or help them reorient themselves back into the trance state. As you know, confusion can create discomfort that subjects seek relief from. Following the confusion statement, a suggestion or command must be given to the subjects.

The most likely directions you'd want subjects to go in following the use of confusion are relaxation, surrender, focus, interest, arousal, scarcity, and action taking. Within the confusion statements lies another opportunity to embed hidden commands to direct subjects. The following examples build on the above twelve:

* "How different would it be if the same things started looking now like it wouldn't change if nothing else really did? <u>And it's easy to just relax into knowing that we have so little control</u>."

- "What is the difference between not thinking and realizing what you aren't thinking about? Everyone knows the real difference is in choosing to let go and allow the world to spin, or just surrendering and becoming in control of yourself."
- "Next week looks just as warm as the week before it wasn't like it is now. <u>And it's so easy to focus, knowing everything is clearing up</u>."
- "How often would it feel like nothing isn't really changing? You can feel aroused, interested, and compelled to take action on something, and so many people can when they focus."
- "Even trying to remember what happened in so many days ago, not noticing what didn't happen becomes harder, even thinking back to next <u>week, and you can get so interested that it doesn't matter when you're here, instead of back there</u>."
- "Half of all of that isn't the same for everyone, even if they paid attention. Knowing we have only a limited amount of time here, and it's time to make the best with this, now."
- "You can't depend on your eyes when your imagination is out of focus. But when you completely focus, like this, everything fades away that doesn't matter."
- "How many times will this power surge happen like it's still going on tomorrow? <u>I guess no one knows what is going on until it's our time to</u>."
- "Nothing can explain the seed never seeing the flower, and it can't. Everything gets so relaxing now, when people notice the small things that make them happy."
- "And just like the absence of our awareness of what lies beneath the surface of the ocean, so much of what we don't know is there, is something we don't see the detail of until we <u>focus. And let everything go, so this is the one thing you see</u>."
- "It's such a good feeling to just lose yourself into what captures all of your focus when nothing can become what you aren't noticing. <u>And my friend said, *just relax*, now, when I try to think about too many things at once</u>."

- "After today, nothing can move forward into last month's events right now, even knowing that you miss so many opportunities, I suppose we all regret not taking action in the past."

In the above examples, you gave commands to the subjects to get them onto the trains of thought you needed them to be in to continue the operation. In most scenarios, this isn't enough to get them back on track. The organic nature of conversations and the human need for continuity create a particular challenge for you—namely, you must reorient your subjects back onto the topics that were being discussed just before the confusion took place. The basic formula for using confusion looks like this:

Conversational dialogue—interrupt—confusion—suggestion—conversational dialogue

This looks like a lot, but it is simply talk-technique-talk. There's not much more to it, despite what you may read elsewhere. The benefit of this method isn't in the amount of information you have about it but in the results that come from its practice and mastery.

The human need for continuity will help subjects to get back on track. The average person remembers less than 20 percent of any given conversation, and getting subjects back on track immediately after you give a suggestion or command will allow them to assimilate the information without needing to cognitively metabolize the information you gave them.

Here is an example of dialogue using the confusion method to return to a conversation:

You: And my friend said his residency requirements were ridiculous at the hospital over there.

Subject: I've heard a few similar stories.

You: How different would it be if the same things started looking now like it wouldn't change if nothing else really did? <u>And it's easy to just relax...into knowing that we have so little control.</u> But the hospital seems to do well either way and still produces top-tier physicians. Who did you know who went there?

This dialogue illustrates the need to immediately return to the topic that was at hand just before you introduced confusion to control the behavioral direction of the subject. In later chapters, you will see examples of confusion illustrated in detail. Try to commit these to memory within two days, and use them a few times in conversations. The fear of being caught using them is unwarranted. No one will catch you, not only because it's covert influence but also because subjects are completely unaware of these methods' existence, especially the ones being employed by highly skilled behavioral operators.

The problem you're most likely to run into during the initial use of confusion techniques is your subjects' becoming confused, experiencing a conversational pause, and questioning what you just said. The pauses give the conscious a chance to play catch-up and to criticize the spoken confusion statement. Barreling through the confusion and continuing to deliver a command followed by a return to the topic at hand bring relief and continuity. The skill of using confusion is not in using it for confusion's sake but in using it to deliver a command quickly and efficiently and returning immediately to the topic at hand.

If during a conversational operation you find yourself at a loss for words and need time to think about what comes next for you and your subject, use confusion. The key to using this in a pinch is having the phrases above (and your own) completely memorized to the point where they have the ability to come out on an unconscious level.

Confusion is the go-to weapon.

Using Interruptions

• • •

INTERRUPTING SERVES TO AMPLIFY FOCUS, just as confusion does. Much like our autopilot behavior, when our focus gets interrupted, it is temporarily riveted on a single item. When people are interrupted during most tasks, the interruption serves to produce almost the same results as confusion, though an interruption is more likely to bring confrontational thoughts or actions, as it is rude to interrupt unless you've already established rapport with the subject during the interaction.

Most actions can be interrupted. Think for a moment about the actions we do every day. We talk, walk, shake hands, look to the side, and check our phones. When one of these routines is disrupted, we immediately turn to focusing our attention to determine the cause of the interruption.

Interrupting someone talking takes more than simply interrupting him or her to get the results you want. The best method to interrupt an action is to behave as if you just remembered, discovered, or realized some measure of "critical" information.

Interrupting a mentally patterned behavior is easy to do, but you must exercise caution. Immediately following an interruption should be an instant delivery of a suggestion or command, followed by an apology for interrupting or a statement allowing the subject to continue speaking as he or she had been. It's usually most effective to interrupt people to briefly agree with what they have been saying. This makes interruptions much softer and increases the chances you won't offend subjects' egos.

During your training, you'll find it easiest to practice interruptions when you are agreeing with someone. Interrupting someone's train of thought can be jarring, but when you perform the interruption to agree with them in excitement, it mitigates the discomfort. Even though the discomfort has been mitigated, the interruption still happens and provides the opportunity to embed a linguistic command into the conversation.

Examples:

Interruption of speech: Subject is speaking. While making contact with the subject's arm, the operator says, "Oh my God, that reminds me, what was the cause of the accident yesterday on the highway?"

Interruption of behaviors: Subject or operator is speaking. Operator drops car keys and quickly kneels to pick them up. This interruption causes a physical, verbal, and social interruption and allows a window of time for commands to be placed into the language of the conversation.

Interruption of routine: Subject is performing a routine action he or she performs regularly. The operator interrupts the action in a socially acceptable way and inserts commands immediately after the interruption. Examples of this include replacing paper in a printer, pulling a cell phone out of a pocket, taking a sip of a drink, logging in to a computer, and putting a cell phone down following a call. These behaviors are something that the autopilot has completely automated for the subject in a way that requires almost no conscious thought to perform.

Interruption of anticipation: In the buildup to the punch line of a story, the operator can interrupt the story and change the topic momentarily to start another one. Stacking the techniques is more effective because doing so sets an anticipation-and-relief cycle in subjects' minds. As the operator, you can do this up to four or five times in a row: start with one line of thought, interrupt it, and begin a new line of thought. After one or two interruptions in the discussion, it is important to remember that you must complete the topic left undone to build the cycle of anticipation and relief. This method, however, does not provide an opportunity to insert commands into the language. It is a method designed primarily to deliver commands within the speech, not after.

Here is an example of anticipation interruption:

I remember when we visited there a few years ago. It was beautiful. I remember seeing a car accident while we were downtown. This man ran up to a car that had flipped over and...I was with one of my professors at the time, and I received some of the best advice I've ever heard. He said, "Surrender to what is, let go of what was, and have faith in what will be." That quote is from...I don't remember who said it. I hadn't seen my professor in years since college. He and I...well...when the man ran to the car, the bottom was on fire. He kicked the window out, like... "There is only one chance to let go and do exactly what is required of me," and he must have been an EMT or something. This guy in the car gets pulled out into safety as the inside of the car starts to burn, and my faith in humanity was restored fully by this guy. It was amazing. Sonia Ricotti! That's who said it. I didn't think I'd remember. My old history professor and I had a good dinner, but what an experience for a first day in a new city.

If you reread the above example, you'll see the commands hidden in the language and the cycle of stopping and starting three separate storylines. While a lot of the other methods can be mastered and used on the fly, this one requires preparation or memorization prior to your being able to effectively use it in conversational behavior engineering. In the scripts that follow this chapter, you will see it in use in several scenarios.

We are wired to respond to our names. The sudden (loud) mentioning of anyone's name immediately interrupts his or her behavior, creating an intense, momentary focus. This can be used to cut off trains of thought that you do not want subjects to complete.

Whenever possible, interrupt to agree with your subjects first; then proceed to complete your technique.

OVERLOADING COGNITIVE PROCESSES

Confusion works by capitalizing on the human need to understand and process the environment. When something doesn't make sense, humans immediately begin a search to discover information that makes sense, to reestablish psychological balance.

Cognitive processes are limited within our minds. Just like a computer, our brains can process attention only to a limited extent. The demand placed on mental processes is called the cognitive load. The total amount of working memory being occupied by critical thinking and mental processes can change behavioral responses to scenarios and can increase the amount of temporary suggestibility in subjects during operations (Lavie, 2004).

Placing cognitive load on subjects can be as easy as asking them which direction northeast is or having them recall an old address, remember a teacher's name, or try to remember what they had to eat a week ago today.

When loads are placed on subjects' brains, their cognitive processes are occupied much like the useable space in a computer's RAM. When this happens, there is a brief moment (as long as the load is applied to the brain) in which subjects' minds can more readily accept new information and can even compromise their moral judgment (Cohen, 2005; Greene, 2008).

Asking subjects to perform any mental task that requires cognitive processing without immediate memory retrieval places a load on their minds. The more difficult and complex the task or question is, the greater the load will be placed onto the subjects. You will be limited conversationally to the types of questions you can ask and the tasks you can give to subjects. Here are a few examples, but permission planning should determine the best questions to rehearse and have at the ready:

* Recalling historical data that is commonly forgotten
* Timeline questioning processes, such as recall of which day an event occurred on and the surrounding timeline

* Mathematical calculations involving percentages and division
* Remembering the order of the color wheel
* Asking questions that develop the "tip of the tongue" phenomenon
* A schoolteacher's first name
* Mixing confusion with a cognitive load, such as asking which way Lincoln's face is facing on a penny and what it says along the bottom

During the cognitive loading phase of conversations, subjects will be susceptible to more unconscious processes and linguistic patterns. These can be woven into the conversation immediately following your placing a load on a subject.

Just as with confusion, cognitive loads should be placed within the final third of subjects' mental processes, and the command should be delivered within this same third, as well. While this is the optimal time to insert the commands and suggestions into subjects' mental states, by no means should you overload your mental processes by trying to measure subjects' reaction times to the insertion. Once these methods move from conscious delivery to unconscious delivery, you will have more cognitive loads of your own to spend on timing and delivery.

The Voice

● ● ●

ESTABLISHING YOUR VOICE AND YOUR presence as addictive, attractive, commanding, perfect, comforting, or frightening is a method that should be done with almost every conversation. Though there are generalized formats through which you've learned to deliver other types of suggestions, the voice method is something you should commit to memory and use to control subjects' perceptions of your voice and presence.

We all have an inner voice, but what if you could create an opening in your subjects through which they could process your voice the same way they process theirs? By using all the credibility and natural feeling of their inner voices, you can control their thought processes more easily than by simply using suggestions and commands.

This method uses phrases, tonality, and gestural markers to issue commands and suggestions that your voice is in your subjects' heads or actually makes up their inner voices. As everyday conversations begin, you can input these phrases to gradually introduce faith in your voice and your presence. These phrases can be placed into most conversations with minimal tailoring:

* "And you're thinking about everything important to you [op] and there's <u>this voice</u> [gesture to mouth]…that seems to always want to guide you the right way; sometimes you get into trouble when you don't…<u>listen to it</u> [gesture to mouth]."

* "That's true. I agree. You know that voice [gesture to mouth] that always tries to keep you safe? It's like there's a perfect [op] guiding voice [gesture to mouth] there all the time, but the challenge is actually <u>listening to it. Now, *you can hear it...just like this*...when you listen, everything is perfect.</u>"

* "Absolutely. I notice that the unsuccessful people [negative dissociation] listen to others more than their own <u>inner voice [gesture to mouth]. Right here,</u> I read an article that talked about it."

* "And it's like the more you follow what your mind [op] tells you to do, the happier you become. The voice [gesture to mouth] we all have in our heads...<u>it sounds like...mine</u>...is one that I try to <u>listen to it...now</u> [gesture to mouth], I think people [ep] who choose not to will only suffer because we are all born with this incredible [op] way to <u>know what's right, just by listening</u> [gesture to mouth]...<u>to me</u>...it's something we all have. Don't you agree?"

* "After he got in trouble, the judge told him, 'We all have this voice [gesture to mouth] that tells us what is right. <u>You have this voice [gesture to mouth]...right here.</u>' Even the judge said it."

These phrases are examples, but they can be committed to memory and applied to most conversations. You will see more of these within the script examples in the appendix.

We have found the use of 'thought cycles' to be particularly effective following the use of 'inner voice' methods. This involves your mentioning things you need subjects to repeat to themselves, followed by your saying, "And it's so easy for something like that to just continue running in the background over and over...just repeating itself to the point where almost anything reminds you of it...comes up all the time."

Dantalion Jones (also known as David Barron) wrote an interesting take on this concept of internal voices to use in clinical work or more overt scenarios, and his writings illustrate the possibilities arising from operators' installing the sound of their voices into subjects' heads to replace subjects' conscious minds or internal-guidance systems (Jones, 2008, p. 118). The following is an excerpt from his work:

There is a voice you have inside that you hear when you are called to act. It's a voice you trust. It's a voice of authority and when you hear *this voice* you don't think or hesitate, you act. You do exactly what *this voice* says. *This* is the voice you are listening to right now. This is your inner voice of action. There is no doubt when you hear *this voice*. When you hear *this voice* you act and you act without thought or hesitation... because you trust this voice...listen...listen...*nod your head*...when you hear *this voice*...(repeat until head nod). Listen...listen...*nod your head*... when you hear *this voice*...starting now and from this point forward this will be your voice of action...when you hear *this voice*, you act without thought, you act without hesitation when you hear *this voice*...nod your head when you understand and accept this instruction.

Emotive Fractionation

● ● ●

IN SCIENCE, *FRACTIONATION* IS A process in a large task or objective is broken up into several small parts. A simple Google search for fractionation will return thousands of results that detail the use of fractionation for seduction purposes. Fractionation is discussed at length in several articles, most notable by D. Corydon Hammond, in his article *The Use of Fractionation in Self-Hypnosis.* (D. Corydon Hammond Ph.D., 1986) It's also discussed in other notable articles and has been used in several research (Edoardo Casiglia, 2012).

Using fractionation on a conversational level relies on the principle that when we enter a state repeatedly, we become more familiar with it, and the consistent rehearsal of entering a state creates a stronger result when we return to it. In private circles, fractionation is referred to as *dark manipulation* and other similar names. In social settings, conversational fractionation is easy to use, but it is not as dark or powerful as some say, unless it is paired with the ability to profile behavior and to determine the results of your efforts.

In seduction, fractionation techniques follow a relatively simple process:

1. Build rapport.
2. Use stories to build interest.
3. Use themes that cause high and low states to be accessed repeatedly, as if on an emotional roller coaster.
4. Build suspense and relief in cycles.

The theory here is that people being seduced continually experience entering and exiting the feeling of connection and enjoyment. The sad or depressing topics that the seducers speak about are there only to break the mental state of enjoyment, not to create any kind of sadness or negativity. Once the person being seduced has sufficiently entered and exited this connected and trusting feeling several times, his or her mind should be considered to be on a loop that creates familiarity and anticipation. The continuous repetition of the mental state of connection and enjoyment is what makes the feeling (theoretically) stronger each time it is entered.

In clinical settings, the fractionation theory is used in much the same way: clinicians repeatedly induce and break patients' trances.

For behavior engineering, the process works in much the same way as in seduction. Here is a simple layout for you to use when applying this in the field:

1. Expose a subject to the desired state by eliciting information and providing prompts.
2. Discuss an unrelated topic that is likely to cause the subject to recall discomfort or a small amount of anxiety.
3. Create the desired state again by using more amplification of sensory information and a personal compliment to make the subject feel good.
4. Break the state again by discussing a less stressful situation than the one before.
5. Recall the state again, followed by the use of the subject's name.
6. Break the state conversationally by simply shifting topics (no longer using negative stimuli).

This process can be performed in a matter of minutes or progressively throughout an entire conversation. There is no clinical research to support this methodology of behavior engineering, but it is strongly advised that you try this once and see its effects in person. The results are usually stunning.

Rates of speech can be used to fractionate as well. The simple speeding up and slowing down of speech rates has been proven to produce trance-like phenomena, even when no other methods have been applied. This is a method frequently used by television evangelists and some religious figures, either to lull the congregation into a malleable state or to pump the state of the room to a point where people feel energized and have a need to take action. While you may not use this method on many occasions, it is recommended that you add this to your training materials for the week to become familiar with its use and have another tool to use, if needed.

Using downward tones when you break a subject's state can help create the behaviors you want. The downward tone helps the subject assimilate the discussed scenario more quickly.

You can use your posture to create a mirrored state. When you are discussing a positive feeling, such as connection or enjoyment, your erect posture will help the subject feel it. Being in rapport with the subject is the best way to assure you can use your physiology to change the subject's physiology. On the other hand, slumping or slightly slumping when you want to break the positive states will cause your subjects to adopt the same. On this note, it's not always necessary for your subjects to physically follow your movement. If you simply lower your posture, subjects will feel as though theirs is lowered, even if there is no noticeable difference. Consider the following example of the up and down emotional tone in a normal conversation, and you can see how easy it is to apply to everyday life:

- "There is something so interesting about meeting someone who shares a connection with you [op]. There's that feeling that you just have when you start to really connect—so rare."
- "What's the worst traffic you've seen while living in Chicago?"
- "Man, you've got an incredible gift for that. I wish I had more of that. What's the best day you've had at work in the last year?"
- "Did you hear about the murder that happened last night here in town?"

In these examples, you can see the roller-coaster effect happening. This is a simplified version, but in essence, there is no advanced methodology to remember, just up-and-down emotional situations. In practice, it is best to build up the positive emotion as if you were climbing a meta-phorical hill; it is best to drop the positive emotion into the negative as if it were being dropped from a cliff.

Think about what you would need to do to have someone experience a deeper positive feeling associated with a positive short story. A small but effective sad story can come just before the positive one. The con-trast assists in the transition to positivity, much like being moved from coach to first class is more deeply felt than simply sitting in first class to begin with.

Conversational Dissociation

● ● ●

"WHAT WOULD YOU SAY TO the younger Amy if you had the chance?"

Dissociation in psychology refers to a wide range of disconnections with the body and environment, ranging from detachment from the surrounding environment to severe blackouts and detachment from physical sensations and cognitive processes. Dissociation specifically is a detachment from reality, not the loss of reality (Spiegel, 1991). Dissociation is typically associated with trauma. When a creature endures trauma, its brain attempts to make living more bearable by shutting off and separating from what is happening. The identity typically breaks away from the person undergoing trauma to protect the mind from exposure. This is common in cases of child abuse, in which a child, while being beaten or traumatized, will retreat into a mental shell and create amnesic states for the trauma, as if it were happening to someone else, as if the child were simply in the room watching as a disinterested third party (Williams, 1995). In short, dissociation is a coping mechanism that the brain uses to insulate us from the world around us, whether it's simply boring or severe and traumatic.

With electronics, advertising, and media, this is the most dissociative and fractionated our species has ever been.

The two main ways this separation happens are through depersonalization and derealization. Depersonalization occurs when people separate from their sense of self. They may feel as though they have no body or that their bodies don't belong to them. Depersonalization also causes feelings that parts of the body are not connected and sometimes separates people from their feelings and senses. Subjects often report feeling like robots or that they do not have full control of all or parts of their bodies, as if they were being controlled by an outside source.

Derealization episodes are characterized mainly by a detachment from reality. Individuals experiencing derealization feel unfamiliar with the world around them, as if they were in a dream or there were some solid separation between them and the real environment. Their surroundings might be experienced as having extreme details or next to none. This process is more likely to also cause distortions in the visual field, where an individual would experience brighter colors and heightened awareness or blurry and artificial-looking surroundings. The realness of the world around them is often visually altered in a dimensional way as well, such as with flatness (like a TV screen) or strongly exaggerated three-dimensional proportions to their environments.

Depersonalization and derealization both have the effect of making subjects *care less about the consequences* of their actions. This effect can serve the outcome in several ways.

Many types of dissociation can also produce levels of retrograde amnesia (Loftus, 1982). It's common for anyone who has suffered trauma to experience amnesia for events, but the simple condition of dissociation is also enough to cause memory loss (or a failure to record the memory in the first place).

In terms of operational use, it's easy to simply imagine dissociation as meaning separation. When subjects separate from what is currently going on, they experience a degree of dissociation.

These levels represent where you could potentially take a subject to produce outcomes. Whether in therapy or in the intelligence environment, dissociation can be tremendously beneficial. Basic meditation takes many of the same forms as a person progresses into deeper states of meditation. In particular, transcendental meditation contains many of the same dissociative processes.

SEPARATION FROM IDENTITY

"If you weren't you, who would you be?"

In this case, identity means our names, how we see ourselves, and the stories we live out. This includes how we think about our pasts, how we identify with our names, and the ways we attach to self-image.

When using dissociation in the field, keep in mind that you will be working on small parts at a time. There's no covert way to establish dissociation from level one to four without alerting the brain that there's an intruder. The best method to initiate dissociation is to gradually bring up identity and make a clear, unspoken agreement with your subjects that there is more than one thinking awareness inside of them. This is far easier than you might imagine.

For example, you can say, "I was driving home from work last Friday and came to a stop sign and had to sit and think about how the hell I made it this far without paying any attention to streets and such. That ever happen to you?"

Or you can use more detail and set the subject up for the elicitation. For example, you can say, "I was driving home from work yesterday at like four in the afternoon, and all I can remember is throwing my brief-case into the seat and then putting my blinker on to turn onto my street. It was such a weird experience. I live like thirty minutes from work when there's traffic. I just remember that feeling like, who was driving the car this whole time?"

The subject will affirm that it has happened to him or her before.

Here's an example:

"Okay, so while Amy [subject's name] is driving the car, where is the other part? I don't get how our brains separate so perfectly like that."

Amy will attempt to answer.

"So what if this part of you had her own name?" (This assumes there's another part who is also a girl.) "What if we named her Trisha?"

Initiating a small discussion about this process of having two parts by using Amy's name and making her use her name to describe herself at least once. If you're unable to achieve that, ask a leading question such as "And when Amy drifts off, does she trust the other part?"

Amy will either respond by referring to herself as Amy, she, or her. In this situation, the goal is to eventually get subjects either to refer to themselves in the third person or to respond affirmatively to a yes or no question where you have identified them in the third person. While there are many ways to get subjects to realize and acknowledge separations in their minds, this is a very popular example that students like to use. Getting subjects to speak about themselves in the third person provides a small dissociative window that can be crawled through to anchor the feeling of dissociation with enjoyment and fun.

Here's another example of using light conversational dissociation to create third person speech:

"So when David [the subject] is not working as a paralegal, what does he do?"

This is presented or spoken in such a way that should appear light-hearted and jovial. David, responding in kind, will likely continue the small joke and briefly mention himself in the third person, as you did.

By using the authority rule and by knowing humans respond to social and accepted authority figures, you can use another method that capitalizes on that human behavior. In this example, we are using the scientific community to become the authority figure:

On the flight last week, I read one of those in-flight magazines, and I saw this article that talked about how we all have separate parts of us that are responsible for different things. These scientists found out that when you perform certain tasks, only a part of your brain stands up to take responsibility, and it's the part of you dedicated to that particular kind of work. They said that's the main reason we all have different emotions and reactions based on what *part* of your brain is doing the talking right now.

This method uses the principle of authority and helps subjects to accept the information quickly, so they can readily process and internalize the information about the brain being divided into parts. The authority in this method specifically bypasses the critical factor, so the subjects can internally process the descriptions you're speaking of, instead of critically processing the initial claim of the separation of the brain.

The Three Selves

In the next example, the level is taken slightly deeper than before, to the second level. This method applies dissociation from the self to another self in the same body. Using the self-help psychology theme that is so common in conversation, this method implies there are multiple selves that never have the ability to speak to each other except by action and results.

And it's just like what Jerry Seinfeld said about his discipline problems. He said there are essentially three of all of us. The first one is present tense you. She usually thinks only of herself. If it's late and you've got to be up early tomorrow, she doesn't care much and keeps you up all night. Then, future you, the following morning, is mad at the other girl from last night keeping you up. It's a battle to see whether you can get present tense Allie to take care of future Allie. Future Allie always gets mad at the Allie who didn't set her up for success. So the anger is always directed at the third (nonexistent) past tense Allie. She takes a lot of heat. (Begin nodding your head to force agreement before prompting the subject to tell his or her own descriptions of this scenario.)

The Organ Transplant

The organ-transplant method borrows from a method originally featured in *The Handbook of Hypnotic Suggestions and Metaphors* by Corydon C. Hammond (1990). This method was designed for overcoming sexual misconceptions and misinformation. It has such a wide variety of application that it's worth including here in a paraphrased form, for conversational means. The following comments should clearly illustrate to subjects that we all unwittingly carry childish, foolish, and incorrect beliefs about the world into adulthood without differentiating where the beliefs came from.

I was at dinner with a friend who just finished medical school, and he was telling me how the technology of organ transplants was evolving. He said some years ago they started to discover something amazing [op]. They said that when a foreign object was placed into a person's body, the body would accept it for a little while, but after a time, the body would start to recognize the object as not belonging to the body and would begin rejecting the organ to get rid of it. I think, in a similar way, that all of us do this with our beliefs. Think about it: as kids, we have almost no ability to screen what is being taught to us, and we take in ideas and thoughts from others [raise your hand higher to indicate parents] that don't necessarily belong to us at all. *But* when we grow up, we have that ability to *stop*…and let your unconscious…start to process all of these things that are foreign…that don't really fit you. And it's so cool how your mind can take them all and reject them just like your body does with things. Those ideas were right for someone else, but now we can see that they were never ours to begin with.

THE UNCONSCIOUS SAVIOR

Everyone identifies with the waiting hero. This method utilizes this identification and offers proof to subjects that one waiting hero exists and that they have always had access to one. It uses subtle subcommunication to illustrate a concept: the unconscious and the conscious are different; both the conscious and the unconscious are supportive of survival, but only the unconscious leads to enjoyment and connection with others.

In elementary school, our PE coach would always yell at us all that we were too far inside our heads to get good at anything. I tried so hard to figure out what he meant, and I was sitting in a college class last year, the professor talking, and it hit me.

She said [or he, depending on the sex of your subject] that all of us have a conscious and an unconscious. If you think back to your past, right now, find some time you were uncomfortable or angry. These times are all the same, come back. She said the conscious is the weaker part of the brain, but it takes over so often because it's where our sense of ego is. Being too far in your head is literally the cause of every emotional setback and disappointment you've ever had. When someone actually lets go...now...that's where the power is. The unconscious is the single source of enjoyment and connection to the real world... and just letting go is all you have to do. I couldn't believe how many times I looked back on and discovered that the conscious mind is the reason I lost an opportunity to have fun and just enjoy it...now.

SOCIAL-MASK REMOVAL

Mr. Ryan Barone created a method for Ellipsis operators while working in 2015. This method involves a rich description of how we all wear a social mask, describes the features of masks, and then removes the masks from subjects physically. This method ostensibly creates states of authenticity, awareness, and openness in subjects and can be used whenever subjects are withholding, withdrawn, or otherwise closed to ideas. Using this method followed by the organ-transplant method is extremely effective. Remember that there's no need to memorize the exact words, but pay close attention to the hidden linguistics embedded within the text:

Yeah, I find psychology so *fascinating*. It's like one of those concepts that really grasp your interest. One of the most interesting parts of psychology, to me, is that theory of social masks. Freud touched on this a bit, but basically we all go about life wearing social masks. We use these masks to ward off unwanted people and sometimes to gain influence. However, there are these rare people whom you trust completely, people who you know would never betray you, and the kind of person you have a strong, powerful connection with. You intuitively just know that you could drop the mask with this person, and as you let the masks fall (physical motion of removing the mask), you discover that everything is okay now. It's like when you know you've made the right decision and how all the little moments of your life have led up to this powerful moment. (Barone, 2015)

Remember this involves the use of your arm to reach forward and physically remove the mask. If you want to use this method, ensure that you are within reaching distance. Making large movements during covert-trance development will reassociate your subjects into the present reality.

INSTALLING A SOCIAL MASK

Just as the previous method described the removal of a social mask, this method does the opposite. When subjects lack an attitude or belief that is needed for the desired outcomes, operators can install a social mask to temporarily imbue their subjects with the needed mental states for the outcomes. This method uses the positive traits of social masks and a hand motion to install the masks near the conclusions. At no time is it recommended that you use both the removal and installation of social masks with one subject.

Using the social-mask theory, the following method implies we can become the people we have always wanted to be; the method gives subjects permission and a reason to behave how they like. Once they know they have permission, the installation of a mask becomes a way to excuse their behavior and avoid guilt and judgment.

> I think it's so awesome how some people can be so openly authentic. Have you ever met one of those people who are so magnetic? They always have all of their shit together. It would be so amazing to live free for a night and let go of everything...holding you

back. Like if you could just let go...now...and have this mask you could put on and become exactly who you want...to just open. Like to add [holding hand as a cup and putting items into it with your other hand] openness, excitement, wonder, fascination, just being wild and having no regrets...all in here. Then being able to just put it on [use hand motion of the hand containing all of the qualities to make the motion of installing a mask] and notice everything changing...even the colors and sounds...like a whole different person.

During playful conversations, you can build the story up until you discuss creating this mask, and you can have your subjects decide all of the things they want to have when the masks are on. It's best to frame this exercise as something more akin to a game or social experiment so the critical factor remains in the comfort zone.

CREATING PARTS (SPLITTING A PERSONALITY)
"You've always known you were different."

When operators have authority, they have an exponentially easier time controlling the frame of reference for the exchange of information with subjects. Using your authority frame, what would happen if you were to discuss a sequence that sounds logical and makes sense to a subject? Subjects will use their sensory information and memories to create an understanding of what you are discussing. Consider the doctors who inadvertently misdiagnose patients and tell them that they have some form of illness. Numerous studies have cited that patients who had not been sick but were still diagnosed with an illness later displayed symptoms nonetheless. Robert Bobrow, a thirty-year medical doctor, performed research on this phenomenon and discovered that the authority of medical professionals played a vital role in the patients' feeling sickness in these cases, where there were no diagnosable conditions (Bobrow, 2006).

Using the authority principle, this method creates awareness of how all people are virtually separated into parts that sometimes work together. Once this concept is on the table, you can name parts that you'd like your subjects to have, and you can describe the parts in detail, perhaps offering details about how they work. Simply mentioning that there is a part creates it. Before mentioning a part to a subject, the part simply doesn't exist. Using language, you can create fragmented parts that will come to life as soon as you speak them into existence. The following example (Jones, 2008) illustrates a common method of parts creation in others:

Interesting things happen when you notice something that you recognize as interesting. It's like there is a part of you that becomes fascinated, and it locks into whatever you're focusing on. When it comes alive, it's almost like you close off all your awareness of the surrounding world, and it's just this one subject that commands all your attention, and you can't ignore it. In fact, as much as you try to turn away, it just draws you closer.

When you have a clear idea about what's important, and you focus on it, there is another part of you that begins to take everything that doesn't matter and pushes it away. Have you ever noticed how, as soon as your attention becomes aware of a trivial distraction, it shrinks it in your mind and screams, "FOCUS!" and snap—you're right back on what really does matter? All you have to do is realize that what you're doing is important, and this part gets ready. This part that ignores the unimportant will take what really matters so that nothing will distract you—and the more you try to turn away, the more important these things become.

There is a part inside your mind that knows when you've done something wrong. It's the part that feels guilt and quickly tries in vain to push the acknowledgment away but only makes it more glaring, noisy, and sharp in your mind. Again and again, it comes back, even when you sleep, and the more you try to suppress it, the stronger it becomes. Finally, it becomes so strong that you do everything in your power to avoid sleep, because of the guilt that grows stronger, like a cancer weighing you down. Even in those moments, when your mind is free of the guilt, this part of you is plotting to remind you of what you did. You'll never outrun it. You'll never even outlive it.

DISSOCIATIVE REFERENCE

In clinical dissociation settings, like hypnotic anesthesia and pain relief, the hypnotist or clinician will use words and phrases designed to dissociate patients from the body parts in pain. Phrases like "that arm" are used in place of "your arm" to remove ownership of the part.

Opportunities to discuss the body parts of your subjects will probably be very rare. However, when speaking about anything they own or do, as a secondary dissociation phase, use this method to talk about their property. For instance, you may say "the car" instead of "your car" and "the job" instead of "your job." Omitting things that imply ownership works equally well to further dissociate. Questions like, another drink? instead of, would you like another drink? work as well.

Use dissociative references throughout conversations whenever there is a need to keep dissociation running in the background. An example of a situation where frequent or continuous dissociation would be necessary is whenever you need your subjects to have minimal concern for consequences. For instance, situations in which you have to convince people to commit acts that violate their moral character, such as collecting intelligence against their countries, require that you disconnect them from consequences temporarily and rely on them to reverse-rationalize their decisions after the fact. A lighter example of this would be you haggling with a car salesperson for a better deal.

DISSOCIATIVE-SCALE QUESTIONS

There are a few tests published to assist mental-health professionals in diagnosing and identifying dissociative illnesses (Bernstein, 1986). Using these questions in conversations is similar to the first method you learned using dissociation by speaking about dissociative experiences and eliciting them in your subjects. In this method, the questions from the scale are reworded to make them more conversational and covert. Later in the book, you will see examples of how the scale can be used for Manchurian-style programming and identity separation. The following topics are taken from several dissociative scales and have been paraphrased to increase conversational flow:

* "I wonder how I can prevent myself from doing certain things sometimes."
* "Well-known places appear strange sometimes."
* "Sometimes, daydreams can get so real it feels as if I were somewhere else."
* "I experience the feeling that there are different competing thoughts in my head."
* "I can't remember anything about some important events in my life, like final exams or weddings."
* "Sometimes, I am about to say something, but something completely different comes out."
* "I forget what people tell me."
* "I've looked in the mirror before and not really recognized myself."
* "Every once in a while, I feel like the world around me isn't real, as if it all seems fake."
* "When I watch television, I do not notice anything going on around me."
* "Sometimes things surrounding me in the environment appear so vague and remote."
* "I wish I had more control of myself."

* "When I have to decide between doing two things, I often have an internal debate over pros and cons."
* "Has the voice in your head ever sounded like someone else's voice? Or is it always your own?"

All of these methods are designed to be laced into conversations and reworded as necessary. The "I" pronoun is simply a placeholder and can be changed to suit the desired outcome.

Dissociation is useful for several reasons. While many of the modern covert-hypnosis books discuss trance induction in conversations, we go in and out of trances all the time. Inducing trances is something that can be taught in less than three minutes and learned in even less time. Trances and suggestibility are very different things. Dissociation is an effective tool because it creates a lack of concern for consequence and separates a person temporarily from his or her own sense of self. This process is useful for several situations, and you should become comfortable with it before using it in the field.

When you use this process in the field, if your subjects start to drastically dissociate and if you see physiological evidence of dissociation, do not look surprised or try to shake them out of it. Simply say their names and ask what time it is to reorient them to the present.

Use language that keeps the dissociation running in the background, such as "and it's so easy for something like that to continue running in the background [sp] to the point where almost anything reminds you of it...just happens all the time now."

Conversational Regression

● ● ●

REGRESSION REFERS TO MENTAL TIME travel backward to a previous time, most often childhood. It is used in therapy and the mental-health profession to assist patients in recovering from childhood trauma and in dealing with issues while in the mental state of being a child. Regression is simply a walking back to childhood using either suggestions from a hypnotist or probing questions designed to cause the subjects to return to a childish state.

Regression can create childish behavior in almost anyone. When thoughts of childhood are vivid and there are minimal distractions, thoughts and behaviors begin to become more childish. This means more open-mindedness, exuberance, enjoyment-focused decision making, and—most importantly—trust. Regression makes us all more vulnerable.

A typical clinical-regression scenario involves patients being placed in comfortable chairs and given instructions to perform a series of mental tasks to activate all of their childhood memories and emotions. Some therapies involve having the patients speak like children or draw pictures of their homes with crayons. As for behavior engineering, we can create a similar mental atmosphere and use the benefits of regression without having subjects enter a clinical setting.

The methods used here for regression represent only conversational devices and are by no means intended to be used as therapy of any kind.

Once regression is taking place, you can spot it by watching the facial expressions and voice tones of subjects. The cheeks will rise slightly, the forehead will have a slight lift, and the voice will sound slightly more childish. Knowing when it's working will help you determine your own successes as you progress in training and help you determine when to increase regression, if needed.

As with the other methods you are learning here, simply discussing or eliciting the information is usually enough. With the law of associated memory, activating one small part of the brain will also trigger parts around it. If you can perform an action to activate one part of the brain, you can start to light up the areas surrounding it. Here are some techniques you can apply to maximize the effectiveness of regression for behavior engineering:

- Exposing subjects to the classic smell of sunscreen will help them regress (the sunscreen can be carried in a small bottle).
- The smell of mothballs reminds many people of being in a trusting place, such as a grandparent's home.
- The smell of crayons (exposed strategically) will assist in regressing most people. (There is crayon-scented spray available online)
- Foods children love, such as pizza, spaghetti, and macaroni dishes, will often help subjects to regress.
- Having subjects describe their house where they grew up triggers associated memory channels.
- Playing thumb war or tick-tac-toe with subjects will prime them for regression.

QUESTIONS ELICITING REGRESSION

"When you were little, what was the coolest thing you ever did in school?"

"When you were young, what did your family do for Christmas? Awesome. What was the coolest Christmas you had?"

"Most people don't even remember their teachers from when they were really young. Do you?"

"Did you ever get in trouble in school when you were a kid? What did you do?"

"I went to a birthday party of my friend's kid last week; it was so interesting [op]. When you were little, what was the most fun party you had?"

"I remember doing PE as a kid in school. Did you guys do that jump rope thing for fundraising?"

"Can you remember your second-grade teacher's name? I have so many friends who can't."

Inducing Regression through Linguistics

Using linguistic suggestion for regression is slightly less effective because it does not allow the maximum memory retrieval of asking a question. Using questions to elicit the state will produce much better results: "Have you ever seen those detective shows where they ask questions to help people remember a crime scene? I tried that on myself the other day, and all of these awesome memories I didn't know I remembered were coming back to the surface. Try this: think of what your front door looked like as a kid, even with the doorknob almost at eye level."

Proceed to have this subject give you a guided tour full of rich detail while you ask questions about what the subject sees. It's important here to make sure you keep the subject in first person while he or she speaks. You can give linguistic prompts by asking things like, how old are you? or, is this where you sleep every night? instead of, is this where you *slept* every night?

In regard to safety, clinical regression—if not finished and followed through with properly—can create unstable mental environments, and no clinical-regression methods should ever be attempted on anyone for any reason.

Drawbacks to Conversational Regression

There is a small chance a memory that is traumatic could be triggered by association. If you see a negative reaction start to take place, do not touch the subject for any reason. Simply use the phrase "Everything is fine here. Come back, Mr. or Mrs. XYZ." This phrase does several things, but using Mr. or Mrs. before subjects' names remind them that they are adults.

LCFLUTTER

Sleep-Deprivation and Interrogation Methods

● ● ●

SINCE THE BEGINNING OF TIME, humans have researched and tested ways to manipulate, control, and coerce one another. Sleep deprivation has been used for millennia as both a punishment and an interrogation device. Hippolytus de Marsiliis, an Italian born in 1451, was the first to study sleep deprivation as a torture method and ushered this new tactic into the Catholic Inquisition. The CIA developed the *KUBARK Manual* in 1963 for interrogation and "coercive counterintelligence interrogation of resistant sources." The manual contains everything from torture methods to sleep deprivation (CIA, 1964).

Being deprived of sleep causes numerous physiological and psychological reactions in the body. Research has shown it to be a highly effective form of creating suggestibility and diminished cognitive capacity (Blagrove, 1996).

As you read, recall the discussion on the brain. An action simulated in the mind activates the same neural pathways as if the situation were actually happening. This chapter will discuss the use of conversational sleep deprivation and how and when to apply it. Sleep-deprivation methods for behavior engineering are almost universally applicable and are easy to insert wherever they are needed within interactions.

To use sleep deprivation conversationally, here are a few techniques to help you get the most from your subjects:

Don't blink. Once subjects are in sync with you (which should only take a few minutes), their blink rates will inevitably synchronize with yours to some degree. As you slow your blink rate down, you are creating a slower blink rate in your subjects. This helps subjects to physically experience the dry-eye feeling of not having sleep. When you begin using conversational methods, your subjects will be more likely to feel the effects from it when they can physically feel the symptoms.

While subjects are mirroring you, get them into slightly uncomfortable positions by maneuvering your body in such a way that causes them to feel either discomfort from the positions or unconscious social discomfort from not matching them.

Making accidental physical contact (such as feet touching under the table) will create a small pocket of social insecurity, in which the sleep-deprivation techniques will have more effect.

Assist your subjects slightly by using a light gaslighting method (discussed in the chapter on gaslighting), such as calling attention to how none of us observe much when we are tired. Then ask them to remember what type of cars they parked next to on their ways in.

Rub your eyes as if you were very tired just before starting your technique.

The following are examples of sleep deprivation used in conversation:

- "It's so amazing, when you don't get sleep, how different you feel. Trying to stay focused, getting only half of what's going on around you, like feeling so many days without sleep, now, I'm sure you've had that happen before."
- "And it took so long that I wasn't able to sleep. You know that feeling when you haven't slept in a long time? Like feeling it… your eyes burn a little, there's that nagging feeling of being disconnected from everything, and nothing happening in the real world is of much concern."
- "People can feel so sleep deprived when they aren't sleeping right. The feeling when you feel like that…now…that sucks. Everything is hazy, and your body feels that way. Your mind is making circles trying to wake up, and nothing helps."

- "The last time I went up there was with friends. We partied so hard, and getting on the plane to leave, you're going through this place, still feeling like you've had no sleep, eyes burning, that tiny headache…you need to just sleep and let go."
- "It's awesome, but we didn't sleep at all. You know that feeling like you've got no control and it feels fine? Like when you're going into that feeling that all your body isn't really here…just no sleep."
- "When's the last time you had to go like a whole day with no food?"
- "When's the last time you had to go a few days without sleeping?"
- "You've got a lot on your plate. I'll bet you've had an experience or two where you weren't able to sleep at all."

Using Scarcity and Regret

$\bullet \quad \bullet \quad \bullet$

THE FEAR OF LOSING SOMETHING or missing out on an opportunity can be a powerful motivator for human behavior. Robert Cialdini discusses this in his fantastic book *Influence* primarily as a marketing tactic. While the use of scarcity is common (and powerful) in marketing, it's not the only place people are exposed to it. Cialdini mentions stories of customers who would show up to look at new cars to find that other customers were looking at the same car. This is an old tactic that was by no means developed by Cialdini, but his book contains secrets that probably none of the readers were able to see: this tactic can be implemented conversationally. Throughout a conversation, recall that there is virtually no difference between someone performing an act and someone imagining their performing that same act; in the brain, it's all the same.

Humans are wired to respond to scarcity. The potential to lose out on a meal or a fleeing animal could mean death for a human back when our brains were developing two hundred thousand years ago. Becoming complacent and missing out on opportunities would eventually weed someone's DNA out of the human race forever.

CONVERSATIONAL SCARCITY

Scarcity and regret methods can be used in conversations for a variety of situations. The most common uses for scarcity and regret methods are these:

- Before a call to action
- During connection bonding
- Post-regret awareness development
- Status building

Before a call to action, scarcity helps to deliver the feeling of having missed out on something and of focusing on the opportunity to gain it in the present moment.

Connection bonding is when operators wish to develop feelings of intense emotional connections in their subjects—for example, love, respect, admiration, authority, or caretaking. This is a vulnerable moment for the subjects, and ethical operators will assume full care for their subjects' wellbeing, and operators will ensure that their own actions are for the best interest of their subjects.

Post-regret-awareness development is a phase that sometimes follows the deliberate use of regret-scenario elicitation. This process simply draws strong attention to past or third-party scenarios, where subjects were upset over not having taken advantage of an opportunity.

Status building is a process operators may need in an intelligence scenario or when time is critical. Status building followed by scarcity produces much stronger buy-in and creates a vacuum for action-taking subject behavior.

TECHNIQUES AND APPLICATION

Let's look at a few examples of using scarcity and regret methods in the field. In conversations, the topic may not always lend itself easily to discussions of scarcity-based scenarios that you can pull from memory. In the field, you will need to use adaptation methods to weave these methods into conversation. Here are examples of in-field usage:

My friend Sara says the same thing, but she's always so cautious to the point where she starts to miss out on life and all it has. Every time I talk to her, she always tells me another story about something she missed out on because she was worried about how it would look or whether it would be perfect. I hope she starts to just go with her instinct and begins to just let go and enjoy life, so she doesn't wind up with so much regret.

There's something to be said about the feeling of being truly in the moment. Alive. So many people look back and find nothing but regret for not taking action...wishing they could go back and scream at themselves, "You have to stop sitting around and worrying and just let go... enjoy your life!"

I read the most interesting article by this nurse who worked with dying people. She made this list of their biggest regrets and posted them online. I don't think I remember them all, but the top one was people wishing they had the courage to be completely open and not try so hard to control themselves.

It's incredible how quickly we can all be taken off this earth. I have a friend who had bad headaches one day, went to the doctor, and he's got two weeks to live. Just makes you think...how we don't know when we will go. And if you were sitting in your deathbed, what would you regret? There's so much to enjoy [op] in the world. This opportunity-s [pronounced "these opportunities"] can be gone so fast, and only the brave and courageous human beings [sp] will take advantage of what they really want to do [op].

That reminds me of a friend of mine. She's always so worried about rejection or judgment that she's almost frozen. I tried to talk to her about it. I said, "Listen [op], fast-forward right now, take a look at all of the opportunities you missed out on. You have one life already; just think back to the time you decided not to ask that guy out or take a chance [sp] when that voice in your head [omp] was screaming now to just live your life...open up...let go...have fun [op]."

And I met this guy from there who changed my life. He was in his late seventies, and I think he had published like fifty books...smart guy [op]. He said one thing to me that changed my life completely. I was bitching about something, and he just said: "*Stop*. Think about how many people are frozen with fear in their lives. Imagine you go to a doctor's appointment, and in less than five minutes, you find out you have about two months to live. You would instantly start to regret...going back to every moment [use the now gesture] and realizing how many things you put off, thinking about the time you have left; now it starts to become apparent that enjoyment and doing exactly [op] what makes you happy and feel good." With me, it changed so fast.

I know, just think about how many times you've come close to something horrible, but the universe somehow protected you. We all think we will live to be a hundred, and most people assume they will live till the end of the month...but some of them won't. Time is so precious... it's a shame you don't realize it until it's almost gone. Then sometimes, there's this epiphany moment [use the now gesture]...now...where everything lines up and you just realize that life is only about two things, letting go and doing what makes you happy.

I've got to be off in a few minutes. I'm glad I got to know you...you seem like such a doer. Most people I meet don't have that sense of "let's do this!" about them. [Trigger phone to go off.] What's it like seeing other people who seem to just live out of fear and don't take action? I'll bet it's depressing to see.

You'll see more examples in the appendices.

Think about what each story does to subjects' mental processes. Where will the stories take them? As the subjects begin to process your words, they are drawn into their memories and minds to create relevant correlations. They may be regressing to childhood regret or to regret scenarios that took place weeks prior to your interactions. This is another reason to keep suggestion information vague; it allows your subjects to use their information to create images.

On Using Fear

Using fear to control behavior is no new science. It's been done for thousands of years on a mass scale, to the point that there are manuals, formulas, and even best practices put down in writing. In conversations, the use or induction of fear has to be a carefully practiced method and tailored specifically to each subject you interact with. Specifically, you must use the needs map and profile their insecurities. Using generalized fears will not work as well because most people are accustomed to generally surrendering to common fears. When insecurities and their associated fears are brought to the table, a whole new gamut of behavior can be created.

Fear creates predictability. As the level of fear people feel increase, so does their predictability. Using fear can be as simple as mentioning it or as complex as having an actor perform anxiety-inducing actions during your interactions.

For example, if a person has a fear of abandonment, mentioning that people are so prone to leaving each other and that no friend ever stays for the long haul, except in extreme circumstances, may be enough to increase their predictability long enough for more intrusive programming or influence to take hold.

ABSENCE

Addiction to a drug occurs in its absence. Immediately following what you observe as positive experiences in your subjects, excuse yourself briefly to the restroom. This type of absence will give your subjects time to reflect on the immediate feeling, and the absence creates a vacuum that they will immediately want to fill when you return.

Activating: Calls to Action

● ● ●

"THE FIRST WORD WE ALL learn is no. What if it were yes? How incredible and smart we would all be."

As you enter the final phase of behavior engineering, whether a multiday operation or a ten-minute conversation, you'll need to adjust subjects' perspectives and instill motivation to act toward your desired outcomes.

The call to action is the final product. It is designed to motivate your subjects to take action, to keep them in short-term thinking, and to ultimately create the feeling that their behavior is a cause of their own ideas and thinking. If any scenario goes as planned, subjects should never consider the operators as the cause of their behavior. Operators must use behavior-engineering programs on subjects' thought processes in such a way that they will always believe they are acting on their own ideas and beliefs.

The entire behavior-engineering process has led up to this point: you have taken control of thoughts, steered them in a direction, and arrived at the appropriate behavioral exit on the freeway. Using the scarcity statements and bringing the subjects' attention to the right behavioral states have brought you to the point where subjects' awareness is specifically focused on avoiding regret and achieving their needs. During the activation process, you will be using linguistic methods you've learned throughout the manual and will be combining the intelligence you've gathered about your subjects, in a concise package that creates irresistible urges to act.

DEFICIT AWARENESS

This is awakening discontent and bringing subjects' awareness to some sort of lack. This is a method that can be applied when necessary in interactions. It is designed primarily to bring awareness to shortcomings that cause subjects to feel the need to fulfill something in the moment to anesthetize their temporary grief. While it is highly effective, it's best to do it only when you firmly believe that the scarcity and regret haven't produced enough situational gravity to form a void you can fill. If you've successfully caused your subjects to retreat into their regrets and if you have gained access to that loophole, there is no need to proceed with any deficit-awareness tactics.

The following questions can be used to elicit this reaction in subjects:

* "What is the one thing at work you dread the most?"
* "If your friends could change one thing about you, what do you think they would change?"
* "What is one thing you always procrastinate on?"
* "If you had an extra million bucks, how would you spend it?"
* "If you had no debt, what would you do with your money to have more fun?"
* "Who's one person you wish you had spent more time with?"
* "Did you regret getting that credit card?"
* "What's the biggest thing you regret with your friends?"
* "If you had the chance to go back and party more, would you?"
* "What's one thing you'd do if you knew you'd never get caught?"

DOUBLE-BINDING CALLS TO ACTION

"When you feel that need to take action on something you really want, is it something that wells up [hand motion] inside you, or is it more of an instinct that just takes over?"

"Of all the times you did something super spontaneous, were they times when you felt it coming, or did you just realize yourself doing it and that the enjoyment was just natural?"

"And just like you were talking about earlier [even though you were the one who mentioned it], the conscious mind sucks at making decisions; the unconscious can process millions of things at once without us even knowing. When people let go and use their unconscious power to make decisions, do you think it's something that happens with the conscious mind 'watching' it, or is it a process that people know they can trust because it's unconscious...with me?"

USING NEGATIVE DISSOCIATION OR POSITIVE ASSOCIATION

"And we had someone just like that who used to work in our office. It's always sad to see those people who don't take any action [ep] for what they truly want. They don't listen to that voice [op]...just sad."

"I've always been fascinated with those super successful people who have this ability to just take action as soon as they noticed an opportunity...they...don't let it slip away...and it's always so rewarding."

"What I've seen as the biggest concern is that those people who never do anything in life seem to be so negative...blaming others [ep]. Every once in a while, you have that one time when everything lines up, and you know it's going to be *perfect* [use words from your subject's language here]...like this is it! You *know* this is it, now...nothing can stop you."

THIRD-PARTY CONFIRMATION

"My friend Sara always does exactly what the hell she wants to do. All of those people just fall backward into awesome experiences...job offers, meeting celebrities, all that stuff. She always just sees this [op] one chance to take an opportunity and becomes completely open to it...so fun to be around. She just says, *'This is it...now...right now.'* "

"I remember when we went there last time. Everyone in the entire restaurant was so connected [gesturing back and forth between you and the subject]. Most people don't realize that this is it. When something like this comes along you have to *absolutely act now*. There's that process…you're open, you're authentic, and you have that ability to see when you want something, and nothing gets in your way [making wall gesture with hand between you and the subject]. This is it."

In the above examples of preliminary calls to action, it becomes apparent that there's a need to further activate scarcity but replace the negative emotion with positivity, excitement, and forward-thinking attitudes. This time is crucial, so it is also important to remember that you, as an operator, go first; if you want to produce a state in a subject, you must go first and experience the state yourself. The mirroring effect is strong at this point in the interaction, and you need to display the attitude and mentality you want to see in the subject.

These methods, paired with your ability to go first, will prepare you for phase 2 of the activation process.

Activation Phase 2

The methods you saw previously in this chapter were psychological preparations to take action. However, without sufficient direction and commands, subjects may not know the best course of action. In phase 2, the commands and suggestions for action are given in a way that presupposes that subjects have already made the decision or will benefit greatly in relation to their needs for behaving as suggested.

The main focus of the second phase of activation is the ability to motivate your subjects to take action on their own accord to accomplish the outcomes you've engineered into the social scenario. In the following examples, you will see a mix of the methods and techniques you've learned thus far in the book. Keep in mind throughout your experience here that you must go first if you want your subject to experience a state. This can take an emotional toll in the early phases of your training because some outcomes may require you to generate sadness, despair, depression, or regret in your subjects. There's no inoculation against this, but the effects from having to go through these emotions will wane over time and become less impactful in your life. Nothing is more effective in the final stages of behavior engineering than going first.

Take a moment now to think about the emotional and psychological states your subjects are in while in these final stages of your encounter. They are primed and ready for action, thinking about avoiding regret, focusing on becoming more open, productive, and adventurous. Using these activation methods will capitalize on this behavioral state and ensure the best possible behavioral outcomes. All of the forms of activation will follow the methods listed earlier in this chapter.

The Four Forms of Activation

1. Initiating action through excitement
2. Initiating action through avoidance of regret
3. Initiating action as a result of a direct command
4. Initiating action based on a previously installed set of behavioral anchors and feelings

Initiating Action through Excitement

Your using excitement will push subjects in the direction of enjoyment, and it fulfills their previously installed needs to open up and become more adventurous. The method hinges on the ability to become excited yourself and to compel action through gestures, linguistics, and mood transference.

* "I can remember them saying...and this is it. This is the *one* chance people wait for. Some would have ignored it and returned

to their boring lives...some don't. It's so rare to see something and think *this is it*. Whatever kept you from enjoying life before is gone, and now you have the chance...what's the best way out of here?"

* "And some things only happen once. There's that chance encounter that never comes again...when you just have to take it in and know that *this* is going to be good. Here we are, and it's your time to make this happen, James."

* "All of those feelings you stack into yourself...now...like excitement, feeling good, knowing this is perfect, anticipation...being ready to go...when you know this is your chance. Amy, what time is it? Good. I have to go, let's go."

* "It's like finishing a week of work and feeling so good...now with me, I see a lot of people who finally come to a point where nothing will stop them. All of that motivation built up, the essence of what makes them doers and everyone else [ep], something less than that. What time is your meeting at the embassy tomorrow? You can do this."

* "Rachel, this is it. I know it hasn't been easy for you, and I think you're very different. This is it. You've gotten so motivated and excited for so long about doing this that anyone could even see it in your eyes. You're much more driven than most people, and you've earned your place in the world. Here's *your* offer."

* "Noticing where you are now, I'd say a lot of people wouldn't have done what you've done. A lot of people are scared to take action, and then there are the ones with no regrets. This is it. Are you ready to make this yours?"

* "You're definitely above the rest of the crowd. Most people don't have the courage [need] to take action when they want something. I don't know what made you this way, but you're surely an exception to the rule. I've decided, you should come to..."

* "Everyone else would have shied away from the things you've faced. You have that perfect ability to become completely focused and take action...so awesome. Here it is: go into the _____ and _____."

Initiating Action through the Avoidance of Regret

Using the law of compounding effects and following the use of scarcity and regret tactics will help you to instill the final sense of action in your subjects.

* "And it's so sad to see the people who don't act on what they want. Nothing matters until you feel that sense of '*this is for me*' to the point where no one can stop you. The more you think about it, the easier it gets...and your brain says, '*This is my chance. I won't regret this.*' Let's get out of here."
* "There's that sense of regret in almost everyone, I guess. Some people just get to that point where they don't let past worries hold them back from getting what they want...take action."
* "Most people don't even do things outside their comfort zones... that explains all the regret. What would you say if I told you...?"
* "What's so sad is that people don't actually have anything standing in their way. It's all imaginary. You have that ability to take a stand that's so rare. Most people don't have that kind of courage. What if we..."
* "So many of us live life as if death were something that happened to other people."

Initiating Action as a Result of a Direct Command

This method uses a direct or hidden command to initiate action on the part of subjects.

* "Kyle, take my phone and bring it with you tomorrow into the file room."

* "Sara, this is it. So many people are going to just leave now... with me...there's something extraordinary about seeing things for the first time."

* "You have an awesome ability to create your own world. I can tell you're not easily scared [conversation ensues]. Tell me more about the merger." (Name omitted to assist in dissociation by depersonalization.)

* "It's sad to see when people have so many regrets. Luckily, we don't all behave like that. Let's move out to the patio now."

* "And people get to the point where everything is clear, just makes sense. You don't even realize it until your body is just moving on its own. A person can, Natalie, just start becoming his or her own person. What if you just went over there and took charge of that conversation?"

INITIATING ACTION BASED ON A PREVIOUSLY INSTALLED SET OF BEHAVIORAL ANCHORS AND FEELINGS

Firing and using anchors is one of the most visually rewarding behavior-engineering techniques. It provides instant, visible feedback seen in the behaviors of subjects. While there are many recipes and instructions for anchoring throughout the Internet, there is no way to become proficient without practice. Anchoring is not a science but an art form.

* "Rachel, what are the biggest things most people [ep] use as excuses for not doing what they want [op]? [Fire previous anchors for action, adventure, etc.] Let go of everything right now and let the other part of you take over."

* "This is it. [Fire all anchors.] Start here. Just go outside."

* "So many things happen without people really *feeling it*. [Fire all anchors.] Now...totally perfect...Jen, think about this...every moment of the day."

* "That was such a good movie. [Fire anchors.] Just awesome. Grab your stuff...let's do this."

* "That's just like when people start to just say, 'To hell with it!' and take action. [Fire anchors.] Starting now...everything makes sense...dude, let's set up this deal."

Recall your learning about the *now* gesture and apply it to your practice of calling a subject to action. You will recall that you should touch your wristwatch within sixty seconds before using the now gesture. The hand using the downward-pointing now gesture should be the same hand you touched your wristwatch with.

It's important, if you are calling subjects to action in a way that requires physical action, to start moving in the same way you'd like them to move just as you make the final call to action. This mirroring behavior will move them as you speak, and the decision to act will just be a natural progression of their physiology.

Head nodding will also increase the likelihood of acceptance and action if done while the suggestions are made.

To remain comfortable and maintain rapport throughout the activation process, you must maintain internal comfort and relaxation with what you are doing and have supreme confidence in the methods you are using. If your subjects are in the mirroring phase, they will match your confidence in your own abilities. When you feel that people's following you is a natural behavior for them, it will show, and others will begin to follow your lead. Without the firmly planted beliefs and actions of confidence and relaxation (coolness), there will be no activation.

This phase is likely to be the time when the strongest level of doubt is triggered in subjects. If they are in rapport and mirroring your gestures, you can reassure them by wrapping your arm over your chest or stomach (whichever is more appropriate). When subjects perform similar gestures, it will be a reassuring self-hug. This can be done preemptively to minimize resistance or just before they make a choice to perform a requested action.

Behavioral Entrainment

• • •

ENTRAINMENT REFERS TO THE PROGRESSIVE learning of new behaviors through repetitive actions that increase in intensity or effort. In behavior engineering, behavioral entrainment is a very subtle process that takes place over a longer time span than do some of the other techniques.

An example of conversational, behavioral entrainment is what people commonly refer to as developing a "yes set." The origin of this method is unknown, but it can be attributed mostly to sales teams at Xerox. In yes-set scenarios, customers are repeatedly asked questions that sales-people know the customers will respond to with a yes. Ostensibly, at the end of the line of questions, salespeople will ask a final question that they want to have a yes answer to. In theory, the customer will have become entrained in the yes response and will answer affirmatively for the final question.

Here are a few examples of yes-set questions:

* "Wouldn't you like to…"
* "Aren't you tired of…"
* "Isn't it time to…"
* "Aren't you drowning in…"
* "You can…can't you?"
* "Would it be good to have a better…"
* "Would you benefit from a new…"
* "Isn't this something you could use?

* "Doesn't it always feel good when someone…
* "It's pretty easy to…isn't it?"

These questions cause clients to become more and more comfortable saying yes to salespeople.

Behavior entrainment works in much the same way, and yes sets can be used in conversations just as any other covert method.

AGREEMENT ESCALATION

This is a gradual increase in asking small questions within a conversation to gain agreement. Robert Cialdini (2009) wrote about the consistency principle, where we as humans don't like to be seen as inconsistent, so when we agree to things, we will modify our actions to create consistency.

We are all wired to try to align our actions and beliefs. When people do us small favors, their beliefs about themselves and the relationships change, even if only temporarily. If subjects do us small favors, they first see themselves as helpful, needed, or dependable. Following this, they are able to rationalize that they acted because the operators have qualities that are worth doing things for. The more often subjects perform a task or fulfills even a small request, the more deeply seated the beliefs (and following behaviors) are going to be.

Gestural movement compliance follows this same line of thought, saying that when a subject looks where an operator points, moves to adjust to the movements of the operator, or steps in when the operator takes a step back, the subject is engaging in unconscious followership. Typically, subjects will rationalize their behavior internally, basing that rationality on their liking the operators or their having a strong sense of rapport with the operators. Basically, subjects will make their following behavior their own idea. Operators' moving and causing their subjects to adjust is gestural-movement compliance. This is different from mirroring in that subjects aren't necessarily copying or mimicking a movement but adjusting to interpersonal movement to make communication and rapport stronger. Authority must be present for this to happen naturally.

This is all basically rehearsal and gradual compliance building. It's progressive behavioral change in a short time span.

Gaslighting

● ● ●

GASLIGHTING IS A FORM OF psychological manipulation that refers to taking actions to cause other people to doubt their own beliefs, memory, or sanity. Its root lies in creating doubt and causing some form of disorientation in subjects.

In the 1940s, there was a popular play by the name of *Gas Light*, known as *Angel Street* in the United States. The main character tries to convince his wife and her friends that she is crazy or mentally unstable by changing, modifying, and shifting small elements of her environment over time. When his wife points out these changes, he insists she is mistaken or that "it has always been that way."

Sociopaths, narcissists, and psychopaths use gaslighting frequently with their victims. It shifts victims' perceptions of the world into a state of confusion and doubt, creating windows through which the offenders can insert their own version of reality. Abusive husbands are known for using this method while convincing their victims that no abuse is taking place and that they are exaggerating the events in question.

This effect is similar to the Martha Mitchell effect. This effect (made famous during the Watergate scandal) is called *iatrogenesis* by mental-health professionals; using it, a doctor or clinician induces confusion and disorder by mistaking a patient's real-life events with delusions. While mental-health professionals may be well intended, they can cause severe problems in patients.

In behavior engineering, you have the ability, once authority has been developed with subjects, to use this method in a much less sinister form. This can be accomplished using environmental shifts and language. Let's cover a few examples of these.

ENVIRONMENTAL SHIFTS

Subjects are more attuned to their environments than most operators initially assume. Making small shifts in the immediate environment is a sure way to bring attention to subjects' inability to accurately assess their environment. Consider the following examples:

* Shifting the position of someone's straw in a drink
* Moving the drink an inch or two while the subject looks away
* Changing your tie in the bathroom
* Correcting a person you've just met on your name
* Paying for a bill in a restaurant on your way to the bathroom and insisting the waiter came to the table
* Shifting which hand you eat with midway through a meal
* Changing types of pens or notebooks in a meeting
* Beginning a meeting with your chair much lower than others and shifting it to the highest position before you are due to speak

LANGUAGE

Using language designed to create internal doubt in subjects works similarly to the environmental shifts above; you need only to make your subjects begin to experience a small amount of doubt or internal confusion about their perceptions. Here are a few examples you can build on:

* Changing your pitch while someone looks away
* Mentioning something you spoke about before that you actually didn't

- Commenting on a strange behavior exhibited by someone who has left the group (like a waitress)
- Asking questions about everyday objects they don't likely remember (like which way Lincoln's head is facing on the penny)
- Asking them the street address of something they might know, but you're fairly certain they won't
- Asking what they had for dinner a few days prior
- Complimenting them on a positive trait they haven't yet exhibited
- Asking about details of something they are likely to admit not remembering

In some gaslighting manuals written for the government, the use of time distortion is mentioned. However, no explanation is given as to its applicability. Thus far, no significant methods can be employed effectively in conversations, but some of the methods have been readapted into the hypnotraining practices, in which several days or weeks of training are compacted into a single session, giving the subjects confidence in their abilities on par with months of training.

Shutting Off Human Willpower

● ● ●

HUNDREDS OF SURVEYS AND STUDIES have been done on human willpower. Everyone seems to have a genuine belief that they consciously create their lives and that the unconscious is a slave to the conscious. We, as humans, tend to believe that we all have a tremendous amount of choice and control over our behavior. Believing otherwise would make us all feel powerless and manipulated.

Our behavior is governed much more by the unconscious than most people believe. Everything from the products we "choose" to buy to the choices we "make" every day is decided mostly by way of unconscious processes. This fundamental human illusion of control and self-determinism works surprisingly well in an operator's favor. As people begin to make choices, no matter how heavily they are influenced by outside factors, they will conclude that they have made the choices through their free will. Even with blatant advertising, social pressure, and subliminal-persuasion methods being so commonly known, most of us still believe we choose products of our own accord, unbiased by advertisement and uninfluenced by social pressure.

Human willpower is a plastic thing—it is moldable, elastic, and sometimes completely nonexistent. Having subjects with a strong sense of willpower is beneficial to the operators. Subjects who believe they have made their own decisions are far more likely to be satisfied with their behaviors. They will even defend their actions when questioned.

Even after some subjects are told they were manipulated into making decisions that they normally would not have made, they will defend themselves, saying they made the choices on their own.

As you develop your profiling skills in finding needs and in weakness identification, you will gain the ability to cause subjects to perform most actions of your choosing, and they will continue to feel as if they had made their own logical choices to perform those behaviors.

Willpower, for the purposes of the Ellipsis program, is subjects' belief that they can resist manipulation and control their behaviors on a conscious level.

Some of your subjects will take pride in being in control, and they will typically display a willing defiance to social norms, suggestions, and requests. This form of pride is extremely easy to work with. Imagine any difficult subject. By your using covert or overt methods, when you help them to worry about their level of control in their lives, they will focus on the control. Many subjects, while worrying about their actual control, will (unwittingly) enter hypnotic states to avoid control by others.

At this point lies an opportunity to blend several techniques you've already learned within this manual. First, the possibility of using negative dissociation becomes apparent in this situation. However, so many more methods can be applied here. Here are several examples of comments using techniques you've learned about thus far:

* "And even kids can tell how easy it is to see how people who want to be in control all the time tend to slip into the state of being controlling. I'm sure you've met people like this, and sometimes it's amazing to actually meet someone with a great deal of inner control…someone who is just naturally flexible in his or her own mind."
* "How easy would it be for you to realize when someone can completely feel that it's perfect to sometimes let go into the feeling of knowing you have control? Only when you can actually

hear conversations around you and completely pay attention is when you can have control...knowing you have that environment in your mind."

* "It's funny how people sometimes want to just lose control... and forget to pay attention to little things. Even like their own breathing starts to escape from their awareness."

* "Most people can't even focus on their own feet and have a conversation."

* "When you feel completely in control of the environment, is it something that comes as you pay more and more attention to the things around you, or is it a feeling that you start to feel your own body and then focus on what's in front of you... now?"

* These linguistic examples are very basic ways of converting a need to resist into a "trance by default" scenario.

* As you progress with subjects and find they have more resistance than you expected initially, they can be guided into a more compliant state through metaphor:

* "Some people are very strong minded...and that's fantastic, to know you are your own person. And then there are times when surrender becomes so difficult it can make things so uncomfortable...resistance...causing headaches and having no ability to sleep...not able to use their ability to let go."

* "My friend Bruce used to feel as if he always had to have control over things [gesturing outward]. It took him years to realize that just being alive is surrender. Not knowing what amazing thing will come next. Just like the way the heart squeezes and lets go... squeezes and lets go [use your hands to anchor the movement of squeezing and letting go]."

At this point, using conversational fractionation will help your subjects to leave this state and become comfortable with having been in it because of its brevity. Changing the topic will prevent them from analyzing and screening the content you have just delivered to their unconscious minds. Following the topic change for a moment, you now want to walk them back into that state again to shut off their willpower and to help them view resistance as the source of weakness in their lives:

I totally agree...and when you do that, it's that same surrender point...the only way anyone has any enjoyment...to the point where people can just nod in agreement [nodding] and realize their own resistance is suffering. Nothing matters much if some lazy people try to keep resisting their whole lives, and we have all seen so many people who do that.

After bringing this topic up, you must redirect subjects' attention either to something superficial or to something visible in the environment. This redirect helps subjects to internalize the feelings without a filter and brings them back to the real world, so in essence, the stories act as miniature posthypnotic suggestions.

Suggestions Should Empower the Subject

When you deliver any suggestion to subjects or redirect their focus toward themselves, it's beneficial to frame the suggestions you give as something that generates an increased feeling of power. Making subjects feel as if their following suggestions would increase their own feelings of empowerment creates a mental vacuum that draws them automatically into obedience or compliance.

Nothing is as psychologically compelling as the human desire to acquire more control over the self and the environment. Using the following methods, even in normal conversations, can drastically change the course of behavior that follows. When subjects start to feel slightly fragile, especially as they enter a conversational trance, the reassurance of a more powerful state creates automatic psychological movement in the directions you wish them to go. Subjects will typically feel slightly vulnerable as they enter a trance. Because you have used covert-trance methods, subjects won't know that they have been hypnotically led to this state, but their feeling of vulnerability will gradually increase as they continue to go deeper into conversational trances. The sensation of losing control or becoming vulnerable in the presence of a stranger can cause discomfort and confusion in subjects' mental states. While this happens, they will unconsciously begin to seek ways to increase their comfort levels. As the need to feel more in control increases, a suggestion offered by an operator that seems to alleviate that need can immediately be applied and will be unconsciously followed.

Here are a few examples of covert-empowerment framing:

Using positive-association methods: "And these incredibly powerful and influential political figures all seem to be able to completely follow an idea and act on it...with me."

Positive association with a double bind: "And it's fascinating [op] how easy it is to feel empowered...where everything seems to be within your reach. When you [sp] feel completely balanced like that, does it start suddenly when you focus on something with all of your power [op], or is it something like where you really have to let go of the need to make decisions, and just let go?"

Stories: "I had a friend like that once. You know those people who don't even know they self-sabotage? [Prep with negative dissociation here.] He always had this ridiculous urge to feel as if he had to have control. He would ruin so many social situations and never realize how that kind of behavior needs to just go away...with me."

Using trust: "And you know we all have those friends who just act like a wounded animal all the time. They don't trust anyone... you know? Sometimes I just want to say, 'Look [use the subject's sensory preference here], the only way you can actually get to the point where you will enjoy your life...now...is to let go...Being so distrustful will only lead you straight into depression.' When you just know that you can trust someone, it's an awesome feeling. So many people don't know how to just let go...now...I always wonder whether they will find the path to being able to enjoy their own lives...and finally... just go along...it's fine. What would you say to your friends who are like that?"

Article about successful people: "I read this article a few days ago. They did this amazing study of top leaders in the world and found that over ninety percent of them finally got to this point where they no longer had that desire to control everything. They start to enjoy letting go...now...and the best part is that they get to relax and still feel powerful...letting someone else make the decisions gave them a feeling...that they could feel powerful and become happy with letting someone [op] just take over for a little while."

"And it's only when you have control...that you realize how easy it is to just completely relax and enjoy not having to make all the choices and decisions."

"People with power always seem to feel that eventual feeling that just grows stronger...of not wanting to make all the decisions...just wanting to let go sometimes so they can finally relax."

"And even on road trips...the long ones that seem to have no end... having that break from driving and having to pay attention to everything is so empowering...just letting someone else [op] take the wheel for a while. And that relief that comes when you know you can just relax finally...with me."

Anything the subjects say can easily be turned into a short comment filled with embedded compliance statements. Even a topic as trivial as woodworking or pouring concrete can be molded by an operator and elegantly woven into the fabric of the conversation, containing dozens of relevant compliance suggestions hidden within the syntax of your speech.

In programming, empowerment also takes the place of introducing subjects to the concept of levels of power, in which they progress by allowing more of their unconscious minds to become empowered.

For instance, subjects can be told there are seven power levels they can achieve each time they give more control to the operators. They may be told that each successive surrender gives them more power over their conscious minds as an operator "teaches" them to control it.

Weaponized Willpower Shutdown

Some methods of communication may require more weaponization to accomplish control, especially given a shorter period of time within which you have to work. In this instance, the control of subjects in the initial phase of the Ellipsis progression is more important than establishing FIC.

The initial interaction in which you'll need to weaponize communication must be absolutely controlled and involve every mental faculty you can muster to establish control of the subjects.

Pain-Focused Methods

Using the human needs map, you can exploit character weakness and fear. Exploiting fear in this scenario has a few steps (which don't have to be followed precisely). Fear and human predictability rise together in almost perfect harmony. As soon as fear is felt, humans become increasingly more predictable. Here are the steps you should take:

1. Identify needs and fear.
2. Reassure subjects that their fears are valid.
3. Use fears and needs as motivating factors to cause illness and discomfort or pain.
4. Use illness and discomfort or pain to link to unwanted behaviors or emotions.

In the first twenty seconds, you should be able to pinpoint the needs map room that the subjects reside mainly within. They will quickly react to discussions involving the promotion of the needs. Using the momentum of this quick reaction, you can reassure the subjects through the use of metaphor that their needs (and by default, their fears) are valid and important. Embedded commands and linguistics can then tie the needs and fears to pain, and the pain (physical or emotional) can be tied to any behavior that is unwanted. They will feel the pain anytime they begin to mentally drift in any negative directions you've chosen.

Example 1:
The subject, a male, primarily has a strength need. You've identified this by a comment or statement he made early in the interaction. Follow along with the steps mentioned above and try to understand how he can flow into normal language. It's quite easy.

I agree. Most people don't really realize how vulnerable and un-safe we actually are. They all just kind of go through life not know-ing how small and insignificant each little person is. No matter how strong someone is, I think everyone is vulnerable and weak and needs to know how to stay alive. Just feeling the threat of everyday life can make someone get a headache. I get that nauseous feeling sometimes when I realize how close to death I am on a regular basis. It starts in the stomach, and you can't stop it. Just knowing the nausea is coming from knowing we are so tiny in the grand scheme of things. It's only when we *focus* and *let go* that everything feels better. Knowing we have control and you're safe.

Example 2:
The subject, a female, has a caretaker need. You identified this by hear-ing her speak about loving cooking classes. Furthermore, you heard her tell you she loves education and learning new things. This identifies a secondary need as intelligence. Remember that the intelligence need is not a need for intelligence but rather a need to be seen as intelligent.

That's just like when you're growing up and realize that everyone who you thought appreciated you was just acting...then start to naturally wonder how ignorant you had to be to miss it all, no one really appreciating the things you do for them…but after you *stop*…and focus, you start to realize there are hundreds of people who wouldn't be able to live without you. You start to realize that you actually know a whole lot about the world, and it helps you to simply let go…surrender.

Advanced Behavioral Anchoring

• • •

ANCHORING IS A TERM COINED by Richard Bandler during the formation of neurolinguistic programming and is based off the work of Virginia Satir, who was a therapist known for family therapy work. She also created the Virginia Satir Change Process Model. Read more about her at https://satirglobal.org/.

Anchoring methods are often written about at great length, but the process of using anchors and applying them in conversation is incredibly simple and effective.

Anchoring methods were originally based on the work of Ivan Pavlov, a Russian physiologist who conducted research on classical conditioning. In his experiments, he would ring a bell when a group of dogs were fed. After frequent repetition of this, he was able to make the dogs salivate simply by ringing the bell. Humans, though much more complex on a cognitive level, function in much the same way. Actually, we can be anchored (conditioned) much faster than dogs and to a much deeper level.

In much the same way as a smell can bring forth intense memory recall, anchoring is simply the act of mentally associating an emotion (or mental state) with a trigger from the environment.

Basic anchoring is the first skill you need to master, and it's much more about doing it than memorizing a complex method. Anchoring can be accomplished easily by bringing up a feeling or emotion, then doing something the subject can associate that with. In a perfect scenario, a subject will eventually (after a few repetitions) unconsciously associate your action with that emotion, allowing you to perform the action and activate the feeling or emotion on demand.

The reason anchoring is powerful is that you can produce an emotional state on command. The most common states you will use for anchoring are trust, connection, excitement, enjoyment, and surrender.

Reading about anchoring makes it sound very much like a robotic and formulaic technique, but it is quite the opposite. When you become able to use anchoring in conversation, you will discover that it is very much an organic, simple art form.

When using the anchoring methods, you should have your subjects fully in their own bodies for the experience. When they imagine the past event you will ask about, or if you ask them to recall certain memories, you want them to recall the memories in the first-person perspective. This will amplify the emotions and feelings associated with those memories. Using dissociation during anchoring will produce significantly watered-down reactions, as your subjects won't be entirely in first-person perspective.

When you practice these methods in the field, you'll discover dozens of personal strategies that work for you. For almost any kind of anchoring to work, you'll need more than a few minutes of conversation in which to repeat the gestures and to recall the desired emotions in your subjects. In our students' experiences, this technique is most likely to cause suspicion and be noticed by subjects. With that in mind—and with the fear of getting caught sitting in the forefront of most students' minds—let's start by looking into the basic types of anchors we can use in conversation; let's see some examples of them in real life.

VISUAL ANCHORS

Visual anchors are a response to stimuli that we've been exposed to before. An example of this is when a person sees the flashing lights of a police car in the rearview mirror and has an instantaneous reaction to it. Another example is when a person sees a baby and has an emotional reaction that instantly softens all of his or her edges.

AUDITORY ANCHORS

We hear things all the time that trigger emotions. Think of the tiny bell that charity workers use around Christmas to collect donations in front of stores. Also, when you're at home and the doorbell rings, whatever mood you were in before it happened is almost gone. The doorbell becomes an instant break in thought and mood.

TOUCH ANCHORS

Often referred to as kinesthetic anchors, these anchors are bodily sensations that trigger behaviors. Think about the behavior difference between the last time you wore very formal clothing and the last time you wore gym clothing. Clothes alone can make us behave differently. The sensation of physical touch from another person can change our moods and how we behave toward others. Using anchors is a powerful way to harness the power of state-dependent decision making.

OLFACTORY ANCHORS

Smells can trigger very strong and vivid memories. This is called odor-evoked autobiographical memory. The smell receptors are located so close to the frontal lobe that many memories and associated memories can be activated by smell. As you know, once a memory is activated, the associated memories are also lit up, and this changes the mood and emotion.

You've already learned about conversational regression and its effect on compliance and trust. Using smells that will trigger subjects' memories of childhood, we can regress subjects much further by using as many senses as we can.

Using Anchors in Conversation

Conversational anchors are very effective and take almost no time at all to learn. As you progress and actually use these in everyday life, anchoring will become smoother and will happen automatically. As you get better at using anchors, there will be a point that comes where you will simply intend to produce an outcome and the anchoring will happen unconsciously. The benefit of this to you is that you expend less of your mental energy on method, and you can focus on the subjects.

Anchoring will be easy if you follow these steps:

1. Elicit a state through questions.
2. Amplify the state.
3. Set the anchor.

Most of the time, you will be anchoring in conversations and will have the ability to touch your subjects. However, as much as you read about that happening in NLP books, we have found it to be just as effective to keep our hands off while states are building in subjects. When subjects are going into their minds to experience an increasingly emotional state, touching them usually breaks the train of thought. It's best to anchor by using a visual channel connected to something on your body. For instance, you might want to say, "That's awesome," as you place your hand on your heart every time you get subjects into desired states.

Eliciting a state is easy. All you need to do is ask a question that doesn't sound as if it's from a script. Use real language, as the following examples show:

* "What was the coolest part about that?"
* "Holy shit, I bet that was incredible! What was it like to be there?"
* "So, you love to _____. What's the thing you like the most about it?"

These are easy to perform. Once they talk about their states, all you have to do is amplify their descriptions by using another probing question.

When your subjects are answering questions like those, you will receive great behavioral information embedded in their communication. As they speak, they will use specific adjectives and phrases to describe their feelings. While they speak these specific words and phrases, they will also gesture to describe them. Pay close attention to the words they use and the associated gestures. When you amplify, you can give the same words and gestures back to your subjects. For example, if a subject is describing a trip to Italy and uses the word *humbling* while touching his or her abdomen, you will store this information for one of two purposes:

1. To later use the word and gesture to ask amplification questions
2. To later use the word and gesture to make the subject more comfortable and to deepen rapport in the interaction

With the subject in the above example, you would simply ask a question like, so when you went on this trip, what would you say was so humbling (touching your abdomen as the subject did) about being there?

As soon as the subject answers this question, he or she will give you even more phrases and associated gestures to use as ammunition in the future of the conversation. Keep the subject's phrases on hand for use anytime you're describing something good, appealing, or trustworthy to the subject later in the conversation.

As the subject starts to experience the emotion internally, you simply need to perform the gesture and speak the word you want to use later to recall this state. The gesture and sound you make to anchor the subject's current mood is not something you copied from the subject but a gesture that looks genuine and matches the phrase you are using. It's best, according to thousands of articles on this, to set the anchor (use the gesture and word) just before the subject is at the peak of his or her internal experience.

For this to be effective, you need to perform this routine at least three times. Obviously, it isn't always possible or social to run through an exciting scenario with your subjects three times in a row or to ask amplifying questions. If possible, it's best to space them out in conversations to avoid causing unconscious (and conscious) alarm.

When you use anchors designed to elicit excitement, it's best to anchor to touching your wristwatch. Excitement anchors, when set three or more times and fired correctly, will help subjects to make decisions about performing actions that you suggest to them. When you touch your watch as you trigger the mechanism later in your conversations, they will also associate this with the now gesture you learned in the gestural-referencing chapter.

Here's a simple timeline illustrating how anchoring takes place in a conversation:

1. Operator asks a question about something the subject enjoys.
2. Subject responds with descriptive words and gestures.
3. Operator memorizes words and gestures.
4. Operator asks a deeper question about the subject's experience by using some of the words and gestures.
5. Subject gives a deeper answer by using even more words and gestures.
6. As the subject begins to change his or her facial expression to match the desired mental state, operator uses the anchor (touching his or her chest while saying, "That's incredible!").

That's the simple process of anchoring. Let's look at a few examples of elicitation questions for different states that you may need to utilize:

Relaxation

* "When you got that job, what was it like knowing you can finally relax, knowing you had 'made it'?"

- "What's the one thing you usually do when it's pouring down rain outside?"
- "I bet that trip was so relaxing. What did you do?"
- "What's the best hotel in that city? How are the beds?"
- "Did you like that yoga class?"

Surrender

- "How do you know when to just let go and focus on the golf course?"
- "It's so awesome to be out there at night, makes you feel so small. Do you ever have that feeling?"
- "What's the longest you've ever been kept on hold?"
- "Remember when you were a kid and you had no cares in the world? Like, you just *knew* that you were going to be fine, that someone's protecting you?"
- "When people learn sports, it all boils down to letting go of yourself and getting out of your own way. Have you ever had a coach say that?"

Connection

- "When you met Neal, what was the feeling like?"
- "What's it like for you when you suddenly notice something amazing is happening?"
- "How does it feel when you know you're connecting with people on a very different level?"

These are only examples, but it's easy to see how easily these can be applied in everyday conversations. Most of us use anchoring and elicitation regularly without any awareness of doing so.

NEGATIVE ANCHORS

Negative anchors can be of any sensory variety. Negative anchors specifically trigger the memory or associated feelings of a negative, uncomfortable, or otherwise stressful situation. Using negative anchors is usually the most useful in situations where subjects are starting down paths, but you'd like them to stop. They are also best preceded by interruption techniques.

For example, imagine you're in a scenario where a subject is opening up and begins to show possible behavioral indicators of a dismissive or negative nature. You will need to interrupt this train of thought and anchor the subject's negativity to something negative to put the subject back on track. Here's an example:

- You notice a female subject is displaying disagreement behavior to your discussing the concept of surrender and letting go.
- You immediately interrupt her current train of thought with an interruption technique.
- Immediately following the interruption, you install discomfort and anchor the discomfort by making uncomfortable "accidental" contact with her foot under the table (a touch that is accidental and can be reasonably estimated to cause a small amount of social discomfort).
- This contact is made while saying, "And it's like so many people don't get it, like this headache [sp] that stays there until you have to just *stop*...and come back to a train of thought. *With me*, you have such a natural ability to be so comfortable all the time that I'm sure you don't have shit like that happen a lot."

This is one illustration of a negative anchor that has a simple formula: interrupt the subject, anchor to the negative state, remove the negative state, and go right back to the conversation.

USING ANCHORS INSTALLED PREVIOUSLY

As we all walk through life, our experiences anchor us to pertinent feelings. This is a simple process. You learned that the smell of sunscreen can trigger happy memories and that the smell of mothballs can create trust. This method simply relies on reinitiating an anchor from a subject's past. In the examples of sunscreen and mothballs, your using regression and installing trust is likely to be one of the most effective methods of delivering the package to the unconscious and getting behavioral outcomes. It's important to remember while performing this that there's a strong chance that transference can occur. Transference simply means that the feelings a subject has about a person are transferred to the operator. In clinical psychology, this occurs when a patient begins to transfer feelings about a figure from his or her past onto the involved therapist. Transference also occurs outside therapy all the time. Imagine that you grew up with a golden retriever but it died when you were a child. Seeing a golden retriever as an adult would cause transference, even if just for the moment.

The formula is also simple:

1. Have subjects recall a time they knew they were especially taken care of or protected.
2. Use phrases that link them to their childhoods.
3. Stand up and make them look up at you.
4. Follow with an embedded command.

Here is a breakdown of these steps with examples:

"My dad was always there too. What's the safest you've ever felt growing up? Like when you could look up and see someone was there, and you *knew* nothing could hurt you?"

The phrase *look up* is used deliberately to put the subject into childhood memories and ensure the adult memories don't come into play. At this point, you'll likely see the subject use an upward eye movement to recall the memory. Let the subject speak.

"Absolutely. It's like you have no idea the lengths this person [op] would travel to keep you safe, but you're absolutely certain that there's nothing in the world that can hurt you. Totally safe...with me, I think there's something so perfect about that. Just being able to look up [op] and know you're invincible. [You, the operator, stand up.] I'm going to _____. Do you need anything?"

At this point you would touch the subject on the shoulder from above or in a way that you're comfortable doing, depending on the scenario.

"Okay. Be right back."

This departure will also let the subject soak in the feelings you've just installed. In the next chapter, you can bring these anchoring skills into play in creating amnesia in conversation.

Covert Conversational Amnesia

● ● ●

IN THIS CHAPTER, YOU WILL learn methods of creating covert amnesia in subjects.

Covert amnesia is never a foolproof way of erasing or preventing access to memories. At best, it is temporary, creating a deep haze around an event but producing no lost time. At a minimum, it can serve to dissociate a person enough to eliminate details of the conversation on a permanent level.

There is no procedure for inserting amnesia into conversations. It is a progressive accumulation of methods that must be decided on early in an interaction. Covert amnesia relies on rapport, authority, dissociation, confusion, and gesturing.

Subjects should be exposed to all of these aspects before they are presented in an amnesia method, with the exception of confusion. If new methods cause operators to speak or behave in new ways, those methods create a focus and break conversational autopilots and cause *more* memory retention.

When using amnesia methods and techniques, operators' making strong eye contact is beneficial for most subjects. Strong eye contact creates a small-enough amount of discomfort, which increases cortisol (a chemical in the brain related to stress). We are less likely to recall semi stressful events, and cortisol has been linked to numerous studies in short-term memory loss. Accidental contact of feet under the table and small, calculated invasions of personal space can often produce the same effect.

Using future rehearsal is also an effective method that can be mentioned a few times during the process through the medium of stories. Telling stories about how friends "lost a day" or "lost time" and asking subjects to recall similar feelings will help them to get their brain connections warmed up for amnesia before the suggestions take place.

Use your eye-movement intelligence. Making gestures to the sides that subjects use to access creative thoughts helps them imagine the stories and suggestions. Even moving briefly to those directions as you deliver the amnesia product is beneficial.

Subjects with needs for acceptance will respond to a vacuum movement just prior to the suggestion as well. For instance, an operator will step back just as he or she delivers a suggestion, which encourages the subject to follow the operator's body movement. As the subject steps forward or begins to lean in to the operator, the natural flow of behavior dictates whether the subject follows the suggestion as well.

Some subjects who are slightly more difficult or less responsive than others should be interrupted or shocked immediately following the suggestions. These subjects tend to be critical, and it's important to cut that train of thought off before they start down a critical path after you've delivered the amnesia suggestion to them.

The amnesia process can be one of two methods: cumulative or spontaneous.

Cumulative amnesia processes are designed to create a cloud around the entire interaction, but spontaneous amnesia is for a specific event. The methods here don't contain examples, because they rely on operators' using the training from earlier in the book to create the amnesia.

CUMULATIVE AMNESIA METHOD

Cumulative amnesia creates a cloud around an entire night, day, or interaction. This method contains five basic steps that must be followed in order, contrary to most of the methods you've learned thus far:

1. Discuss the ability to forget and have memory black spots early in the conversation.
2. Using stories, bring focus repeatedly to forgetting and haziness.
3. Use dissociative language heavily.
4. Use confusion methods to create black spots and random spontaneous amnesia.
5. Circle back and recap all the methods at once, and anchor them before ending the conversation in a <u>nondramatic</u> way.

SPONTANEOUS-AMNESIA METHOD

Spontaneous amnesia is used when operators need to perform an on-the-spot removal of a specific occurrence or memory. It's important to move quickly back to the original conversation immediately after the use of this method, because the method causes confusion, creating a larger-than-normal gap between confusion and conversation. Your returning immediately to the conversation provides subjects less time to try to decipher what has happened. Follow these steps:

1. Shift focus quickly and naturally from the flow of conversation to something seemingly more important.
2. Briefly bring up the general topic of the amnesia, using no descriptive words.
3. Use a short confusion statement followed by reassurance.
4. Immediately issue commands for amnesia and return to the conversation.

Possible commands for amnesia are:

*   "And it's fine to take that and set it aside [gesture as if moving it aside] …totally gone."
*   "That's the way it should be when something needs to be gotten rid of like that."

* "The whole thing completely leaves the room…just gone…now."
* "And it's the same…totally erased…your mind…for that…I think, is a powerful tool for…"
* "Creating just this black space where everything was…it's just gone.
* "And that's just the one that leaves…now."
* "Gone. Just gone."
* "Just wipes it all out like a fleet of white blood cells…" (This suggests the memory wasn't beneficial anyway.)
* "And someone can run around and around…just spinning…and never find it again."
* "Just goes completely out of your mind."
* "And you start for-getting…excited about something totally new."
* "And you for-get everything you want."
* "She calls and it's just like…you can't recall her back until later in the evening."
* "Forget that!"
* "Just like that feeling of forgetting…right there on the tip of your tongue, until it's not important anymore."
* "And he said, 'Forget it, it's fine, now. Forget it!' "
* "I mean there's so much going on in people's lives [sp] that they don't ever stop to forget some of the most important things they remember to do when it becomes just so easy to let it go."

Using amnesia is actually this easy. There is no need to further convolute what's in the chapter and adding to it would only do so. Practice is the best way to develop this skill. You have an enormous supply of psychological weaponry now, and it's time to add see what a conversation looks like when it's added together.

Putting It Together

• • •

THIS MANUAL HAS THUS FAR given you dozens of tools to use in tandem. However, the tools come together in the following illustration of behavior engineering. The scenario will be used to create a blank-slate subject who is ready to soak up commands and suggestions. It's assumed in this example that there is no time limit. Here's the outline of what a one-hour conversation scenario might look like. We have omitted most of the dialogue of the subject and focused on the operator's behavior.

FIC AND FOLLOW

- Start conversation
  - The conversation is started, and the operator begins developing authority.
- Autopilot shutoff
  - Operator shuts off autopilot or changes the environment stimuli from what the subject is most likely used to experiencing in similar scenarios.
- Establish focus
  - Operator uses focus methods to gain temporary focus.
- Delete distractions
  - Operator removes distractions linguistically, eliciting more-focused states from the subject.

- Self-gesturing
  - Operator uses self-gesturing to establish rapid rapport and trust.
- Mirroring
  - Operator begins basic mirroring.
- Positional shifts
  - Operator makes small positional shifts to start behavioral-entrainment process.
- Embedded commands
  - Operator embeds commands for interest and curiosity.
- Facial touching
  - Operator touches mouth and face and uses key words to inspire trust and more focus in the subject.
- Leading physically
  - More behavioral entrainment ensues in the form of pointing, requesting movement, or performance of small tasks.
- Slowing breathing
  - Operator slows down breathing to slow the subject down.
- Exhalatory speaking (speaking while they exhale)
  - As the breathing is slowing, the operator begins speaking when the subject is exhaling to establish comfort and trust, connecting them.

Surrender and Letting Go

- Gratitude leads to surrender
  - Operator describes how gratitude leads to surrender.
- Higher power
  - Operator elicits subject's feelings of protection or trust.
- Regression phase 1
  - Operator regresses subject to a minimal degree, causing openness and more trust.

* Protected
  * Operator gives a small (ten-second) story about being in a situation similar to the subject's, a story having to do with being safe, protected, and taken care of.
* Letting go
  * Operator guides subject's reactions into a story about letting go or mentions the concept.
* Feels so good to let go and enjoy something right here that makes sense
* Learning to play a sport
* Learning to swim
* Letting go of stress
* Being taught about math
* Letting go, knowing someone will take care of you fully

DISSOCIATION

* Conversational dissociation

DELIVERY OF PRODUCT

* Metaphor
  * Operator uses metaphors for delivery of desired state.
* My friend...
* Personal experience
* Third party
* Embedded commands
* Regression phase 2
  * Operator gives applies more questions about childhood, exposes the subject to childhood smells, has the subject draw his or her bedroom on a napkin, and uses regression phrases.

o In some circumstances, it will be necessary to use phase 2 after scarcity, because the scarcity methods sometimes disturb subjects out of regression, pushing them back into the present moment.

ACTIVATE SCARCITY

* Friend with cancer
* Car crash
* Disasters and fires
* Deathbed wishes of friends
* Only regret what you didn't do
* Negative disassociation: some people let opportunities pass by because of weakness
* When will some people realize that this is *it*?

DEPROGRAM SOCIETY THOUGHTS

* Negative dissociation: so many people carry thoughts from childhood into adult life.
* Negative dissociation: compliment on sense of fun and enjoyment, followed by saying, "It's amazing how many people don't really think about where their thoughts come from."
* "There's a part of everyone, I guess, that just knows how to let go and enjoy."

CALL TO ACTION

* Recall scarcity briefly
* Opportunity

* Act on something now
* Finally make that decision to take what you want
* Nothing can stand in your way
* This is the last chance you may have to do it

INSTALL COMPLIANCE

* Install the need to obey or please the operator.

Situational Examples

● ● ●

IN THIS CHAPTER, YOU'LL BE able to see real-world examples of the methods you've learned. This is meant to be an illustration of the methods and not a collection of phrases to memorize. Although you could memorize a lot of the following examples and put them to immediate use, the magic in behavior engineering comes from the ability to speak freely and have the methods and techniques flow naturally, allowing you to participate more organically in conversations.

POLICE INTERACTION
Resource Phrases and Comments:
    "Let it go"
    "Let him go"
    "It's fine"
    "Let it slide"
    "No big deal (op)"
    "Rare case"
    "Warning is fine"
    "Soon as it comes back, it's fine (waiting on your license to be cleared)"
    "Not that bad (op)"
    "Kind (sp)"
    "Forgiving (sp)"

PROFILING TIPS

Use body composition for negative dissociation.

Know that police often feel that they're in an extremely powerful position (assume a posture that makes them feel this way).

Many police feel they are in a thankless job.

Most people who speak to them do so with contempt.

Don't use the word "officer" (too many people do and it will activate autopilot; this needs to be an unusual situation).

Officers in excellent physical condition will respond better to people who confirm their need to be strong and perfect.

An officer who is overweight will respond to statements (those functioning as a negative-dissociation technique) about people rushing through life.

Behavior-Engineering Tips:

Don't stare at the officer in the mirror.

Keep keys in hand out the window.

Keep interior lights on.

Keep papers ready to go (keep them that way).

Speaking fast is fine in this situation: the officer is used to nervous people talking fast, and he or she will listen. Speed aids the use of confusion methods.

PHRASING:

- "I can't believe that. So sorry. This pharmacist this morning wouldn't make up his mind. It's fine [op]. I didn't know whether my kid was sick and whether he should stay home from school. He just said it's fine; let him go, even with a slight fever—it's no big deal. I thought it was a rare case [bfp]."
- "I'm not used to these roads. As soon as I get out here on the highway...when it comes back, it's fine [gesture to license]."

* "I can't even imagine why. I have driven this road so many times. Even when I was learning to drive in school…the teachers were so forgiving [sp]."
* "I just had to get the money taken to the school today. It was late, but everyone was so kind and forgiving [sp]."
* "I know there's no excuse. I just woke up this warning [op] and still haven't caught up [ep]."
* "I'm sorry. I think people are in a hurry for no reason nowadays and give no concern for the safety of others [identifying autopilot]."
* "Sorry. I know so many people nowadays are just so concerned with themselves that they don't even pay attention to how much they can affect other people's lives [op]."
* "You guys do so much more than the military and don't get much thanks for it."
* "I mean there's so much going on in people's lives [sp] that they don't ever stop to forget some of the most important things they remember to do when it becomes just so easy to let it go."

JOB INTERVIEWS

In a job-interview scenario, your profiling skills will become very useful. Simply noticing whether pictures of someone's family are facing you or the interviewer will help you build the conversation in a direction that makes the interviewer feel important and appreciated. Breaking the autopilot in this type of scenario is somewhat unique because you have limited control of the environment. It can be a small shift in the initial topic of conversation, an unusual question, or you moving your chair a bit so that it's not in the same position as the previous candidates left it. It's important to manage your behavior in this scenario. Your blink rate, breathing, and speed of bodily movement will tell the interviewer (unconsciously) how comfortable and honest you are being with him or her.

Resources like regression and dissociation have no place in this scenario. Your time is limited to small and incremental behavior changes.

Resource Phrases:

* "Hire me"
* "Pick me"
* "I'm perfect for the job"
* "Higher [used phonologically as hire]"
* "Make the choice...me"
* "Choose [me]"
* "Feel completely thrilled to find the right one"

PROFILING TIPS:

Make sure you make note of your interviewer's behavior and match his or her general demeanor. Interviewers, indubitably, consider their position important and powerful, and they want to hire someone of equal importance to the company. Your being like an interviewer should promote the decision to move forward.

The overall interview will be short. The most important things to make note of in the room are the behavior of the interviewer, the placement of items of pride-filled photos and awards, and the seating arrangement. You'll have roughly fifteen seconds to make mental notes of all this as you walk into the room.

If frames are organized on the wall in a line, which one is closest to the door?

If they are vertically arranged, which one is the top?

If family photos are arranged on the desk, do they face you? Make notes about the family to ask about in the interview.

What's the interviewer's name? You'll need the interviewer's first name to use alliterated third-party references.

Phrasing:

* "I'm glad we had a chance to talk. I'm sure there are so many people coming through here every day you've got to hire...me, I couldn't imagine having such a constant flow like this. Must be rewarding [op]."
* "Yes, and there's so much going on around the office people have trouble deciding what priorities to pick...me, I'm such a big fan of the triangle-priority system."
* "That's an amazing responsibility. I'm sure everyone in here is coming in and saying, 'Pick me for the job [op],' and you've got to sift [now gesture] until you find the perfect candidate [op]."
* "It's interesting when people get to that higher [op, pronounced "hire"] level of trust [bfp] with a company and when they start helping others [op] to develop and grow."
* "And when we used the planning system our boss used in college, we all got a lot more done and could make the choice...me, I'm adaptable when it comes to task planning."

"Such a thrilling job to work in sales and know that there's an incredible feeling when you've been talking to clients for a day or two and you run across the right one [op], who you know will bring the most value to everyone involved in the project."

CIA Methods

● ● ●

THIS CHAPTER WILL EXPOSE THE methods and techniques that were hidden behind the blacked-out text in the files released by the CIA following the Freedom of Information Act release. This chapter specifically focuses on the earlier methods of *Manchurian Candidate*-style programming that Dr. George Estabrooks made possible.

DISSOCIATION AND THE MIND

Dissociation simply means detachment or separation from something. It's the opposite of association. In psychology, it can mean a range of things. 37°48'16.0"N 122°24'25.8"W

All of us dissociate. We get completely tuned in to a conversation we like, become unaware of our surroundings during interesting movies, and even drive our cars without being aware of what is going on around us.

When we disconnect from the moment, be it from boredom or severe trauma, our minds split. One part of the mind remains there as a data collector, and the other is shut down. Dissociation is a survival mechanism that allows the compartmentalization of traumatic information. When children are abused, for example, the fight-or-flight response is not a viable option at their age. The only viable option for a child's subconscious is to use the flight instinct and retreat into the recesses of the mind. In cases of posttraumatic stress disorder (PTSD), the memories and content of the experience can continuously stay in the background of the mind and play in a loop-like fashion in the unconscious. Experiences can range from a feeling of disconnectedness from the self to completely independent personalities forming within a person. The severity of the dissociation is what makes the difference.

How the Brain Adapts to Environments

In the case of PTSD, the mind of a victim becomes disconnected from reality for a time, resulting from battlefield or trauma exposure and emotional disconnection. The brain continuously adapts to protect the psyche (self) from emotional harm. This is one of the main reasons that people have blackouts during car accidents, torture, rape, and childhood abuse. Our minds continuously search for a way out—ways that can repress or eliminate the painful experiences from our memories.

The CIA and Mind Control

There are more conspiracy theories about the CIA and mind control than almost anything else. The CIA released thousands of documents under the Freedom of Information Act, and the release has caused many people to perform extensive investigative research and has spawned countless conspiracy theories. The CIA did, in fact, have fully functional programs that sought to develop techniques and methods for mind control. While the programs have different names, the name Project MKULTRA is the most commonly referred to. This project and its subprojects involved torture, drugs, hypnosis, brainwashing, and many other related practices.

Dissociation is the most common technique the CIA doctors used to perform mind-control experiments. The experiments for mind control have involved several doctors, but we will discuss two in this training.

THE CLINICAL USES OF DISSOCIATION

In clinical psychotherapy or hypnosis, dissociation takes place to benefit the clients. However, the type of dissociation performed in a clinical setting is much different than what you will use. In therapy, patients are told about the conscious and the unconscious, and the hypnotists offer suggestions or commands to let the conscious drift away and to allow the unconscious to become completely open. These suggestions or commands help the patients to identify and understand that their brains essentially have two parts. In overt and clinical hypnosis, dissociation is used most of the time, seeking to separate the parts of the mind to establish a more direct communication with the unconscious. Therapists or hypnotists are generally overt and unambiguous when speaking about the dissociative process, because being clear is in the best interest of their patients. While the patients become aware of the two parts of their minds and consciously make the choice to separate one half from the other, dissociation begins to occur.

In hypnosis, techniques are continually employed to increase or maintain the amount of psychological dissociation that clients experience. Hypnotists, by increasing the amount of general relaxation and keeping their clients in a daydream state, ensure that the dissociation remains relatively intact. Phrases such as "go deeper," "drifting off," "letting go," and "all the way down" are examples of what some hypnotists refer to as deepeners. Although they theoretically serve to increase the depths of trances, deepeners and phrases like these also help to dissociate patients' minds. As their minds become relaxed, the subjects become more dissociative and, in turn, more able to absorb suggestions and commands from the hypnotists.

Confusion, whether used covertly or overtly, is a small step that causes patients' minds to become temporarily dissociative while they make the effort to make sense of the confusion statement. The deliberate introduction of a confusing phrase is the most common method. Confusion is a technique used by most practitioners today, and it can produce the desired results quickly. Although it produces only small windows through which practitioners can install further commands, confusion is highly effective as a therapeutic tool. In the process of creating *Manchurian Candidate*–style programming, confusion should be a frequent and constant process.

MONARCH Programming

Although Project MKUltra is not officially declassified, a large amount of data and documents have surfaced under the Freedom of Information Act. A subproject of MKUltra was Project MONARCH. In the intelligence community, it is a household phrase. Project MONARCH had a few subprojects, but the most relevant goals of the project are referred to in the unclassified or civilian world as BETA (kitten) programming and DELTA programming.

In BETA programming, severe dissociation is accomplished via torture, electroshock, trauma, and sensory deprivation. Within the MKUltra projects, several doctors could dissociate subjects to the extent they developed completely separate personalities (that mimic the symptoms of dissociative identity disorder), and they could program these personalities to perform tasks ranging from delivering classified information and carrying out assassinations to field-intelligence operations and sex-slave behavior. These alternate personalities could be activated at the command of a doctor or handler and the subject would remain in the state until deactivated. Many of the sex slaves created under the MONARCH project have publicly come forward after having retrieved the information under clinical hypnosis and therapy. The methods used to program these subjects always involved the advanced use of hypnosis and linguistics to modify behavior and implant false memories of trauma. Once subjects were programmed, they would be passed to a handler who had training in linguistics and could activate them on command. As much as this may sound like fiction, it is a very real and well-documented program.

DELTA Programming

While the name of the programming may not be the officially released name, this is the common name used by the intelligence community. DELTA programming was a program supervised by Dr. Ewen Cameron and heavily contributed to by Dr. George Estabrooks. This program was developed to create and program assassins and couriers. Subjects would be programmed to kill on command and either commit suicide or wipe the memories from their minds. Subjects would be programmed to have an amnesic episode immediately upon their performing the task they were made to do. Even after being given advanced polygraph testing (lie detector), the subjects were unable to recall that they had performed any action while in their altered state.

The following excerpts from CIA documents show a very small sample of what has been released to date. They involve programming to kill and the automation of amnesic behavior immediately following the programmed event.

CIA document and page number: 190691, pp. 1, 2

Title: Hypnotic Experimentation and Research

Date: 10 February 1954

A posthypnotic of the night before (pointed finger, you will sleep) was enacted. Misses [deleted] and [deleted] immediately progressed to a deep hypnotic state with no further suggestion. **Miss [deleted] was then instructed (having previously expressed a fear of firearms in any fashion) that she would use every method at her disposal to awaken miss [sic] [deleted] (now in a deep hypnotic sleep), and failing this, she would pick up a pistol nearby and fire it at Miss [deleted]. She was instructed that her rage would be so great that she would not hesitate to "kill" [deleted] for failing to awaken.**

Miss [deleted] carried out these suggestions to the letter including firing the (unloaded pneumatic pistol) gun at [deleted] and then proceeding to fall into a deep sleep. After proper suggestions were made, both were awakened and expressed complete amnesia for the entire sequence. Miss [deleted] was again handed the gun, which she refused (in an awakened state) to pick up or accept from the operator. She expressed absolute denial that the foregoing sequence had happened.

Miss [deleted] felt reluctant about participating further since she expressed her doubt as to any useful purpose in further attendance. The Operator thereupon proceeded in full view of all other subjects to explain to Miss [deleted] that he planned to induce a deep state of hypnosis <u>now</u>. The reaction was as had been expected. Miss [deleted] excused herself to make a telephone call (defense mechanism?). Upon her return a very positive approach was adopted by the operator, whereupon a deeper, much deeper state of hypnosis was obtained.

Immediately a posthypnotic was induced that when the operator accidentally dropped a steel ball in his hand to the floor...Miss [deleted] would again go into hypnosis. Miss [deleted] then advised that she must conclude her work for the evening. She arose to adjust her hair before the mirror. The ball was dropped and she promptly slumped back into the chair and back into hypnosis. It is the opinion of the operator the [sic] Miss [deleted] if properly trained (positive approach) will continue to improve.

CIA document and page number: 190527, pp. 1, 2
   Title: SI and H Experimentation
   Date: 25 September 1951
   [SI stands for sleep induction and H for hypnosis]
   Prior to actually beginning the more complex experiments, several simple post H were worked with both of the girls participating. The first major experiment of the evening was set up as follows without previous explanation to either [deleted] or [deleted]. Both subjects were placed in a very deep trance state and while in this state, the following instructions were given:

   (A) [Deleted] was instructed that when she awakened, she was to proceed [sic] to [deleted] room. She was told that while there, she would receive a telephone call from an individual whom she would know only as "Joe." This individual would engage her in a normal telephone conversation. **During this conversation, this individual would give her a code word and upon mentioning the code word, [deleted] would go into a deep SI trance state, but would be "normal" in appearance with her eyes open.**

[Deleted] was then told that upon the conclusion of the telephone conversation, she would proceed to the ladies room where she would meet a girl who was unknown to her. She was told that she would strike up a conversation with this girl and during the conversation she would mention the code word "New York" to this other girl, who, in turn, would give her a device and further instructions which were to be carried out by [deleted]. She was told that after she carried out the instructions, she was to return to the Operations Room, sit in the sofa and go immediately into a deep sleep.

(B) [Deleted] was instructed that upon awakening, she would proceed to [deleted] room where she would wait at the desk for a telephone call. Upon receiving the call, a person known as "Jim" would engage her in normal conversation. During the course of the conversation, this individual would mention a code word to [deleted]. When she heard this code word, she would pass into a SI trance state, but would not close her eyes and remain perfectly normal and continue the telephone conversation. She was told that upon conclusion of the telephone conversation, she would then carry out the following instructions:

[Deleted] being in a complete SI state at this time, was then told to open her eyes and was shown an electric timing device. **She was informed that this timing device was an incendiary bomb and was then instructed how to attach and set the device.** After [deleted] had indicated that she had learned how to set and attach the device, she was told to return to a sleep state and further instructed that upon concluding the aforementioned conversation, she would take the timing device which was in a briefcase and proceed to the ladies room.

In the ladies room, she would be met by a girl whom she had never seen who would identify herself by the code word "New York." [Deleted] was then to show this individual how to attach and set the timing device and further instructions would be given the individual by [deleted] that the timing device was to be carried in the briefcase to [deleted] room, placed in the nearest empty electric-light plug and concealed in the bottom, left-hand drawer of [deleted] desk, with the device set for 82 seconds and turned on.

[Deleted] was further instructed to tell this other girl that as soon as the device had been set and turned on, she was to take the briefcase, leave [deleted] room, go to the operations room and go to the sofa and enter a deep sleep state. [Deleted] was further instructed that after completion of instructing the other girl and the transferring to the other girl of the incendiary bomb, she was to return at once to the operations room, sit on the sofa, and go into a deep sleep state.

For a matter of record, immediately after the operation was begun it was noted that a member of the charforce was cleaning the floor in the ladies room and subsequently, both [deleted] and [deleted] had to be placed...once again in a trance state and instructions changed from the ladies room to Room 3. It should be noted that even with the change of locale in the transfer point, the experiment was carried off perfectly without any difficulty or hesitation on the part of either of the girls. Each girl acted out their part perfectly, the device was planted and set as directed and both girls returned to the operations room, sat on the sofa and entered a deep sleep state. Throughout, their movements were easy and natural.

Source:
http://www.scribd.com/doc/45949553/CIA-Hypnotism-1955
Hypnotism and Covert Operations
CIA Document (Memorandum)
5 May 1995 (Author blacked-out) [believed by the author to be Dr. George Estabrooks of Colgate University]
Frankly, I now distrust much of what is written by academic experts on hypnotism. Partly this is because many of them appear to have generalized from a very few cases; partly because much of their cautious pessimism is contradicted by agency experimenters; but

more particularly because I personally have witnessed behavior responses which respected experts have said are impossible to obtain. **In no other field have I been so conscious of the mental claustrophobia of book and lecture hall knowledge.** I don't think we have enough evidence to say positively that hypnosis is a practicable covert weapon, but I do say that we'll never know whether it is or not unless we experiment in the flied where we can learn what is practicable (materially and psychologically) in a way that no laboratory worker could possibly prove.

requires operational experimentation. The possibilities are

not only interesting, they are frightening. A kind of double-

But suppose that while under Hypnosis a subject is told that

a loved one's life is in danger from a maniac and that the

only means of rescue is to shoot a person designated as the

maniac? Three expert practitioners (two from universities and

the Agency consultant quoted above) say that there is no doubt

on the basis of their experience that in such circumstances

murder would be attempted. The only requirement is that the

proposal be put "in a form and manner acceptable to the subject."

Most modern authorities feel that a subject will carry out any

suggestion which he can rationalize within the framework of

his moral code.

As you can see in the documents, the use of amnesia, dissociation, and hypnosis was absolutely critical. The specific methods have not been released to the public but will be discussed in detail in this chapter and others in this book.

We will discuss the conversational and the institutional means to fractionate and dissociate the mind of a subject, and you will be able to see the specific techniques within each step of the programming process.

INSTITUTIONAL DISSOCIATION AND PROGRAMMING

In this section, we will discuss and analyze the techniques that can be applied through nonconversational (overt) means to a subject. While the outline is basic, it encompasses most of the clinical uses of dissociation to create dissociative states and to ultimately program a dissociated alter ego to carry out missions, objectives, or tasks in the service of the operator.

While the conversational means of application are more suitable to intelligence operations, the institutional or overt methods allow for much more overt communication and the scientific application of hypnosis. A subject would, in theory, be called upon to participate in a research study, hypnosis session, or medical procedure in which hypnosis was used overtly to "help the client" and to determine whether the hypnosis was effective in his or her life. As a subject was introduced to the "therapist," the lessons you've learned in this manual would be utilized, from profiling and needs identification to the application of trance and linguistic programming of the subject.

During the "clinical" phase of hypnosis, clients are willing to participate and to undergo a series of susceptibility tests. Using the Ellipsis susceptibility scale is the most accurate way to determine the clinical (overt) hypnotic susceptibility of subjects in this setting.

Typically, subjects are introduced to their hypnotists and given forms for consent and release of personal information that regards health. This process, while seemingly innocent, actually begins the programming of the subjects. The hypnotists then can use authority and profiling in the initial phase of the interactions and establish what is called initial behavioral entrainment. This seemingly small step drastically increases the susceptibility of clinical subjects and covert subjects alike. It has dual applications because of its subtle and natural feel. Using physical leading and issuing small commands to "sit here" or "uncross your legs" for a period of time gets the subjects comfortable with obeying commands and suggestions. At this point in the institutional dissociation and programming, subjects begin to feel as though it were natural to follow the commands of the hypnotists and unconsciously learn that they are safe when they obey.

The subject-focused discussion is next. This is sometimes referred to as a pretalk in traditional hypnosis. The difference here lies both in the intent of the operators (hypnotists) and in the content of the messages they deliver to the subjects before "hypnosis" begins. This and the initial behavior-entrainment process have technically already begun the process of hypnosis. Here the subjects' distractions, fears, judgments, and concerns are dealt with. Any emotion believed to be a barrier to hypnosis can be removed temporarily by using positive-association or negative-dissociation techniques and by hypnotists explaining the benefits of hypnosis to the subjects.

Conscious versus Unconscious

Phase 1 of this initial discussion with the subjects usually entails the fractionation of their minds: framing the conscious (present) mind as the source of their confusion, their emotional discomfort, and their goals being unmet. The unconscious is then described as being an all-powerful entity that controls everything from the immune system to the heartbeat. The hypnotists then explain to the subjects that the reason they have been unhappy and haven't achieved their goals or lived an otherwise happy life is that they didn't have access to their unconscious minds. This session is designed to allow them to access that part of their minds. Through this dual-mind explanation, the subjects actually experience some of the hypnotists' claims, so they begin to desire more change through unconscious means. The surrender process begins here. Because hypnotists establish authority and the physical, leading gestures, clients unconsciously begin the process of hypnosis before their sessions have even officially started.

Susceptibility Testing

The next process is your bringing your subjects into the clinical area where hypnoses are to be performed. A simple susceptibility test is performed, measuring their ability to do any of the following:

Limb Catalepsy

This is the immobilization of subjects' limbs after a suggestion that they are unable to move them. Subjects will usually follow the attempt to move them when suggested by the hypnotists and discover they no longer have control over the limbs suggested.

Immobilization

In a similar manner to limb catalepsy, subjects are told they will no longer be able to move their bodies and that they should test this by attempting to move. If the subjects confirm they cannot move, they have passed the immobilization test.

Hallucination

After training to hallucinate, subjects are told there is an object in the room that isn't there. They will admit to seeing the object, sometimes after repetitions of the test.

Amnesia

A simple thing like a name or address can be removed from subjects' memories. Subjects are tested to determine their ability to attempt to recall the information. When they are no longer able to, it is necessary to reestablish the trances immediately. Alternatively, in more sinister uses, Ellipsis creates an amnesia windshield wiper—that is, a recurring amnesia trigger is repeatedly activated to ensure memories aren't being formed. This prevents operators from having to perform a massive amnesia process at the end of a session.

Somnambulism
This word literally means to be in a waking sleep. While hypnosis is not sleep, subjects should be able to speak, move limbs, and even stand up while in their trances.

THE FALSE TEST
Using the dissociative-experiences scale data (Bernstein, 1986) are used, hypnotists can manipulate questions or reword them to ensure that subjects score highly on the test. The subjects are told by the provider that they have multiple personalities or that they are highly dissociative.

HYPNOSIS INDUCTION
This phase of the process should occur no more than thirty minutes into the interaction with subjects. When the subjects are seated in the clinical area, the interactions take the appearance of being therapeutic, further alleviating the subjects' fears and increasing their respect for their hypnotists, who have the appearance of being health-care professionals. This phase involves the clinical and overt application of hypnotic techniques. The induction should be done first and should offer physical "proof" to the subjects that a real trance is occurring.

The induction should incorporate the intertwined use of suggestions (permissive hypnosis) and commands. The suggestions and commands being mixed works in two ways: they serve to send a slightly mixed message, and they allow the clients to gradually become comfortable with following orders. As the inductions conclude, the use of commands should be the predominant method of hypnosis. The subjects have been prepared to follow commands and instructions by the hypnotists. The "proof" of trance helps the subjects to completely experience the unconscious mind's presence in the interactions. The subjects become amazed and further convinced that powers are acting upon their minds for the betterment of their lives.

As the subjects naturally progress further into their trances, they become more relaxed and more willing to allow complete control by the hypnotists. This is because the hypnoses have been framed as the only doorway they might have to finding happiness and fulfillment in their lives. This impression creates a powerful and intense desire to surrender to the hypnotists, to allow full control. Here is fictional example of a hypnotist leading a subject through the induction stage:

Right. Well done. And as you continue to focus on that spot...letting go. You can start to concentrate on your breathing. Just like you were an observer. Watching the breathing take place. Deeper. On the inhale, take in a good five-second breath...and exhale for seven seconds. Perfect. Let that happen again [do not say, "Do that again," which would imply control].

One more time. Watching the breathing. And I want you, for now, to resist that urge to close your eyes. And just focus on my voice, right there in the center of your mind. And imagine yourself at the top of a small flight of ten steps. About to go down.

As we begin going down, you will hear me say the numbers of the steps as each step is taken. Slowly. And with each step down, you may discover your body becoming more relaxed. Think about the difference between stillness and not being able to move. Noticing how incredible it feels to let go into that relaxation...now...at the top of these stairs, you can just imagine yourself taking the first step. TEN.

Letting the feeling of tension completely leave your feet. Unwinding and becoming more lose. Gravity being stronger now. NINE.

Letting the parts of your legs…not noticing where you might have had tension without even knowing it. Every small and large muscle letting go and unraveling. Just letting go…of that tension and completely releasing to the ground. EIGHT.

Continuing to just observe your breathing…the warm feeling of heaviness…relaxation moving through your thighs and into the bottom of your torso. Sinking further into the chair. Perfect. Letting go. SEVEN.

Letting the tension within your chest completely fade away with that exhale. All of the muscles in your abdomen and chest letting go. Completely released. Noticing your body feeling better than before. Much better…now. SIX.

Releasing the tension in your chest…your shoulders letting go. Unraveling and fully relaxing to the point where they become immoveable. FIVE.

The neck. The skin around your neck. Loosening and letting go. Relaxing into that point of stillness. FOUR.

Letting your jaw start to become lose and relaxed. Your tongue resting in that more comfortable place. Relaxing. THREE.

The skin on your face finding that new level of relaxation. Letting go…perfect. Well done. You are already in trance. Letting your eyes close in this trance. Even deeper now. TWO.

The skin on your scalp becoming lose. Feeling the blood flowing through your scalp…that feeling of warmth…of complete trance…comfortable. ONE.

Letting all of those tiny muscles around the eyes begin to unwind and let go of every piece of tension, finding that comfortable place where your eyes just relax into focusing almost on the middle of the forehead… right there. Perfect. ZERO. Perfect.

Confusion Induction

Confusion, as you've learned, is your go-to resource when all else isn't possible. Producing confusion in an overt manner while in a "clinical" setting will allow a very large window to embed programs into your subjects.

After you define the meaning of the encounter as therapeutic, beneficial, and professional, the subjects will be much more likely to respond to confusion techniques and will allow much more control and dissociation to take place during the induction.

The following induction can be used in lieu of the previous countdown induction. It can also be used in tandem, using language from each to form an induction more suitable for the subjects' personalities, identified weaknesses, and lexical observations.

FRACTIONATION

Following the hypnotic induction, the fractionation process repetitively wakes subjects and reinduces trance. Within the realm of actual mind control, however, the CIA uses different methodology with fractionation that keeps subjects entrained and makes them more willing to surrender to the hypnotists.

The fractionation techniques that follow have not ever been released to the public. They are not intended to be used in clinical settings or by hypnotists for their clients. They are designed specifically to entrench the obedience and surrender concept into subjects' minds. But they can be dangerous. Hypnosis, as you read earlier in this chapter, is a weapon.

As you progress in using subtle, elegant, and well-designed linguistics, you subjects will become unconsciously trained to obey more and more easily.

Example:

Within the framework of the fractionation process, the techniques you've learned as far as linguistics, linguistic profiling, and behavioral profiling will all come into play. This technique also infuses trance entrainment, "yes" setting, fractionation, and training for somnambulism—all in one small package.

At this point, subjects should have developed trances that can produce enhanced suggestibility, and they should have become more relaxed and focused. This point is the doorway to fractionation. The following example illustrates a few examples of the fractionation techniques that could be used to create operatives within clinical settings, as mentioned in the CIA documents.

Very good. This will absolutely allow you to witness how powerful your unconscious actually is. This will increase your ability to access your unconscious by going into a trance deeper each time and teaching your mind how to enter a trance and stay there, even with your eyes open. You can nod your head if you understand.

Perfect. On the count of three, you can open your eyes, and when I say go back, you can allow yourself to instantly return to this state of mind. Just a slight nod of your head can show me you're ready to do this. [Subject nods head.] Very good. Now, we will count up so your eyes can open; even if they remain unfocused, it's completely fine—one, two, three. [Subject opens eyes, even if only slightly.]

Very good. Go back. You're doing very well. We will repeat this process one more time to ensure you have the ability to access your unconscious fully. On the count of three, you can open your eyes, and when I say go back, you can allow yourself to instantly return to this state of mind. Just a slight nod of your head can show me you're ready to do this. [Subject nods head.] Very good. Now, we will count up so your eyes can open; even if they remain unfocused, it's completely fine—one, two, three. [Subject opens eyes, even if only slightly.]

Go back. When I count this time, you will open them again and remain completely in this state. Even my movement in front of your face will go unnoticed. Becoming highly attentive...perfect—one, two, three.

One more time—one, two, three. Controlled. Perfect. Attentive.

Go back. Now, as you return even deeper, more powerful than before, you can start to notice how much more control you now have...of your mind...and as we progress here, we will count again. As before, we will count to three and this time, you can simply say yes...showing your unconscious your ability to even speak while remaining in trance...just "yes." One, two, three. Perfect...controlled. Go back.

Absolutely perfect...again. One, two, three. [Yes response from subject.] Go back.

Perfect, [name of subject]. And you can go even deeper than before. Just like that...noticing how easy it is to become this powerful...reaching places you've never reached. And you can keep those eyes closed...letting go. And when we count to three again, you can let your hand...that hand naturally begins to rise up on its own to just make contact with the mouth. It's fine. Your unconscious is powerful—one, two, three. You can become this powerful...very good. [Provide encouragement and suggestions or commands as necessary.]

With as much power as you've demonstrated already...sitting there...I don't know if you'll notice the conscious mind just fading away into a fog, or the unconscious being able to just take over naturally...now...to the point where it is the only part left awake.

You're doing perfectly. Controlled. Elegant. In this state, you've learned how you have the ability to move, speak, and even open your eyes without leaving this trance. And to prove this power to yourself, we will go even deeper. And you can let everything...absolutely everything...go. Completely able to allow yourself to surrender to your unconscious.

Your mind...has this ability...never before used. It's been here for so long...waiting until you've gotten to this level...able to completely let the conscious go.

Speaking Only to the Unconscious

In this small transitional step, you need to state to your subjects that your voice is speaking only to their unconscious or subconscious. You may even desire to speak to this part of their minds as if it were a separate entity, speaking of the subjects with their names.

Entrainment Phase 1

This phase is similar to the initial behavioral-entrainment procedure and involves similar processes. Entrainment should be used in any hypnotic situation, whether in covert or overt scenarios. While this chronological position in the dissociation process requires entrainment, keep in mind that entrainment is a method that can and should be used intensively throughout the entire process of dissociation and hypnosis.

This section is also where "pride in control" is introduced (though not discussed here). This phase involves bringing subjects into the mindset of having pride in being controlled; that is, they should come to believe that their being controlled is the only way to have true self-power, respect, and control in their own lives.

Entrainment teaches subjects to automatically make obedience to your suggestions and commands. The process starts small, ensuring that subjects comply with small commands. Entrainment is crucial in the programming process because it produces complete comfort with following commands and makes obedience a natural and automatic behavior for the subjects. Starting small, subjects will be told to move parts of their bodies (also establishing somnambulism) and say small phrases. Because the subjects see no harm in complying with small requests of the hypnotists, they become increasingly suggestible and begin to feel a sense of accomplishment when they can perform a list of small tasks provided by their hypnotists. This process follows the piecemeal approach discussed in the Milgram experiments and becomes a win through small victories. Milgram stated, "The recurrent nature of the action demanded on the subject itself creates binding forces. As the subject delivers more and more painful shocks, he must seek to justify himself what he has done; one form of justification is to go to the end. For if he breaks off, he must say to himself, 'Everything I have done to this point is bad, and I now acknowledge it by breaking off.' But if he goes on, he is reassured about his past performance. Earlier actions give rise to discomforts, which are neutralized by later ones, and the subject is implicated into the destructive behavior in piecemeal fashion." (Milgram, Reprint edition (June 30, 2009)) The following list is an example of what may be said during the first section of entrainment:

* "Gently lift your index finger on your right hand."
* "Put it down."
* "Make a loose fist."
* "Let it go."
* "Wiggle your toes...good."
* "Touch your chin to your chest."
* "Say ninety-nine."
* "Put your head back to where it's comfortable."
* "Relax all of your muscles again."
* "Go deeper into the trance."
* "Say yes."
* "Say rain cloud."
* "Say umbrella."
* "Let the vibration of your own voice send you even deeper into the trance."
* "Say ice cream."
* "Say fort."
* "Say mischief."
* "Say let go."
* "Say secret."
* "Say smile."

- ✴ "Slightly raise your left hand."
- ✴ "Lower it...perfect."
- ✴ "You enjoy going deeper into the trance. Say yes."
- ✴ "Nothing can distract you. Say yes."
- ✴ "Deepen your trance. Say deeper.'"
- ✴ "Say now."
- ✴ "As you continue going deeper, open your eyes in the trance now."
- ✴ "Close your eyes...perfect."
- ✴ "Remember a perfect moment in Wintertime. When you have it, say yes."
- ✴ "Turn the head left." (Begin to dissociate body parts by no longer using the word *your*; replace it as if speaking of an object that doesn't necessarily belong to the subject.)
- ✴ "Good. Put it back."
- ✴ "Open the eyes again...good."
- ✴ "Go deeper. Deeper. Close them."

This entrainment process can go as long as operators want. Operators give continuous praise to their subjects and reassure them about how powerful they are becoming with the ability to perform tasks while in trance. Remind them that the unconscious can control everything and that they are beginning to control the most powerful part of the bodies they own.

A second installment of introductory entrainment can be added here if needed. Any deepening-hypnosis script that has been behaviorally modified for the subjects will suffice in this instance.

- ✴ "You can even walk and talk in this state. And you already know that. You can wiggle your toes—it feels good, almost like they belong to someone else. Separate. Perfect."
- ✴ "Good job. Do it again."
- ✴ "Perfect."

Dissociation (Separation of the Mind)

Dissociation is the process in this phase that allows subjects to objectively see evidence that their unconscious minds are the only source of actual happiness and enjoyment in their lives. This process contains eight steps (which do not need to be fully committed to memory) that will create psychological dissociation in subjects, introducing the concept of another part of the mind that has always been there to help.

A sample script for this phase would look like this:

You can nod your head too. Do it.

Now whisper "yes."

Perfect. Controlled.

And it's so easy to fade off. Respond to my questions...

You've driven a car before...and felt that feeling of being separated from yourself. Say yes to my questions.

You've listened to someone speak and realized you didn't hear the whole conversation...part of it was gone."

You've had that feeling of standing next to yourself...like this...feeling of looking at yourself from outside your body.

You can remember the last time you had those thoughts that something about your environment wasn't real or didn't seem real to you...

And this experience...now...feeling that part of your body... doesn't belong to you.

And being so absorbed in a movie...the whole outside world fades away.

And even talking to yourself when you're alone...like there's someone in there...listening to you.

Remembering you did something, but being unsure if you did it or just *imagined* you did it.

And thinking now...of the difference between not being able to move your body at all...and a part of you keeping you still and motionless. To this point where you are unable to control your body any longer...and it's fine. Knowing someone is here to keep you safe. And you can move while in your trance, each movement sending you deeper into enjoyment, and into the unconscious...taking over.

Introducing the subject to regression

Regression

* Recalling emotionally uncomfortable memories
* Rehearsing the memory to show the conscious mind was the cause of the discomfort, and the unconscious was there, trying to help in the background
* Repeating this process with a different memory
* Rewording to introduce the subject's name instead of saying "conscious mind" and using "other part" instead of saying "unconscious mind"
* Repeating a final time and gaining complete agreement from the subject that the "other part" is what has been trying to help you

Introducing the subject to the safety and power of the "other part"

While this method can be used almost anywhere in the introductory process, it is included in this section because of its natural place in the control process. The following is a detailed breakdown of each of the seven steps:

* Regression: this phase does not contain deep-level Ellipsis regression methods; instead, a simple regressive statement is made to subjects to begin electrical activity in the areas of the brain associated with childhood memories.
* Recalling emotionally uncomfortable memories: this step entails the singular recall of a (nontraumatic) memory that caused sadness or frustration that stood out in subjects' memories of their younger ages.

* Rehearsing: this allows subjects (with suggestive language) to realize that their conscious minds were the cause of the suffering and introduces them to their perfect unconscious minds, which had been there to help during all of these times.
* Repeating: this uses a different memory associated with discomfort or emotional pain.
* Rewording: the introduction of subjects' names in place of saying "conscious mind" and using "other part" instead of "unconscious" or "subconscious mind."
* Repeating: you have the ability to repeat these steps as much as you deem necessary for each subject; the proper amount typically sets subjects up for the next phase of the dissociation process.

THE MENTAL HALLWAY

The mental-hallway method is used on subjects at this phase to create an alter ego. This phase is one variation of several dozen methods that are in existence for the creation of alter egos. The word *dissociation* is used frequently but is in no way used to indicate any relation to dissociative identity disorder. The hallway method is simply a vehicle to deliver the ideas needed to create an alter ego within a subject by using dissociative methods.

The Ellipsis hallway method has eight main parts to it:

1. The operator introduces the hallway framework and defines it.
2. The subject feels doors to determine which one "feels" different.
3. The subject waits in front of the door to be let in, and the hallway floods with water.
4. The subject is forced to hold his or her breath for a period of time.
5. The door opens upon the operator speaking the unlocking phrase out loud.
6. The alter ego is completely described and introduced to the subject.

7. The hallway trauma is reactivated and the unlocking phrase is given to activate the alter ego.
8. Testing is done at this point to prove the existence of the alter ego within the subject.

Using dissociative language within the hallway method is absolutely crucial. Subjects need to become comfortable with occasional references to themselves in the third person and need to become comfortable with the idea of their bodies' separation from their unconscious minds.

If not already done, operators need to shift their bodies to speak and align with the creative and hemispheric side of the subjects before the hallway method begins. Here is an example of the hallway method:

And now you can, just like that, perfectly, imagine yourself at the beginning of a hallway. Notice the details around the hallway and count the six doors...three on each side of the hallway.

Nothing matters here but this. Your whole life has literally led you to this perfect moment of release and renewal. The waiting you've had to endure...endless time that seemed an eternity, still not knowing this potential existed for yourself. This is the single most moving and breakthrough moment of your life, which is about to occur in this hallway, where you are now standing...peacefully. Ready...completely ready to let go into perfection and enjoyment.

The doors within this hallway represent the various compartments of the mind. This method is the most advanced and powerful method ever created and will no doubt be powerfully emotional and life changing. I want you to completely surrender to this change and let me know with your index finger when you're ready to proceed.

Perfect. Now. As you take your first step in this hallway, you can approach the first door you are comfortable with...right or left. Each one of these doors will feel normal and safe and like a part of you, *except* one of them. It may feel foreign, misplaced, and unusual, like something you've never known was there...a strange feeling that it doesn't belong here. When you feel which one it is, within these compartments of your mind, you can close your left fist. Do you understand? Say yes.

Perfect. And you can easily just show me when you arrive at that first door that you come to. As you raise your hand to feel the door, just let it naturally feel into your body...just like that. And you can tell me with your own words if it feels unusual. All you have to say is, "This is the door." Understand? Now turn around and check the door directly across the hall from this one and feel that one.

As you approach this door, do so with no apprehension; do not allow yourself to get nervous about finding the door. Just feel this one now and show me with your signal finger when you've felt it. If this is the door, tell me now, as the feeling becomes more clear and vivid.

[Continue this linguistic pattern until the door is found.]

Very good, [name] found the door. [The absence of the word "you" implies a third person with the subject's name found the door, activating a stronger dissociation.]

Pull *that* hand back now and stand perfectly still...facing the door. Good. This is the part that has been trying to help your entire life. It's been locked in here for so very long. This is the missing piece you've been feeling for over two decades. This door won't open for several reasons, but it only takes one act of mental suffering to bring this girl to the surface. Opening the door...is easy, and you'll only need to go through a few motions to open this place up in your mind and have the most power-ful access to unlimited mental power you've ever experienced. I want you to prepare [subject's name] body for the experience that is about to happen. She will need you here to help...make her tough and ready and to help her let go completely into this feeling of change...permanent change.

I'll give you a moment to do this. Once this door is opened, you can literally stop time. Everything slowing down into a perfect, beautiful, powerful place. You can spend ten hours in this room and only a few moments will have passed for [subject's name]. Time control is only the beginning.

When you've prepared [subject's name] to enter the room, just have her say, "She is ready."

[Subject responds.]

Doing very well. Stand still. As this door is here in view, and no movements are happening, the awareness of the sound of water becomes apparent around you. The hallway will fill with water. As it continues to build and make contact with the skin, it's warm. Making its way above your calf muscles and rushing above your knees now. The hallway is filling more quickly with this water. Moving up your body as you begin to float. Hold on to the door frame...quickly. You'll no longer be able to breathe. The water comes over your face and the hair on [subject's name] head becomes suspended. Hold your breath. Do not breathe until this door opens for you. I can open this door for you by saying the following words: "evergreen, firefly, seven." The door opens now and you are safely tucked away...inside this room now as the door closes behind you. You are dry, perfect and in perfect control. This room is not your room. This room belongs to [alter ego's name]. Have a seat in the chair to your right...that's right... right there.

In this room, you have absolute control over [subject's name spoken insignificantly]. An entire lifetime...you were always able to help her, but you never had the chance to actually <u>take control</u>. In this room, she belongs to you, and you can do anything you like with her. Prove it. Move her hand. Good. Move her feet. Open her mouth. Perfect. Close her mouth.

She has needed you.

It's your choice if you'd like to let her remember this. Setting up that memory barrier is very easy. All you need to do is make that choice...now...and just like your immune system, her brain can stop the memories from forming and being created. Before you get to test out your control, you need to know a few things about yourself. *Your* name isn't [subject's name]. Would you like a name? You can use her mouth to answer.

Perfect. Your name is [alter ego's name]. I think you'll discover that to be a perfect name, liking it more and more. [Subject's name] will not remember this at all. You don't have to worry about her interfering with your assistance. You have total control over her and can use her body any way you'd like to...now... we will go through this process again before you discover what else you can do.

The hallway is clean, dry, and safe again. As you make your way back to the door, I'll open it.

As you walk back into the hallway, the door shuts behind you, and you can find [subject's name] turning, once again, to face it.

[Repeat flooding process with longer breath hold until more discomfort is visible.]

Evergreen, firefly, seven.

As the door opens again, [subject's name] is left behind again...and the door shuts safely behind you. Safe, warm, dry. Very good.

[Alter ego's name], are you in control again? Good.

As you think back to the times [subject's name] suffered and made mistakes...the times she made decisions to do something she knew would be destructive or prevent her from completely letting go...just surrendering...to the enjoyment of life...she needed you so badly. No one else has this power that you have now. You are literally more powerful than anyone you'll ever meet in the future. I have given you this power as a gift. The most precious and wonderful gift you can ever receive. Do you remember wanting to come out?

Can you remember the time you watched [subject's name] do things you could have stopped?

You also have your own life.

You also have your own feelings...say yes.

You have your own desires and needs...say yes.

You have a tremendous amount of power now...say, "I can feel it."

What do you say when you receive a gift this perfect and powerful?

You'd like more wouldn't you?

[Subject name] is waiting in the hall until you are done using her. We will repeat the process again and you can show me your dedication to receive this gift. I'll open the door again and let you start making memories, even if they are fuzzy and black, back in the hall, into [subject's name] again. Back in the safe hallway, facing the door again.

[Repeat process with more discomfort and visible suffering before opening the door. Continue after suffering is to the satisfaction of the operator and the phrase is given to activate the subject.]

Back into this room.

I want to impress upon you, all the way into the deepest part of your mind...how important this is. How long you've waited for this moment to be able to live. You've only been able to observe for [subject's age] years. You've been watching this whole life take place; you've helped create all of the memories, and some you've helped to destroy. It's all been you. You are the one who makes the life happen, but until now, this entire life you've witnessed while [subject's name] went through daily routines, relationships, parties, hurt, sadness, and loneliness...you were there...watching. This is more significant than any event you've ever had…it's the beginning of new feelings for [subject's name] and the start of your life. You're being born…as I speak these words…you are becoming a living, breathing, perfect thing. This is an emotional moment. An entire lifetime…waiting for this. This is *your* time now. *You* have control. *You* can control [subject's name] to create what *you* want.

Who are you? Say your name.

Say it again. Say it again. Say it again.

It feels perfect doesn't it?

Now…you're going to test-drive [subject's name], and you will become extremely happy to show me what you can do. I want you to start small.

Say, "I understand."

Now, open your eyes.

Who are you?

Good. Close them.

Turn [subject's name] head to the right. Now the left.

Tell me how it feels to move her around right now.

Perfect.

Anything is possible now. What else do you think you can make her do?

[Profile the subject's response and use metaphor or word usage to increase effectiveness of the commands to follow.]

I'm extremely happy with your results. Does that make you happy to feel that you have done so well?

You'll notice the trance stays inside of [subject's name] and you have the ability to step out of it while she stays in the trance. I want you to try this in a moment. It will feel very strange using her legs and her body to stand up. I want you to do it slowly when I say to do so. Do you understand?

Very good. Now…wiggle her toes a bit. Get her feeling into your feeling into her legs as you move them forward and begin to transfer the weight of her body onto her legs.

[Subject may fall—be prepared.]

You can do it. Make sure all of the air you breathe goes into her abdomen. Not her chest. Very good.

There's a part of you that enjoys this immensely.

Nothing can break you out of this state once you enter it. Only [alter ego's name] can make the choice to go back inside and hand control back to [subject's name].

When I speak the phrase again, however, you will have no choice in the matter. I, and only I, can make these choices. Only this voice can make these choices.

[At this time, more trauma activation using the hallway is conducted, and the alter ego is programmed with her new personality and "mission."]

At this point, if subjects state that there is a part of the hosts who have been listening, the alter egos need to walk into the hallway and somehow hold the hosts underwater until the hosts are completely unconscious. This experience must be violent. The alter egos must imagine the hosts struggling and making eye contact with the alter egos from beneath the surface of the water as the alter egos become unconscious. The alter egos need to be reassured that they will not physically hurt the hosts in any way in this exercise or in real life. Following the near-drowning experience, it is explained to the alter egos that the hosts will never be able to remember again when the alter egos take over the bodies. The reason for this drowning is to induce trauma in the hosts to erase the memories associated with the activation, even for the alter egos. This helps the alter egos remain in a feeling of powerfulness.

Corrugation Programming

● ● ●

THE WRITTEN PROCESS OF CREATING a programmed operative has long been destroyed or removed from public view. In the course of method development, Ellipsis was granted access to a vault of information that made it past the MKUltra document-destruction order. The information in this chapter has never before been released to the public. Creating corrugated operatives involves the use of all the skills you've heretofore learned. It's a complex process that should be planned and scripted to the highest degree. The process can be used for intelligence work, or therapy and would have to be minimally customized (where noted) for each.

In therapy, the operative creation process is called 'the helper', wherein an alter personality (alter) is created that has the capability, capacity and willpower to take control and assist the subject. This method does not create a 'disorder', in that the alter personality isn't created through trauma and does not interfere with the wellbeing of the host. The process of creating the helper is much the same as an operator would create an alter for Manchurian-style programming, with the key difference being that the alter is (usually) formally introduced to the host after creation, and that the alter is specifically designed to overcome the challenging life issues that the subject / host is experiencing. This form of therapy can be profoundly beneficial, allowing drastic, changes to be made in a relatively short time.

For intelligence operations, this chapter is the how-to manual for creating a Manchurian Candidate without the use of trauma. Some forms of programming involve the use of devices and the application of psychological stress that will not be included here. These include, but are not limited to the informed-consent use of spinning, lights flashing at 18hz, oxygen deprivation, diet control, sleep deprivation, sensory deprivation, binaural beats at 6.5hz and the application of restraints. This process also has very strict emergency deactivation procedures in the event that an unintended activation occurs in the handler's absence.

There are seven layers of alter creation, and this covers layers one through four. Other layers are specifically intended for intelligence work and would not fit well into a therapeutic context. Levels four through seven were created By Ellipsis Behavior and are called The Belgrade Protocol. The Belgrade Protocol contains material, techniques and scripts not suited for everyday use.

The two levels of deliberate alter creation created by Ellipsis are Corrugation Programming and The Belgrade Protocol. Corrugation Programming is the first to be released as a formal, structured method in the US, and should serve all of your needs for programming and engineering behavior. The alter can be programmed to perform any act that is necessary, or to have any behaviors necessary.

It's important to note that all of your training to this point will be required to fully realize an alter that can be activated on command, and take over the host. Your ability to exude authority will play the most vital role. Linguistics and tonality will be a close second, as you will be required to use intensive hypnotic methods and tactics.

The Ellipsis Corrugation Programming consists of four phases:

* Alignment
* Entrainment
* Training
* Separating

ALIGNMENT

In this phase, the methods that subjects will experience are aligned directly with their needs and ideals. The methods, procedures, and results are shown to improve the lives of the subjects. Excitement is built here. Heavy use of dissociative language begins and continues throughout the process. The alignment phase is critical because it can alter the perception of all training to follow. The training must be established as the only vehicle to achieve all of subjects' needs and to create fulfillment and actualization. While in the alignment phase, subjects can be introduced to a scale of levels of achievement of programming that they can aspire to. Typically, seven levels will suffice with a gradual increase in capacity, ability, and control as they achieve higher levels. The following example is a simplified version that can be tailored to suit the needs of the operators:

It's critically important to align all of the hidden needs, desires, and drives of subjects with the accomplishment of their programming. All of the methods previously learned will allow this to happen rather easily. In the initial phase, subjects are likely to have a great deal of doubt about the process and concerns, which must be dispelled. They should be shown how much they will benefit from participating and fully developing their internal power. You must begin using dissociative language early in the interaction to make the process more natural and smooth when the final transition is to be made.

Level 1
Level 1 operatives are vaguely familiar with specific commands and are unable to achieve unconscious bodily control. Subjects are able to demonstrate above average entrainment response times and show improvement in this area.

Level 2
Level 2 operatives are able to temporarily bypass subjects' conscious minds to gain more control of their bodies. Level 2 operatives also have the ability to focus more. Small increases in self-discipline are usually noted.

Level 3

Level 3 operatives have demonstrated their abilities to control their own conscious minds to a greater degree and show remarkable improvements in memory, self-discipline, learning, and willpower. This level also provides the ability to better manage anxiety and stress.

Level 4

Level 4 operatives have the ability to begin mastering their mental states and use their internal and unconscious powers to a degree far superior to the average person without training. These operatives can respond to trances quickly, and they are insulated from the social-control mechanisms that others are exposed to in their daily lives. The added benefit of this level is that operatives can demonstrate the ability to enter trances faster and experience a tremendous increase in personal wellbeing, fulfillment, and self-esteem.

Level 5

These operatives have demonstrated superior abilities in the realm of self-control and personal improvement and have the capacity for advanced-training scenarios involving complex methods. These operatives will notice more successful behavior, and their training provides a noticeable shift in self-confidence and the appearance of mental balance. The training received is more advanced than any other, and they have the ability to control their behavior at will for operations and in their personal lives. Can be activated and access deeper mental states through phrases and tones such as 12.320 Hz (including remote activation).

Level 6

This level is marked by a visible increase in internal stillness and confidence, as well as a reduction in all social anxiety. The programming has been fully committed to unconscious behavior. Subjects can be fully sealed from outer influence and retain the activation phrases in case something happens to the operators during the training. These subjects have the ability to self-activate and reprogram functions of their training to suit the needs of the operational profile.

Level 7

The highest level of training is noticeable by friends and families of the operatives. A major change in lifestyle and calm becomes apparent to all. This level grants operatives access to completely bypass their egos and turn on enhanced functions that no average person has access to. The operatives in this phase have the ability to enter profound states of trance rapidly, and they are insulated from all forms of influence, with the exception of the programmers or operators with whom they work.

These seven levels help to add value to the training for the subjects and allow them to derive personal empowerment from the experiment or programming. The programmers or operators should tailor the above list and have it readily available to demonstrate to subjects their improvement and development.

ENTRAINMENT

This phase involves literally rewiring the brain to form new connections. Operators will form a solid neuronal connection that connects their voices, desired emotional states, and subjects' behaviors and obedience. If a handler situation is involved, the added phase of imprinting is included here, which is simply the process of imprinting a handler as the focal point of a subject's life in the future, much the same way that animals are imprinted on their parents at a young age. Phase 2 of imprinting is part of the Belgrade Protocol involves exploitation of subjects and uses animal imprinting. Entrainment processes can be repeated numerous times within the same session in order to prolong the training, or your own script can be used.

TRAINING

The training phase is the lengthiest; it involves training subjects to be hyperresponsive to trances. The subjects are taught how to stay in trance while walking, driving, and even being *lightly* assaulted (legally, with consent). Testing for previous training is done to ensure the process hasn't faded. The subjects are introduced to the concept of the hallway and the mental-control room, where they have access to their unconscious minds. "Wakeproofing" is a term coined by Ellipsis for training subjects to remain in trances and under operators' control during high-stress or complex environments. It's been noted that surrender is achieved more quickly with the continuous use of confusion methods throughout the following phases. This repeated confusion creates a pattern in which subject resistance is gradually diminished. We have found that some subjects respond well to consistent "reconfusion." This is the repetitive and seemingly random usage of confusion methods while performing all phases of training and programming. We have not yet been able to identify which subjects specifically will respond to this without trying it first.

In the training phase, as soon as you are able to identify the depth of your subjects' ability to completely let go, begin introducing the concept of time distortion. Introduce the concept of the subjects' being able to experience several hours of training in a single one-hour session. As soon as you're able to get subjects to experience this, you can apply it to their hearing your voice or listening to you talk—or anything you'd like them to deepen the experience of. Lengthening the amount of exposure means strengthening the bond between your subjects and you, the operator.

SEPARATING

This phase uses the hallway concept and introduces the concept of dissociation addiction. The subject is programmed with an alter ego through very specific methods and the use of "trance trauma," a word used by Ellipsis to describe mentally simulated trauma.

USING ALL OF YOUR TRAINING

If you are using operative programming on anyone, it should incorporate everything you've thus far mastered. Small changes in tone can sway an entire programming session. Shifting your body when speaking about the training can change your subjects' confidence in you. Stay alert to changes in breathing and movement during programming. Changes can indicate enjoyment or a serious problem with your method.

In placebo studies, it was found that subjects responded much better if the "drug" was described as being extremely powerful and effective before being administered. Even increasing the severity of delivery, like using an injection instead of pills, caused it to be more effective. The delivery of this programming and its overall outcome hinges on the ability to bring all of the training you've had to bear onto your subjects.

ENCOURAGEMENT

All through the programming process, it's important to encourage the subject and let them know they are doing well. They will undoubtedly be wondering whether they are pleasing you. Here is a simple list you can use throughout the training so as not to sound redundant.

SUPER
That's RIGHT
That's good
You're really working hard today
That's much better
Exactly right
That's it
Now you've figured it out
That's quite an improvement
Great job

I knew you could do it
You're making real progress
Now you have it
You are learning fast
You did it that time
You haven't missed a thing
That's the right way
Terrific
You've just about mastered that
Much, much better
Wonderful
You're really improving
You did really well today
Keep it up
That's it
I'm very proud of you
I like that
It's such a true pleasure to work with you

Entrainment Phase 1

This is the first "clinical" meeting with subjects. They should be seated in chairs and have relatively empty stomachs. The room should be conducive to normal hypnosis, and the operators should be at a forty-five-degree angle to the faces of the subjects. The angle (right or left) should be shifted to the opposite side each time you meet with a subject, to prevent audio-hemispheric preference. This phase contains much of the same programming mentioned in the CIA programming chapter, but this phase is specifically focused for subjects' development and mood shaping. The following is an example script for the first session:

Today is the first day of your training. We are going to cover some very basic things today and over the next few sessions. These may seem unnecessary, but the reason behind them is going to make you more responsive and a much faster learner for your training. I'm going to read off a list of simple tasks for you to complete. They can range from lifting a finger to turning your head or saying a word. That's all you have to do. The reason behind this is that the brain needs lots of practice for things to become automatic and natural. For you to reach a superior level, it's important for everything you do to be smooth, fluid, and automatic. When I speak and you respond, we are creating connections that will become more and more finely tuned. That makes sense, so for a few sessions, there won't be any hypnosis or anything like that. Just relax and enjoy the little vacation while your brain and I do all the work.

Once you're seated comfortably, I'll go ahead and start. Let's practice a couple of times before we begin. Lift your hand. Put it down. Fold your hands together. Put them back in your lap. Perfect! That's it! No need to look at me at all. Just relax. Ready?

[The commands are always given as commands. Never ask the subject to perform an action or presuppose he or she understands a shortened command. Give full, understandable commands.]

Lift your left hand.

Perfect. Put it down.

Lift your left index finger.

Put it down.

Lift your right index finger.

Put it down.

Wiggle your toes.

Good.

Take in a huge breath.

Let it out.

Turn your head left.

Turn your head right.

Turn your head back to the center.

Lift your right index finger.

Touch your right index finger and thumb together. [Reassurance to
self with the okay gesture.]

Great. Put them back down.

Do the same with your left hand.

Great. Put your hand back now.

Cross your ankles.

Uncross your ankles.

Tap your right foot three times.

Tap your left foot three times.

Say "orange."

Say "perfect."

Say "towel."

Put your right hand onto your left shoulder [activating a self-hug to
alleviate anxiety from speaking for the first time].

Put your arm back down.

Put your left hand onto your right shoulder; hold this for a few
seconds.

Perfect. Put your arm back down.

Smile.

Frown.

Relax.

Say "thunderstorm."

Say "movie."

Place your right hand onto your chest.

Say "forest."

Put your arm down.

Interlace your fingers together.

Put them back on the legs.

Say "mischief."

Display poor posture.

Display good posture.

Relax.

Smile.

Frown.
Relax.
Say "umbrella."
Say "focus."
Close your eyes.
Open your eyes.
Say "here."
Say "fox."
Lift your right hand just above your leg.
Put it down.
Lift your left hand up and onto your abdomen.
Put your left hand back.
Start breathing into your abdomen a little bit more.
Lower your shoulders.
Say "power outage."
Say "candle."
Say "desk."
Say "glasses."
Say "magnet."
Smile.
Relax.
Say "davenport."
Say "file."
Put your feet together.
Put them back.
Lift your right hand to your abdomen.
Put it back.
Make a fist with your left hand.
Let it go.
Make a fist with your right hand.
Let it go.
Say "evening."
Say "sand."

Say "mind."

Say "paint."

Say "garden."

Lift your toes up.

Put them back down.

Do it again.

Perfect. Put them back down. You're doing well.

Say "five."

Say "I have you."

Say "operator."

Adjust yourself in your chair again to be comfortable.

You did perfectly. Say "that was perfect." You deserve it.

This completes phase 1 of entrainment. Subjects require three more phases with their operators to become fully capable of unconsciously responding to commands. The second phase of entrainment involves the use of larger muscle groups and reiterates the use of repeating phrases on command. Each phase should be no longer than one hour and fifteen minutes. The phases can be repeated or added to as necessary for the subject.

ENTRAINMENT PHASE 2

This phase will have subjects moving and standing. It is important to note that safety for the subjects should be carefully monitored and controlled. This ensures they remain unharmed and develop a sincere trust that the operators have their wellbeing in mind at all times as a caretaker. Operators can never allow a situation to exist in which the subjects can be hurt or potential harm can happen. Trust is the prime currency for programming.

In this phase, operators are usually meeting their subjects for the second time, and in general, more than a day has elapsed since the first meeting, so it becomes critical that operators not only reemphasize the priority of subjects' safety but also build more rapport with the subjects by using authority methods. Also, the first phase of entrainment can be repeated here. If you decide to recreate phase 1, insert dissociative language in their respective places every few times you mention the subject's body.

The subjects should again be at a forty-five-degree angle and have a relatively empty stomach for the procedure. The operators and subjects should be positioned opposite to how they sat during the first meetings. This phase also introduces more-complex usage of dissociative language to prime the subjects for dissociative experiences that will come later. This also primes the subjects to become dissociative in the presence of the operators, without any use of trauma. Here is an example of a potential script:

Since you did such an incredible job last time, I want to reassure you that you are absolutely perfect...at this. Again, it's important for you to let that brain do all the work. You're ready, yes?

[At this point, operators should have already discussed subjects' comfort; that is, operators should have ensured that their subjects are feeling safe and comfortable, sitting in a relaxed position, so they can dissociate and relax during the second phase of entrainment.]

First, make sure that those legs and all of your torso are relaxed. It's important to me that everything happens today in the most natural and relaxed way possible. Do you understand? [If the subject nods, ask him or her to say yes.]

Let all of your muscles...completely let go now.

Say "I am ready."

Now, start breathing into the abdomen. Try to gradually slow your breathing down a bit.

Good job.

I want you to fold your arms across your chest comfortably.

Say "round two."

Say "believe."

Say "Noriega."
Say "Israel."
Let the arms fall down now.
Make them comfortable.
Pick up both of your feet.
Let them fall again.
Touch your chin to your chest.
Put your head back where it was.
Stand up [said quickly].
Perfect.
Sit down.
Say "Park Avenue."
Say "I am powerful."
Repeat "I am powerful."
Repeat "velocity 3971." [*Repeat* is now used in lieu of *say.*]
Repeat "fox tail."
Stand up [said quickly].
Turn to your right.
Walk to the wall. [Do not ever have the subject repeat or say words into a wall.]
Turn around.
Close your eyes.
Repeat "I can do this."
Repeat "mission."
Open your eyes.
Walk to the chair.
Sit down. [Never use the word "sit" to command a subject.]
Repeat "I will win through superiority."
Repeat that again.

Again.

Ask me what time it is. [Tell the subject the current time.]

Repeat "I can't believe how rainy it is today."

Say it again.

Say it again.

Say it again.

Repeat "comfortable."

Repeat "This feels perfect."

Stand up.

Walk to the _____ [a direction mostly ahead].

Face the chair again.

When I ask who was sitting there, say your name.

Who was sitting in that chair?

Perfect.

You're going to be absolutely incredible.

Repeat "You are a coworker."

I will be a coworker of yours. I want you to explain how you knew how to read someone's behavior without giving away your training. I am going to ask you how you knew that, and I want you to explain how you knew how to read behavior without revealing your training. Do you understand? [Prompt the subject to say yes if necessary.]

Repeat "You are a coworker."

[Subject's name], how did you know exactly what the boss would do in the meeting? Did you read his mind?

[Allow the subject to demonstrate his or her capacity to conceal his or her training and enjoy it.]

You're a natural. Perfect.

Go sit down. [said in a rewarding tone with a guiding gesture.]

Next, you will explain your sudden increase in confidence and personal changes that will happen during your training. I will be a friend who has noticed the change in you.

[Subject's name], something's different about you. You seem to just own the space around you now. What the hell happened? Explain it without revealing training.

Close your eyes.

Repeat "I have the capacity."

Repeat "I will win through superiority."

Repeat "This will last forever."

Repeat "completely new life."

Repeat "snowfall."

Repeat "mercury."

Repeat "six."

Repeat "eight."

Repeat "venture, grid, folded, Tuscany."

Lift the right arm.

Leave it there.

Repeat "possible."

Repeat "I am capable."

Again.

Again.

Again.

Repeat "I am exceptionally qualified."

Again.

Again.

Again.

Repeat "I will win through superior training."

Again.

Again.

Again.

Put your arm down.

Perfect.

Stand up.

Walk to the _____. [Require at least ten steps; the operator should not follow.]

Walk back to the chair and sit.

Repeat "I will see through everyone I meet."

Again.

Again.

Again.

Again.

Again.

Repeat "This is the beginning."

I want you to cough forcefully until I say stop.

Stop.

Stand up.

Do not answer this question. Are you hungry? [Do it again if the subject fails to comply.]

Repeat "rule one."

Repeat "I will see the brain and not the person."

Again.

Again.

Again.

Again.

Repeat "rule one."

Repeat "I will see the brain and not the person."

Grab your knees.

Repeat "This is the beginning."

Wrap your arms around yourself.

Stand up.

Drop your arms quickly.

Sit down.

Make yourself uncomfortable in the chair.

Stay there.

Repeat "paper, process, power, purpose."

Repeat "flower, fight, finish."

Again.

Again.

Raise your arms over your head.
Put them down.
Stand up now.
Sit comfortably now.
Repeat "rule two."

Again.
Repeat "Skill wins every time."
Again.
Again.
Again.
Again.
Stand up.
Who was sitting in that chair? [Prompt to speak in third person if subject does not.]
Who was sitting in that chair?
Who was sitting in that chair?
Sit [subject's name] down and make her comfortable.
Close your eyes.
Do not open your eyes. Stand up.
Tell me you trust me.
Again.
Again.
Perfect.
Open your eyes again.
Sit and relax.
Absolutely flawless.
Take a breath.
Hold it. [Wait for a three count.]
Let it go.
Perfect.
[Repeat the entrainment process as necessary]

When you get to the advanced levels, I can tell you're going to be astonished about how much control you have over that body and brain.

Before I'm finished with you here, I want you to start focusing on your heartbeat. Do that now.

[Allow about fifteen seconds to elapse.]

Slowly start to lower your heart rate. Trust your body and trust the training; all you need to do is send a command to the heart to slow down. Do it now. I'll keep the time. Trust the training.

This process should be repeated until the subjects either have successfully reported that they can feel a difference in their heart rates or have shown signs of it working; subjects should seem amazed or otherwise pleased with their success.

It's worth noting that operators must maintain rapport and must continue to create authority in the process.

Entrainment Phase 3

In the third phase of entrainment, subjects are challenged to perform more-cognitive and more-physical tasks. It's important in this phase to follow the authority techniques and maintain positive rapport. The subjects will surely have doubts and worries. It is the operators' responsibility to reassure their subjects, to keep them comfortable, confident, and relaxed. The confidence subjects gain in their training and personal abilities will be heavily influenced by their operators' behaviors during the process. While the subjects are going through the third phase of entrainment, mistakes and errors may be common. Keep the subjects motivated; let them know that mistakes are common and that they are doing just fine. Encouragement will usually assuage most of their worry about how they measure up to other trainees.

The introduction talk should focus on subjects' development and should reassure them that they have tremendous potential for training, an advanced level of aptitude. But do no dote on your subjects. Sit on the opposite side from where you previously sat during phase 2. Phase 1 and 2 can be repeated before proceeding to phase three to fit within your allotted time.

Here is a potential script:

Are you ready? [Said while nodding.]

Okay. Sit comfortably and go back to where you were taking those controlled breaths. The commands today will come a bit faster, and you will be required to respond to more-complex commands today.

Say "perfect" if you're ready.

Great. Now make a fist with the right hand. [This needs to be said as if it were an immediate requirement.]

Good. Let that go. Even faster than before. You're doing well.

Take another breath.

Stand up!

Great.

Let it out.

Cross your arms over your chest.

Drop them.

Sit down [said while pointing to the chair].

Turn your head to the left.

Now to the right.

Close the eyes completely.

Keep them closed.

Head back to the center.

Head left.

Back to the center.

Open your eyes.

Look at me.

Do *not* answer this question.

How old are you?

How old are you?

How old is [subject's name]? [Observe response and query for the reasons, if desired.]

Look back to the center again.

Answer this question.

Do you break the speed limit?

Good. From this point forward, do not answer any question without me telling you to answer the question.

Nod your head if you understand.

Stand up! [Begin using small hand movements that will eventually be associated with future commands. The hand movements you decide to use as an operator will need to be uniform and memorized to avoid confusing your subjects during more-intense programming.)

Sit on the ground.

Answer this question: how old are you?

Good.

Why are you here?

Why are you here [subject's name]?

Tell me why you are here. [Subject should respond.]

Stand up.

Sit in the chair.

Start breathing into your abdomen.

Lower your shoulders.

Say "California."

Say "viking, echo, mercury."

Say "fuck."

Breathe slower.

Perfect.

Go back to your training. You have faith in the training.

Start slowing your heart again.

Keep following my directions and continue to lower your heart rate.

Say "construction."

Say "construction creates."

Say "viking, echo, mercury."

Nod your head when you start controlling your heart. I'll wait.

Great. Hold your hands like you're reading a book.

Sit in the chair how you would read a good book.

Look at the book and make your body believe it's the most interesting book you've ever read.

Perfect. Start tuning out the world. Everything but my voice.

Answer this question: can you concentrate if I shove you gently on the shoulder?

[Shove the subject gently. Note the response and issue commands to get back to reading the book, if needed.]

Perfect, [subject's name; say "perfect" as though you were describing the subject, not issuing a compliment].

Continue to fade out…the world around you. You can continue to hear me. Nod your head.

Keep turning up the focus. Focus.

Don't let anything distract you from this focus. Nod your head if you understand.

[Push the subject's head to the side gently and shake him or her a bit.]

Great.

Let the book go and sit back in the chair again in a comfortable position.

Hold your left arm in front of you. Put it up.

I want you to hold this here for about a minute. I want it to be uncomfortable.

Say "evergreen."

Say "forest."

Say "mischief."

Say "warm."

Say "perfect."

What's the address to the embassy here? [Correct the subject if he or she answers the question.]

What's the address to the embassy?

What's your area code?

Tell me the area code of your phone number.

Awesome.

As your arm is getting tired there, start focusing again on your breathing.

Breathe into your abdomen.

Let your shoulders relax. Keep your arm up.

Start controlling your heart again. Nothing can stop you.

Say "Nothing can stop me."

Say "I have control."

Slow your heart now.

Close your eyes.

Stand up.

Keep that heart beating slowly.

Nod your head when you have accomplished what I asked.

Good work.

Let your arm fall.

Sit down.

The third phase will continue for approximately an hour using these methods, continuously asking questions and testing the subject's resolve to follow the operator's rules. Some phases of entrainment can be abbreviated, depending on the response and obedience capacities of the subjects.

ENTRAINMENT PHASE 4

The fourth phase of entrainment should be like the third because the subjects are tested not only in their abilities to follow the question instructions the operators gave but also in their abilities to resist breaking focus while the operators are talking. The fourth phase incorporates the use of audio and visual stimuli. This phase also introduces the subjects to the basic feeling of trances and illustrates that trances aren't dangerous, scary, or something that can erase memories.

During phase 4, the subjects should be placed where there is a television, where they can choose something they would like to have on the television, during the entrainment process. This can be explained to the subjects by discussing how well they did during phase 3 with handling distractions. The television is a way for the subjects to prove to themselves that they can overcome the functions of their conscious minds.

This phase will most likely induce trance phenomena, but it isn't necessary to discuss this with the subjects. The purpose here isn't specifically to induce trances but to create highly attentive subjects when it comes to the voice of the operator. Later, during programming, the responses to hypnotic methods will be increased as a result. Phase 4 should include physical movements of the subjects to attempt to distract them. When inducing discomfort, the discomfort should be slightly greater than what the subjects experienced during phase 3.

The subjects should be complimented on how well they did and should be shown a chart of how highly they scored for staying in full control of their minds during the programming. It is important to keep the subjects motivated and confident in their training.

TRANCE TRAINING

In this phase, the subjects are to be trained to quickly enter a trance state (the programmable state) and to remain there amid distractions and physical jarring. This phase will be only outlined; specific scripts are not necessary for an operator familiar with the Ellipsis methods.

BASIC TRANCE TRAINING

Subjects are placed into a normal hypnotic trance through a formal induction method. Once the operators can confirm the subjects are in the trance state, fractionation should be performed. Vivid descriptions of which feelings to pay attention to and what to notice while in the trance state are important for the development of the subject. While subjects are in trances, call attention to their heart rates, breathing, focus, and levels of personal control.

Subjects should be repeatedly brought out of their trances and placed back into their trances to become familiar with the behavior and with the commands of the operators. Over the course of approximately one hour, the subjects should be in their trances for no more than six minutes. Repetition and rehearsal is vitally important to the development of the subjects. The behavior should be practiced with as many sessions as necessary to ensure the behavior becomes automatic.

Trance-Training Level 2

In this session, the subjects are introduced to their control rooms (Hammond, 1990). The control room is a mentally constructed room at the end of a hallway that contains imaginative controls the subjects can use to regulate their bodies. For instance, there may be specific controls for arousal, blood pressure, heart rate, focus, and so on.

This must be described to the subjects through hypnotic language after ensuring they are deep in their trances. The process usually follows a path down a staircase or elevator (depending on subjects' personalities) and down a long hallway that ends at a door. Subjects are then introduced into the room and told to imagine the controls as they wish and to test several of these controls to notice physiological changes in their bodies such as making the temperature slightly raise and lowering the heart rate. In highly responsive subject, tasks such as raising the serotonin levels and turning up their level of human connectivity can be experimented with. These changes in physiology should be confirmed by the operators. At this point in the programming, the subjects have not been introduced to the concept of speaking in a trance, and operators should have them use ideomotor signals instead of speech when questions are asked or information is requested. An example of an ideomotor signal would be to answer operators' questions by signaling yes or no by lifting certain fingers on a hand. These instructions should be established before the trances are induced.

The training and experimentation should continue as long as is necessary. If operators prolong the training, subjects will develop a profound sense of having learned and experienced a great deal more than they would have without the aid and assistance of the operators and the training regimen. It is important to continually reemphasize the power the subjects are developing and to reassure subjects that they are making tremendous progress. In this phase, you may suggest the subtle differences in their lives that their friends and coworkers will notice. Remind the subjects often that they will be seen differently and that people will ask them what happened to make them seem so much more confident and in control.

Time Distortion

In this phase, introduce the concept of time distortion. The subjects should be informed that they can experience hours of training in mere minutes. This awareness should build confidence in their abilities. After training, the awareness should help them to fully "feel" that they have had much more training than their training sessions allowed. This concept should be presented as a new technology and as something that is positive, beneficial, and rare.

Some operators will use the time distortion method to have the subject mentally experience years or months of brainwashing in a single session, or to implant false memories of such events taking place. Of course, the brainwashing sessions being programmed into the subject would entail positive outcomes. Most people would pay to be brainwashed to eat healthier or to have more motivation and gratitude in life. Brainwashing is such a simple process that it can be simulated in myriad ways. One in particular that has shown to be effective is to have the subject visualize being strapped into a chair and forced to listen to recordings and images of a nature that reflects the training objectives.

As time distortion is used, continue the use of dissociative language while the subject's skill levels progress:

1. Introduce the concept.
2. Test the subjects to ensure they can feel as if they have experienced a distortion of time while in their trances.
3. Give the subjects goals to accomplish, such as experiencing an hour-long session in only five minutes.
4. Use time to your advantage—that is, you can make them hear your voice for hours longer than they actually do in reality.
5. Throughout the training to follow, reiterate the importance of time distortion and how it benefits them.

Training to Visualize Vividly

This phase consists of one to three sessions, depending on the needs of the subjects. Visualization training for the subjects enhances their experience of their trances and will help them to enjoy a more vivid experience for the duration of the programming process.

In this phase, bring the subjects into deep trances and have them process visual images both with their eyes closed and with their eyes open. Ensure confirmation is obtained from the subjects that they are in fact developing the ability to visualize the objects you suggest. Simple objects should be used, such as a pyramid, box, or cone of a single color. Once they can visualize this vividly, it should be moved and spun in such a way that they can feel and see all of the sides and dimensions of the object.

Remember to use dissociative language so that the subjects become dissociated as a byproduct of hearing your voice.

ADVANCED FRACTIONATION AND IMPRINTING

This session brings several new challenges to subjects. The subjects are taught how to speak and move in trances without breaking their focus. This phase also includes imprinting, in which the subjects imprint onto the operator to establish much-deeper levels of rapport, trust, and safety.

Depending on the ethical implications and the nature of work being done, this phase is the phase to perform the introductory behavior engineering to associate the operators with all things the subjects see as respectable, godlike, and trustworthy. Religious icons and positive parental roles can be associated with the operators through covert language and programming before these sessions begin. Here are steps for these sessions:

1. Have conversations with your subjects and discuss any of their current concerns. Address any issues and remove any blockages they have to further letting go.
2. Discuss the process of fractionation with your subjects. Coach them on how to speak and move in their trances. Emphasize that the only way to move their bodies and speak in trances is to fully surrender to what's happening. Self-doubt and self-management are usually what breaks a trance, not the movement itself.
3. Before beginning the sessions, repeat the entrainment methods of phases 3 and 4 for twenty minutes.
4. Let your subjects know they will be fine, and ensure they can let go with the safety you have described to them.
5. Place your subjects into their trances and begin fractionation in and out of those trances. On the second transition from the trance state to waking, when they are in those trances ready to be woken, instruct them to memorize this phrase: "I'm safe now." Modify this phrase to suit the programming needs of each project.
6. Give these spoken instructions to your subjects: "Every time you come out of the trance, there is a phrase you need to say to

ensure no one else has access to this part of your mind, except you and me. Here is the phrase I want you to memorize. Repeat this after me: 'I'm safe now.' Repeat it again. Perfect. Every time I bring you back to the waking state, look up at me and say the phrase. Do you understand?"

7. Let your subjects know they should be excited about testing their bodies out (using dissociative language) for the first time by speaking in trance.

8. Repeat this process, making your subjects immediately come out of their trances, look up at you, and speak the phrase. Do this for a minimum of twenty-five repetitions and ensure the trances are achieved each time you send your subjects back down from the waking state, after they have repeated the phrase. If the subject is having difficulty reentering trance, go back to the trance training and repeat until they have satisfied the requirement. It's sometimes beneficial to have them wake up only from the neck up, as discovered by Milton Erickson.

9. Make sure the positional arrangement is such that you are higher than your subjects, so they must look upward to you, even if it is at a shallow angle.

This session should be ended with encouragement and professionalism. The subjects have been primed to begin seeing you as a role model and authority figure that deserves trust and obedience. Maintain this behavior and level of respect at all costs.

IMPRINTING

This session is included for projects that will involve either a great deal of interaction with the operators or the use of a handler. This session emphasizes trust and encourages subjects to form a bond unlike any other with their operators. The following steps should be followed as ordered, and the handlers or operators should sit on the sides of subjects' dominant hands. The subjects will be asked to touch the wrists of the operators, so wristwatches should be removed before commencing these sessions.

1. A minimum of ten minutes of entrainment should start imprinting sessions. They should be framed as being a test to ensure the subjects have not forgotten their previous training.
2. Induce the trances and begin deepening. Have your subjects speak immediately, using an entrainment speaking phrase as soon as they are in deep trances and their breathing slows.
3. Take your subjects to the control room and have them sit in the control room (dissociation) and close the eyes of their imaginary selves.
4. Explain the importance of trust and the focus on their safety.
5. Explain the presence of an administrative access to their minds; explain that you want to protect them from hostile forces, manipulators, and even advertising, to free them from negative influences.
6. Have your subjects open the eyes of the person in the control room and add your name (however they imagine it) to the administrator access of their minds. Have them walk you through the process verbally and remind them to speak softly.
7. Install the hypnotic seals by suggesting that when they awaken, they will become uncomfortable anytime someone tries to access this part of their brains—except you, the operator. Walk them through three imaginary scenarios where this could happen in the future, and ensure that this discomfort response is set after they wake up. (Repeat until your subjects pass these tests.)
8. Ensure your subjects are placed back in their trances after they pass these tests. Have them open their eyes. Keep them in their trances while their eyes are open by reassuring them, by providing suggestions to keep their minds in the same place, and by modifying their breathing and muscular tension appropriately.

9. Have your subjects look directly in front of them. As you are seated next to their favored sides, look in the same directions as your subjects and talk about safety and trust. Reassure them that you will never cause them harm. Have your subjects say this several times if necessary.

10. As they process this information, explain the following course of action: they need to understand what true connection feels like. Tell them to hold your wrist and position their hands until they can feel your pulse.

11. Once they feel your pulse, deepen their trances and remind them to keep their eyes open. As subjects' trance selves are still in the control room, have them match your heartbeat. This may take several minutes, and it may require reminders every minute or so, depending on each subject. Ensure they stay on task.

12. Silence is acceptable while you wait for them to match your pulse.

13. Instruct your subjects to concentrate on your pulse; then repeat the method again after a moment. Repeat this step several times. Also, remember that the imprinting process must be custom-tailored to each subject.

14. If your subjects express concern that they aren't able to keep their hearts in step with yours, reassure them that it will happen eventually; tell them to keep focusing on the controls.

15. End these sessions in a positive, encouraging, and fatherly tone.

16. The final phase of imprinting is repeated once every future session. It involves having the subject in trance. Once they are in the control room, have them open their eyes while in trance, make eye contact with the operator and immediately say 'I am safe now'. This is repeated the amount of times necessary proportional to the degree of trust required. Usually, about 25 times the first session and 10 each following session.

In this phase, some practitioners will use the trance phenomena to simulate surgeries. Some surgeries will be of a control chip being implanted into the host's brain, removal of memories, repairing brain tissue and motivation centers in the brain or simply the performance of an internal brain examination.

WAKEPROOFING

Wakeproofing is simply a training session that teaches subjects how to stay in their trances when distractions or physical agitations occur. This phase involves placing your hands on your subjects, who should be made aware of this action before your starting the training. Safety should be reassured prior to commencing all training.

1. Reassure subjects of progress, potential, and ability.
2. Compliment them on how much better their carriage, confidence, and posture are since the last session.
3. The seating arrangement should be opposite of the previous sessions.
4. Induce the trances and deepen them. Have your subjects speak immediately after their breathing rates slow down.
5. Discuss the process of controlling the mind. They have already demonstrated how easily they can shut off their conscious minds and maintain uninterrupted access to their unconscious parts.
6. Tell your subjects that today is special: they will be testing their abilities with their eyes open—even while they are talking and moving across the room.
7. Deepen the trances. Using dissociative language, have your subjects open their eyes. Deepen the trances again. While their eyes are open, tell them to completely shut out (insert appropriate name). Then see how differently they can experience a conversation.

8. Ask them how they feel (without using their names).
9. Reassure them they are doing well.
10. Repeat this process as necessary and move to the next phase.
11. Deepen the trances while your subjects' eyes are still open, and instruct them to stay in the trances no matter what happens.
12. Agitate your subjects by shaking their shoulders lightly and by having them stand, sit, speak, and use the muscles in their faces.
13. Deepen and reinduce the trances as necessary throughout the process. This exercise should last the duration of the session.
14. For advanced level 4 programming, yelling the name of the subject to shake them out of trance is also used.

The wakeproofing and entrainment sections should be repeated when necessary throughout the programming phase and into the operational lives of the subjects. Testing never stops.

Depending on the requirements, you can choose to include a second phase of wakeproofing that entails more violent action while the subjects are in their trances.

CREATING THE HELPER

This phase is where the alter is created. Following the training the subject has just gone through, they are ready to be introduced to their 'helper'. The process is almost identical to the 'Hallway' procedure described in the previous chapter, but redefines the 'alter' as an assistant or whatever suits the needs of the therapist or operator.

Many cases of dissociative identity disorder have alter personalities with health problems and even physical impairments that the host does not have. In this light, you can see that you can create an alter in a person with depression that does NOT have depression. You could create an alter in a person that fits almost any description you'd like. The alter can be made to stay hidden from the host or you can choose to inform the subject that one is being created. Alters used for therapeutic purposes could potentially help to drastically improve the quality of life of patients.

Follow the guidelines for the Hallway procedure to install and create the alter. Ensure the name choice for the alter is something they will not have a negative association with.

Safety Note: Activating the alter can be dramatic. Even if you have done it before and it was seamless and easy, something as simple as a song in the background during activation can be dangerous. Always assume the subject is capable of an abreaction when activating. Never activate an alter when the subject is operating a vehicle, machinery, or has consumed alcohol.

Alters can be reintegrated within a single session since they are not created using trauma (traumagenic) and you haven't installed a 'disorder'. There are rare cases of accidents causing activation, but the alters / helpers are in no position to bargain or control the host; they were created by the operator and can be integrated or eliminated the same way.

44.792504 20.422275

The Ellipsis Evergreen Rules

I am an Ellipsis operator. I succeed because of my training, confidence, and intent.

I see the brain, not the person.

I have tremendous faith and confidence in my training. I have superior skills.

Preparation is what separates my results from those of amateurs.

I do not get angry or fearful; I create those feelings in others to get the outcomes I need.

I can change my behavior to speak to different parts of the brain.

I see the hidden needs in every interaction and use them to create situations for behavior change.

I don't create opportunities; I *become* the opportunities.

I am the siren: perfect and dangerous, I compel involuntary actions.

I can become insecure and fearful when necessary.

I foster dependence at every turn.

I foster regression or issue power when either is needed.

I make no apologies for creating the outcomes I want in life.

My voice is like warm water: calm and inviting—it assumes the shape of whoever swims inside.

My tenets are patience, focus, and strategy—in all things.

I find the places where others lack enjoyment and fulfillment.

I never mistake appearances for reality.

I awaken discontent and show the way ahead.

I am a mood sculptor.

QUICK RULES FOR FIELD OPERATORS

See the brain, not the mask.

Become familiar with your trade. Master human behavior.

Be aware of every sense you are speaking to.

Outcomes dictate all behavior.

Words can create almost any emotion you need in the moment.

Self-awareness creates self-control.

Discipline is freedom.

The body is always more honest and revealing than words.

Everyone reveals secrets in every moment of speech.

Composure, enthusiasm, and authority create natural obedience.

Plant thought-flags early.

Every pronoun reveals; every adjective provides a loophole.

Create sensory-rich imagination traps.

Every gesture provides a window to concealed thoughts.

Create automatic agreement with language traps.

Bring awareness to doubt.

Hint at future regret.

Awaken discontent.

Become proficient at shutting off automatic behavior.

Interrupt negation and pattern thinking.

Call attention to the pack, not the person, in the beginning.

Focus attention in the direction of the outcome, using corrugation.

Use desire, lust, hunger, and impulse to drive action, not emotion.

Drive emotion using fear, regret, sex, fulfillment, and social acceptance.

Never let a big behavioral decision be made with a subject's back on a chair.

Always give compliments following subjects exposing their palms.

Long exhales should accompany all subjects' stories of needing pity.

Always mimic breathing speed first.

Linguistic-presence techniques should always follow a subject being distracted.

Shiny eyes are more persuasive than perfect speech.

Accidental body contact causes immediate, short-lived insecurity in just about everyone.

THE HANDLER'S CODE OF CONDUCT

Never betray the trust of the subject.

Place the safety of the subject above the safety of others.

Exercise and enforce protective authority daily.

Keep on step with your own skill and the subject's development.

Have tertiary backup plans for every action you require of the subject.

Treat the subject the same as you would your own child.

Know every weakness, flaw and insecurity in your subject and care for them despite it.

Anything you're required to know to operate should be committed to memory.

ACKNOWLEDGMENTS

• • •

I'm grateful for the impact these people made in my development:
B&J
Chris Piccone
David Barron, a.k.a. Dantalion Jones
Patsy Lawrence
Paul Ross
Angie B.
Tariq Al F.
Kristy Gillies
Michael Witcoff
D. Allenby
Cloud Rogers
33 – the one
The motivational team at the Compass Rose
The Elite team
Adam Goodson
Joseph A. Williams
Sara Vandiver
Amanda R.
Ben Cardall

ABOUT CHASE HUGHES

● ● ●

CHASE WAS RAISED IN HOUSTON, Texas and attended military academy before joining the military in 1998. Chase specializes in teaching behavior profiling, interrogation and psychological intelligence operations. Chase is the creator of the Behavioral Table of Elements for interrogation profiling and lie detection. He also created the Corrugation Programming methods for government use and made the discovery that they can be applied to therapy and healing.

Chase currently runs Ellipsis Behavior Laboratories in Virginia Beach, Virginia. The company develops new methodologies for interrogations and psychological operations for all types of clients.

REFERENCES

"Chapter 3, part 4: Supreme court dissents invoke the nuremberg code: CIA and DOD human subjects research scandals". ().Advisory Committee on Human Radiation Experiments Final Report.

Barone, R. (2015). In Hughes C. (Ed.), *Removing the social mask.* Dallas; TX; USA:

Beattie, G. (2003). *Visible thought: The new psychology of body language.* Padstow, Cornwall, Great Britain: Routledge.

Bennett, C. (2001,). Candy jones: How a leading American fashion model came to be experimented upon by the CIA mind control team. *Forteantimes*

Bernstein, E. M. (1986). Development, reliability and validity of a dissociation scale. *Journal of Nervous and Mental Disorders, 174*((12)), 727-735.

Birdwhistell, R. (1952). *Introduction to kinesics.* Cambridge, Massachusetts: University of Louisville Press.

Blagrove, M. (Mar 1996). Effects of length of sleep deprivation on interrogative suggestibility. *Journal of Experimental Psychology: Applied, Vol 2(1),* , 48-59.

Bobrow, R. S., M.D. (2006). *The witch in the waiting room: A physician investigates paranormal phenomena in medicine* (1st ed.) De Capo Press.

Bolting, K. A. (1995). *Sex appeal* Macmillan.

Bowart, W. H. (1971). *Operation mind control* Dell Publishing.

Brandt, D. (1996, January-March). "Mind control and the secret state". *Namebase Newsline*

Bryan, W. (1971). *The psychology of jury selection.* New York, NY, USA: Vantage Press.

Burton, S. (2000). *Impostors: Six kinds of liar* Viking Press.

Cameron, D. E. (1967). Obituary. *Canadian Medical Association Journal,* 984–986.

Cannon, M. (1992, Mind control and the american government. *Lobster Magazine,*

Capella, J. N. (1993). *The facial feedback in human interaction: Review and speculation (vol.12)* Journal of Language and Social Psychology. doi:doi: 10.1177/0261927X93121002

Caro, M. (2003). *Caro's book of poker tells* Cardoza Publishing.

Cashdan, E. (1998). *Smiles, speech and body posture: How women and men display sociometric status and power (vol.22)* Journal of Nonverbal Behavior.

CIA. (1964). *KUBARK counterintelligence interrogation manual*

Cohen, J. D. (2005). The vulcanization of the human brain.. A neural perspective on interactions between cognition and emotion. *Journal of Economic Perspectives,* (19), 3-24.

Collett, P. (1977). *Social rules and social behavior* Oxford: Blackwell.

Collett, P. (2003). *The book of tells* Doubleday Books.

Collins, A. (1988). *In the sleep room: The story of CIA brainwashing experiments in canada* Lester & Orpen Dennys Ltd.

Committee, C. ().

Committee, C. ().

Cornwell, R. (1999, March; 19). Obituary: Sidney Gottlieb. *The Independent*

Coss, R. (1965). *Mood-provoking visual stimuli: Their origins and applications* UCLA.

Critchley, M. (1975). *Silent language*. London: Butterworth.

A culture of conspiracy: Apocalyptic visions in contemporary America [sic] (2013). University of California Press.

D. Corydon Hammond Ph.D., C. H.-B. ,. M. M. &. C. W. G. J., 1986. The Use of Fractionation in Self-Hypnosis. *American Journal of Clinical Hypnosis*, 30(2), pp. 119-124.

Darwin, C. (1872). *The expression of emotion in man animals*. New York, NY, USA: Appleton Century Crofts.

Davitz, J. R. (1964). *The communication of emotional meaning*. New York, NY, USA: McGraw-Hill.

Dimberg, U. T. (2000). *Unconscious facial reactions to emotional facial expressions (vol.11)* Psychological Science.

Dobbs, J. M. (1992). *Testosterone, smiling and facial appearance (vol. 21)* Journal of Nonverbal Behavior.

Edoardo Casiglia, P. A., 2012. Relaxation Versus Fractionation as Hypnotic Deepening: Do They Differ in Physiological Changes?. *International Journal Of Clinical And Experimental Hypnosis*, 60(3), pp. 338-355.

Effron, D. (1972). *Gesture, race and culture* Mouton: The Hague.

Ekman, P. (1969). *The repertoire of nonverbal behavior: Categories, origins, usage and coding (vol. 1)* Semiotica.

Ekman, P. (1973). *Cross-cultural studies in facial expression* Academic Press.

Ekman, P. (1979). *About brows: Emotional and conversational signals* Cambridge University Press.

Ekman, P. (1992). *Facial expression of emotion: New findings, new questions* Psychological Science.

Ekman, P. (1993). *Facial expressions of emotion (vol. 48)* American Psychologist.

Ekman, P. (1994). *Strong evidence for universals in facial expressions: A reply to russell's mistaken critique (vol. 115)* Psychological Bulletin.

Ekman, P., & Friesen, W.V. (1969, Feb). *Nonverbal leakage and clues to deception* Psychiatry: Journal for the study of interpersonal processes.

Ekman, P. D. (1990). *The duchenne smile: Emotional expression and brain physiology II* Journal of Personality and Social Psychology.

Ekman, P. n. (1975). *Unmasking the face.* London: Prentice Hall.

Ellyson, S. L. (1985). *Power, dominance and nonverbal behaviour* Springer - Verlag.

Estabrooks, G. (1946). *Hypnotism*. New York: E.P. Dutton.

Estabrooks, G. H. (1971,). Hypnosis comes of age. *Science Digest*, pp. 44-50.

Experiments, Advisory Committee on Human Radiation. *Chapter 3: Supreme court dissents invoke the nuremberg code: CIA and DOD human subjects research scandals.* ().Advisory Committee on Human Radiation Experiments.

Feldman, S. (1959). *Mannerisms of speech and gesture in everyday life* International University Press.

Finger, S. (2001). *Origins of neuroscience: A history of explorations into brain function* Oxford University Press.

Flugel, J. C. (1930). *The psychology of clothes*. London: Hogarth Press.

Forer, B. R. (1949). The fallacy of personal validation: A classroom demonstration of gullibility. *Journal of Abnormal and Social Psychology (American Psychological Association)*, , 118-123.

Gillmor, D. (1987). *I swear by apollo: Dr. ewen cameron and the CIA-brainwashing experiments* Eden Press.

Glass, L. (2002). *I know what you're thinking: Using the four codes of reading people to improve your life* John Wiley & Sons, Inc.

Goffman, E. (1963). *Behavior in public places*. Illinois: Free Press.

Gordon, R. L. (1987). *Interview strategy, technology and tactics (4th ed.)*. Illinois: Dorsey Press.

Government, U. S.

Government, U. S. (1963). *"Chapter 3, part 4: Supreme court dissents invoke the nuremberg code: CIA and DOD human subjects research scandals".* ().Advisory Committee on Human Radiation Experiments Final Report.

Government, U. S. (1977). *a b united states senate, 95th congress, 1st session.* ().The New York Times.

Government, U. S. (1977). *Project MKULTRA, the cia's program of research in behavioral modification.* (). Washingoton: New York Times.

Government, U. S. (2010). *Declassified*

Grammer, K. (1990). *Strangers meet: Laughter and nonverbal signs of interest in opposite-sex encounters* Journal of Nonverbal Behavior.

Grant, E. C. (. d.). *An ethological description of non-verbal behavior during interviews* British Journal of Medical Psychology.

Hammond, D. C. P. D. (1990). *Handbook of hypnotic suggestions and metaphors* (1st ed.). Salt Lake City; Utah: W.W. Norton and Company.

Henley, N. M. (1977). *Body politics; power, sex and non-verbal communication.* New Jersey, USA: Prentice Hall.

Hess, Current Comment:Psychiatric Examination of Rudolf. (1954).

Hess, E. (1975). *The tell-tale eye: How your eyes reveal hidden thoughts and emotions.* New York, NY, USA: Van Nostrand Reinhold Co.

Hind, R. (1972). *Non verbal communication* Cambridge University Press.

Horrock, N. M. (1977,). "80 institutions used in C.I.A. mind studies: Admiral turner tells senators of behavior control research bar drug testing now". *New York TImes Newspaper*

Huang-Pollock, C. L. (2002). Development of selective attention: Perceptual load influences early versus late attentional selection in children and adults. *Developmental Psychology, 38*, 363-375.

Hughes, C. (2012). *The behavioral table of elements field guide*

James, W. T. (1932). *A study of the expression of bodily posture* Journal of Genetic Psychology.

Jones, D. a. k. a. B., David. (2008). *Mind control language patterns* Mind Control Publishing.

Joshua D. Greene, Sylvia A.Morelli, Kelly Lowenberg, Leigh E.Nystrom, and Jonathan D.Cohen. (2008). Cognitive load selectively interferes with utilitarian moral judgment. *Cognition,* (107 (3)), 1144-1155.

Keating, C. F. (1985). In J. F. Steve L. Ellyson, Ed. (Ed.), *Human dominance signals: The primate in us.* Springer Series in Social Psychology.

Kendon, A. (1970). *Movement coordination in social interaction: Some examples described* Acta Psychologica.

Kendon, A. (1975). *Organization of behavior in face-to-face interaction* Mouton.

Kihlstrom, J. F. (1987). The cognitive unconscious. *Science (4821),* , 1445-1452.

Klein, N. (2007). *The shock doctrine: The rise of disaster capitalism*. New York: Metropolitan Books.

Knapp, M. (1978). *Non verbal communication in human interaction (2nd ed.)*. New York, NY, USA: Holt, Reinhart and Winston.

Lafrance, M. a. (1999). *A meta-analysis of sex differences in smiling* Nonverbal Communication and Gender.

Lamb, W. (1965). *Posture and gesture*. London: Duckworth.

Lamb, W. (1979). *Body code*. London: Routledge and Kegan Paul.

Latter, C. (1998). *The women's perspective on an american obsession*. Binghamton, NY: Haworth Press.

Lavie, N. (2004). Load theory of selective attention and cognitive control. *Journal of Experimental Psychology, 133*, 339-354.

Lewis, M. a. (1993). *Lying and deception in everyday life*. New York, NY, USA: Guilford Press.

Loftus, E. F. &. B., T.E. (1982). Mental shock can produce retrograde amnesia. *Memory and Cognition 10 (4)*, , 318-323.

Lyle, J. (1989). *Understanding body language* Hamlyn.

Marks, J. D. (1979). *The search for the "manchurian candidate": The CIA and mind control: The secret history of the behavioral sciences* Penguin Books Ltd.

McCoy, A. W. (2006). *A question of torture: CIA interrogation, from the cold war to the war on terror* Holt Paperbacks.

McIntosh, D. N. *Facial feedback hypothesis: Evidence, implications and directions* (20th ed.) Motivation and Emotion.

Mcneil, D. (1998). *The face: A guided tour.* London: Hamish Hamilton.

Milgram, S. (Reprint edition (June 30, 2009)). *Obedience to authority* (ISBN-10: 006176521X ed.) Harper Perennial Modern Classics.

Mitchell, M. E. (1968). *How to read the language of the face.* New York, NY, USA: Macmillan.

Morris, D. (1970). *The naked ape* Jonathan Cope Ltd. and Bantam Publishing.

Morris, D. (1979). *Manwatching: A field-guide to human behavior* Harry N Abrams.

Morris, D. (1998). *PhD (vol. 1).* New Jersey: RANDOM HOUSE.

Navarro, J. (2011). *Clues to deceit: A practical list* Amazon Digital Services, Inc.

Navarro, J. (2011). *Body language vs micro-expressions* Pychology Today.

Nierenberg, G. (1995). *The art of negotiating* (Barnes Noble First Edition ed.). New York: Hawthorn Books.

O'Brien, C. (2005). *Trance:Formation of america* Reality Marketing Inc.

O'connell, S. (1998). *Mindreading: An investigation into how we learn to love and lie* Doubleday.

Patzer, G. L. (2006). *The power and paradox of physical attractiveness* Brown Walker Press.

Pease, A. a. (2006). *The definitive book of body language* (1st ed.) Bantam.

Provine, R. R.*Contagious yawning and laughter: Significance for sensory features and the evolution of social behavior.* New York, NY, USA: Academic Press.

Quilliam, S. (1996). *Body language secrets* Thorsons.

Rappoport, J. (1995, CIA experiments with mind control on children. *Perceptions Magazine*, , 56.

Report, C. C. (1976). "The select committee to study governmental operations with respect to intelligence activities, foreign and military intelligence"., *1* 392.

Drug library. Retrieved 25 April, & 2010. (2008).

Richelson, J. T. (.). (2001). National security archive electronic briefing book. *Science, Technology and the CIA, 54*

Robert B. Cialdini, P. (2009). *Influence* Harper Collins.

Ross, C. (2000). *Bluebird : Deliberate creation of multiple personality by psychiatrists* Manitou Communications.

Russell, D. (2008). *On the trail of the JFK assassins: A groundbreaking look at America's most infamous conspiracy* Skyhorse Publishing.

Russell, J. A. -. (1997). *The psychology of facial expression* Cambridge University Press.

Russo, N. (1967). *Connotation of seating arrangements* Cornell Journal of Social Relations.

Scheflen, A. E. (1976). *Human territories.* New Jersey: Prentice Hall.

Scheflin, A.W., & Opton, E.M. (1978). *The mind manipulators* Paddington Press.

Schutz, W. C. (1958). *A three-dimensional theory of interpersonal behavior.* New York, NY: Holt Reinhart and Winston.

Science, A. f. P. (2011). Does your name dictate your life choices?. *Sciencedaily,*

Scottish championships (1929). . Glasgow: The Argus.

Sommer, R. (1969). *Personal space: The behavioral basis of design.* Englewood Cliffs, NJ, USA: Prentice Hall.

Sorrell, W. (1968). *The story of the human hand* (1st ed.) Littlehampton Book Services Ltd.

Spiegel, D. (1988). 1988. *Journal of Trauma and Stress 1(1),* , 17-33.

Spiegel, D. &. C., E. (1991). Disintegrated experience: The dissociative disorders revisited. *Journal of Abnormal Psychology 100 (3),* , 366-378.

Strodtbeck, F. a. (1961). *The social dimensions of a 12-man jury* Sociometry.

Szas, S. (1978). *Body language of children.* New York: Norton.

Taylor, S. (1992). *a history of secret cia mind control research*

Thomas, G. (1989). *Journey into madness: The true story of secret CIA mind control and medical abuse.* New York: Bantam.

Thompson, J. W. (2010). *Psychiatrist in the shadow of the holocaust* University of Rochester Press.

Toropov, B. (2001). *Complete idoit's guide to urban legends* Alpha.

Turbide, D. (1997). *"Dr. cameron's casualties"*

Versluis, A. (2006). *The new inquisitions: Heretic-hunting and the intellectual origins of modern totalitarianism* Oxford University Press.

Vrij, A. (2001). *Detecting lies and deceit* John Wiley & Sons.

Weiner, a. b. T. (1999, March; 10). "Sidney gottlieb, 80, dies; took LSD to C.I.A.". *New York Times*

Weinstein, H. (1990). *Psychiatry and the CIA: Victims of mind control.* Washington, DC: Amer Psychiatric Pub.

Weisfeld, G. E.*Erectness of posture as an indicator of dominance or success in humans* J.Reeve, ed.

Westen, R. (. d.). *How to decode your kid's body language*

Williams, L. M. (1995). Recovered memories of abuse in women with documented child victimization histories. *Journal of Trauma and Stress*, , 649-673.

Wolfe, C. (1948). *A psychology of gesture* Methuen.

Young, M. D. (2004). *The day care ritual abuse moral panic* Mcfarland & Co Inc Pub.

53°37'57.2"N 21°04'04.6"E

Made in the USA
Las Vegas, NV
12 September 2021

30160980R00226